AT · RISK
FAMILIES & SCHOOLS
BECOMING PARTNERS

Lynn Balster Liontos

Foreword by Don Davies

1992

ERIC Clearinghouse on Educational Management
College of Education, University of Oregon
1787 Agate Street, Eugene, Oregon 97403

Design: LeeAnn August

International Standard Book Number: 0-86552-113-1
Library of Congress Catalog Card Number: 91-77519
ERIC/CEM Accession Number: EA 023 283

Printed in the United States of America, 1992
Second printing, September 1992

Conversion to Adobe Acrobat format, 1998

ERIC Clearinghouse on Educational Management
University of Oregon, Eugene, OR 97403

Prior to publication, this manuscript was submitted for critical review
and determination of professional competence. The publication has
met such standards. The publication was prepared with funding from
the Office of Educational Research and Improvement, U.S. Department of Education, under contract no. OERI-R 188062004. The
opinions expressed in this report do not necessarily reflect the posi-
tions or policies of the Department of Education.

No federal funds were used in the printing of this publication.

The University of Oregon is an equal opportunity, affirmative action
institution committed to cultural diversity.

Mission of ERIC and the Clearinghouse

The Educational Resources Information Center (ERIC) is a national information system operated by the U.S. Department of Education. ERIC serves the educational community by disseminating research results and other resource information that can be used in developing more effective educational programs.

The ERIC Clearinghouse on Educational Management, one of several such units in the system, was established at the University of Oregon in 1966. The Clearinghouse and its companion units process research reports and journal articles for announcement in ERIC's index and abstract bulletins.

Research reports are announced in *Resources in Education* (*RIE*), available in many libraries and by subscription from the United States Government Printing Office, Washington, D.C. 20402.

Most of the documents listed in *RIE* can be purchased through the ERIC Document Reproduction Service, operated by Cincinnati Bell Information Systems.

Journal articles are announced in *Current Index to Journals in Education*. *CIJE* is also available in many libraries and can be ordered from Oryx Press, 2214 North Central at Encanto, Phoenix, Arizona 85004. Semiannual cumulations can be ordered separately.

Besides processing documents and journal articles, the Clearinghouse prepares bibliographies, literature reviews, monographs, and other interpretive research studies on topics in its educational area.

PREFACE

*T*he benefits of parent involvement in education are now well known. When families become involved in their children's education, the children's academic achievement rises and their motivation, behavior, and attendance improve. Other benefits accrue to the parents themselves and to teachers and the school.

For these reasons, educators in many school systems today are renewing their efforts to reach out to parents. New books and articles on parent involvement appear daily, and new programs are begun. But as we survey all this activity, our attention in the end comes to rest on a sobering irony: most parent involvement programs aren't reaching the parents who need it most—those whose children are most likely to fail or drop out.

In values, expectations, and environment, most schools are reflections of middle-class families. To communicate with and involve parents who are poor, nonwhite, or speak a language other than English, educators must be able to bridge the cultural gap.

To help educators meet the challenge of involving parents and extended families of at-risk children, the ERIC Clearinghouse on Educational Management is pleased to offer this comprehensive, practical report. Like other publications of the Clearinghouse, this book uses the technique of "information analysis." It is a summary and synthesis of the most pertinent ideas from literature and practice, spelling out the steps that can be taken by teachers, administrators, policymakers, and others.

This report owes its existence to several people. It was conceived by Stuart Smith, director of publications, who collaborated closely with the author, Lynn Balster Liontos, on its scope and structure. Liontos is a research analyst and writer who has been commissioned by the Clearinghouse to write several syntheses of literature on parent involvement, collaboration between schools and social services, and at-risk students.

Successive drafts of the report were edited by Smith and associate editor Linda Lumsden. Deborah Drost, assistant editor, also contributed to the editing and proofreading. Lumsden and Drost assembled and verified the information in the Appendix and the bibliographic citations. Design and layout of the report was the responsibility of graphic designer LeeAnn August. Drost,

August, and word processing specialist Meta Bruner carried out the data entry and revision.

In the final weeks before the report went to press, Smith and Lumsden incorporated into the text the most recent data on dropout rates, poverty status, and racial/ethnic composition of the population obtained from the U.S. Bureau of the Census and the Western Interstate Commission for Higher Education.

We are indebted to many organizations that supplied us with complimentary copies of publications used for this report, as well as those that gave us permission to print excerpts or adaptations of their publications in sidebars.

Finally, we are grateful for the contribution of Don Davies, president of the Institute for Responsive Education and codirector of the new National Research Center on Families, Communities, Schools, and Children's Learning, for his critique of a draft of this report and for his insightful Foreword.

An earlier version of the first seven chapters, which compose part 1, "Background, " was published by the Clearinghouse in January 1991 as a Trends and Issues paper titled *Involving the Families of At-Risk Youth in the Educational Process*.

Philip K. Piele
Professor and Director

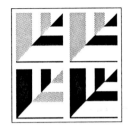

CONTENTS

INDEX TO SIDEBARS

FOREWORD

*W*hy has parent involvement become such a "hot ticket"?

Why is there so little of it—despite all the talk—in so many American public schools?

These are interesting questions for readers to ponder as they dig into the full helping of good material in this book by Lynn Liontos from the ERIC Clearinghouse on Educational Management. In this foreword I will sketch some brief answers that may suggest why this book can be useful to those concerned about school reform today.

There is no doubt that parent involvement has become a fashionable and important topic; it is now a part of nearly every new reform proposal or report and has a spot in nearly every conference and speech touching on school reform in some way. There are several visible and well-funded national projects—Comer's expanding school development program, Levin's accelerated schools program, Ziegler's Schools for the 21st Century, the Institute for Responsive Education's League of Schools Reaching Out—that focus specifically on family and community-school collaboration. Several of this book's chapters describe and draw on these efforts.

The announced plans for the New American Schools research and development program have a parent and community emphasis. And the Department of Education's 1990 expansion of the national network of research and development centers includes a five-year, more than six million dollar commitment to the topic in the form of the Center on Families, Communities, Schools, and Children's Learning.

Clearly there has been a big change in the perceived importance of the topic since the early seventies when the newly formulated and renamed National Committee on Citizens in Education and the Institute for Responsive Education were created and struggling to gain attention and financial backing. The topic was seen as peripheral at best. Then as now there were hundreds of thousands of parents and community groups struggling to participate in the schools, but their efforts were not given the kind of notice and respect as they are now.

Why? Among several plausible reasons for today's renewed interest in parent involvement, three deserve special mention. First, there is *competitiveness*: the deep concern of policymakers, economists, and corporate leaders about the country's ability to remain economically competitive with Japan, Western Europe, and other countries emerging as economic powers. Every drop in SAT scores or report on cross-national achievement studies highlighting the low performance of American students on measures of school learning heightens this concern. Increased parent and community participation in children's learning is easily grasped as related to the need to increase the productivity of education without the kinds of large increases in costs that are politically unacceptable these days. Now more people realize that if the schools are to become more productive and produce more students who are able to contribute to the closing of the competitiveness gap, they will need help from parents and the community.

Second, there is *social inequality and instability*. Many policymakers, social analysts, economists, and corporate leaders are concerned about the development of a two-tiered society of haves and have nots, with a large number of people consigned to a seemingly perpetual underclass. The failure of public schools to serve the urban and rural poor adequately is viewed as one important part of a deteriorating situation in which crime, violence, drugs, and health crises such as AIDS are a threat to social stability as well as to the nation's aspirations to be just and equitable. Moreover, the threat of social inequality and instability is closely linked with the issue of competitiveness.

Third, there is *political reality*. The growing consensus about the importance of parents in the education and development of their own children feeds on itself, and the idea becomes entrenched in public opinion. Ideas such as "parents are the child's most important teachers," "community resources are needed for at-risk children and families," and "the schools can't do it alone" become widely repeated and accepted. These ideas are then reflected in the expressions of public opinion and "leader opinion," which in turn influence elected policymakers.

School officials and organizations read the same polls and hear many of the same messages; by and large they respond to the political reality. It would be hard to imagine an urban superintendent talking publicly these days without considerable bows in the direction of the importance of parent involvement, business community support, and collaboration with community agencies and organizations.

The research, theory, and demonstration projects sketched and synthesized in this report have played and are continuing to play an important role in creating new public and policymaker acceptance of the importance of the topic.

Given the new visibility and significance of the topic, one might expect widespread, nearly universal shifts in practice in the relationships among schools, families, and communities. Clearly, this hasn't happened yet, as some of the data Liontos presents later reveal. What is also revealed clearly and helpfully are hundreds of good examples of schools and communities that *are* working hard, often with considerable success, to create new collaborative relationships among the various key parts of the world of at-risk children.

But the nagging question remains: Why so little shift in the day-to-day practices of most schools? Let me offer three possible answers.

First, the traditional mindset (set of attitudes, ways of viewing the world) of those who most affect the day-to-day life in schools—principals, teachers, school specialists—about school-family-community relationships still dominates. This mindset is reinforced by the traditional school culture and by teacher and administrator training programs and educational organizations wary of too much perestroika too soon. This traditional mindset divides responsibility among educators, families, and other community organizations and sees clearly marked and well-protected boundaries as being in everyone's best interest.

A different mindset is clearly required if significant moves toward partnerships are to be made. These moves require an acceptance of the idea of shared and overlapping responsibility for children's learning and development.

This book can be very specifically helpful as a tool in the hands of those involved in changing traditional mindsets, because it lays out briefly and clearly the theoretical and practical case for shared responsibility, supported by plenty of research evidence and expert opinion.

Second, changes in front-line practice always lag behind changes in public and professional opinion, research, and the political mood. It is one thing to do studies, issue reports, give speeches; it's quite another to change one's own behavior, especially when the work conditions and rewards for risk-taking for front-line teachers and administrators often inhibit and penalize efforts to change.

There is also a big gap between the general theory and the specific "technology" (organized mechanisms of systems) of how to create and sustain school-family-community collaboration aimed at increasing children's social and academic success.

This book makes a major contribution in filling this gap by providing good descriptions of how educators, family members, and community people are actually collaborating and by offering many practical, how-to-do-it suggestions. Although the book falls short of being a complete "tool-kit," it makes a good beginning.

Third, in all the current discussion of parent involvement, there is still missing the kind of authoritative, comprehensive policy framework that will induce institutional behavior to more quickly catch up with the new rhetoric and widespread acceptance of the parent involvement/partnership ideas. There are many policies at all levels now in place—school level, district, state, federal—and new ones arriving in a steady stream.

In a current survey of the effects of policies in schools that are reaching out for new partnerships, we found multiple, fragmented, sometimes conflicting policies—budgets, laws, grant requirements, regulations, union contracts, administrator intentions—in many schools. A more comprehensive, systematic, and authoritative policy framework would be useful to parents and educators trying to sustain new partnerships and to buck institutional traditions.

This book can be useful to both the soft-liners (the majority of educators, policymakers, and parents) who are willing to work along on a more piecemeal basis and the hard-liners who are seeking more profound restructuring and a more authoritative policy framework. The book provides help to those who want to build a case for comprehensive change, but it also gives practical directions to those who want to do what they can while "waiting for the revolution."

What the book offers to both camps that sets it apart from some other similar volumes is that it provides a detailed context—a theoretical and research backdrop. Liontos pulls together and describes the various strands of theory, research, and demonstration that are necessary to understand and properly use the practical examples and how-to-do-it advice that are offered.

The explanation of the context of research and theory is a great and welcome gift to all of us who have been involved in the past two decades of work in this arena. For this reason, I hope that many will find this book and put it to use, and that they then will help take further steps to move the now fashionable idea of partnership into practice in most American schools rather than in a few shining examples.

Don Davies
Director
Center on Families, Communities,
* Schools, and Children's Learning*
Boston University

INTRODUCTION

"*I* never see the parents I need to see," more than one teacher has complained, calling them hard-to-reach or saying they don't care about their children's education.

These are the parents of children at risk—at risk of failing, of dropping out, of having what in today's world accounts for no future at all.

And it's true that, as a rule, these parents aren't very involved with the schools. The Carnegie urban schools study tells of a high school in New Orleans, which, like others in the city, requires parents to pick up their children's report cards. At one school, located in a low income area, 70 percent of the cards remained unclaimed two months after the marking period (Reeves 1988).

A first-grade teacher in Cleveland told the Carnegie researchers:

> You send notices home, there's no response. You ask parents to come to conferences, they don't come. You send homework home, you can see that parents aren't paying attention to it. They aren't helping their kids. (Reeves)

Is this true? Well, yes and no. Many parents simply don't know *how* to help their kids. But most do care. Grace Godinez, interpreter for the Northwest Regional Parent Involvement Project, says, "The principal and the teachers—I think they are more aware of us now.... I think for awhile they thought we didn't care, that we didn't have the same concerns and hopes for our children. Now they know that we do" (Kneidek 1990).

This report will attempt to explore the reasons why some parents traditionally haven't been involved with their children's schooling. These are children who have the most, perhaps, to gain from parent and family involvement. There are reasons why schools haven't done their part either.

It may not be easy to reach parents. In fact, most project coordinators working with "at-risk" families report that it takes a great deal of time, creativity, patience, and commitment. But there's no alternative when we consider that these children are our future.

Literature on At-Risk Family Involvement

The literature that targets at-risk family involvement is sparse. Ironically, in most publications on family involvement, I often found only a paragraph or two that talked directly about at-risk parents. Even when documents did mention at-risk families, most had little to say about the process of reaching them. It is ironic because many of the research studies were carried out in inner-city schools where the populations are largely poor and nonwhite. Yet the literature on parental involvement—which is abundant—is filled chiefly with prescriptions or ideas that are most effective with middle-class parents and families.

Reasons for This Lack

Why is there so little information about involvement of poor and nonwhite families? Part of it may simply be tradition. Our schools have traditionally been part and parcel of the middle-class value system, and teachers are used to dealing with middle-class behavior and expectations. Also, much of the information on parent involvement has come from short-term research projects conducted by doctoral students, where there is no followup and where at-risk families and other cultures are simply part of a larger educational package. Finally, many programs that are working with at-risk families may not publicize their efforts in papers or journals.

Cultural Differences

To date, say Diana T. Slaughter and Valerie Shahariw Kuehne (1987-88), we've paid little attention to cultural differences in parent involvement. We know little about how different subcultures and groups adapt to diverse family involvement programs. As John Ogbu, anthropology professor at Berkeley, has said about the Accelerated Schools for students (Freedberg 1989): You don't just lump all the kids together who are at risk and provide the same program for them. Ogbu claims that to be effective the Accelerated approach must carefully differentiate between student groups. My review of the research suggests that the same principle applies to at-risk families and parent involvement programs.

Considering the fact that a larger proportion of our children will be nonwhite or nonmainstream by the twenty-first century, it is prudent to learn more about different subgroups of at-risk families and how to involve them in our schools.

Pioneers

I am indebted to three pioneers on this path, each of whom has contributed much to my attempts to fit together pieces of the puzzle of how to work with at-risk families.

Don Davies

In his research and with his project Schools Reaching Out (SRO), Don Davies of the Institute for Responsive Education (IRE) in Boston has been working exclusively with low-income families. His two lab schools in New York and Boston have been grappling with putting into practice what his research in three countries has indicated as possible directions for working with at-risk families. The assumptions that underlie all his work—and that are included in this report as well—must be the foundation for involving at-risk families with schools, if the undertaking is to succeed.

James Comer

James Comer, professor of psychiatry at Yale University who established the experimental School Development Program (SDP) in New Haven, has also been working largely with lower-income families and students. He has a particular interest in black families.

His work on empowerment, which includes involving families in the decision-making and governance of SDP schools, stands out. Most importantly, SDP schools work; they are successful and have been replicated in about 100 schools around the country. And parent involvement in decision-making is a key element. Comer's work, because it involves actual schools and deals with a form of the parental involvement process that many writers only give lip service to, has also been very useful to me.

Hispanic Policy Development Project (HPDP)

The Hispanic Policy Development Project (HPDP) is the only detailed source on the process of actually recruiting at-risk parents. HPDP sponsored various projects involving different ways of attempting to work with Hispanic families; some worked and some didn't. The result was the publication *Together Is Better: Building Strong Partnerships Between Schools and Hispanic Parents* (Siobhan Nicolau and Carmen Lydia Ramos 1990).

If other cultures and other at-risk groups, such as teenage mothers and single parents, went through a similar process that resulted in a similar publication, we'd certainly further our understanding of how to work with different at-risk populations.

Although Hispanics have their own particular history, lifestyle, and values, many ideas, concepts, examples, and conclusions that worked for them can be adapted and used in working with other groups.

A Note about Ethnic Terminology

Currently, preferred designations for some ethnic groups are in a state of flux. As everyone knows, ethnic labels can have positive or negative associations. Over time, ethnic terms tend to undergo evolution; one term loses acceptance as another rises to replace it.

Black or African-American?

One area where change is occurring is with the terms *black* and *African-American*. *Black* appears to be losing ground to *African-American,* primarily because the latter emphasizes one's cultural heritage whereas the former does not. In this publication, therefore, I decided to use the term *African-American.*

Hispanic or Latino?

Likewise, the terms *Hispanic* and *Latino* are spawning debate. When several Hispanic/Latino organizations were asked which term they preferred and why, responses varied. Many expressed a sincere desire to be not only "politically correct" but culturally sensitive as well. Yet many also acknowledged confusion and uncertainty.

One person reported alternating between the two terms in written works; another policy was to use *Hispanic/Latino* on the first mention and then continue with one term or the other for the remainder of the document. Yet another organization reported using *Hispanic* exclusively, noting that they have not seen widespread use of *Latino* in written materials.

Several people felt that each term has limitations or drawbacks. One indicated that *Hispanic* does not technically include people with Indian or black blood; on the other hand, objections have been raised to the term *Latino* because it is viewed as being too narrow in scope, technically referring only to those of Latin descent.

Those who prefer *Latino* say that it emphasizes the native character of the people. The term *Hispanic* may be problematic for some, stated one organization, because of its "associations with Spain and the conquest." Another organization indicated that a weakness of the term *Hispanic* is that it stresses those of European origin, even though only a small percentage of people classified as Hispanic are of European heritage.

A representative of one organization made an interesting point—that very few people actually use either term in reference to themselves. Instead, people tend to identify with the country from which they are descended. For example, a person would be more apt to describe himself or herself as a Mexican-American or a Puerto Rican, not as a Hispanic or a Latino.

When consensus did not emerge from my conversations with representatives of various Hispanic/Latino organizations, after much deliberation I opted for using *Hispanic* instead of *Latino* when referring to Mexican-Americans, Puerto Ricans, Cubans, or others with Central or South American or Spanish origins. In part, the decision was made for the sake of consistency. Because references to U.S. census data are sprinkled through this publication, and the U.S. Bureau of the Census uses the term *Hispanic*, in the interest of reducing confusion, it seemed to make sense to stick with the same term for all textual ethnic references. It is my hope that readers who prefer the use of *Latino* will understand that an effort was made to learn about and weigh disparate definitions and viewpoints regarding use of the two terms.

Who This Report Is For

This report is for everyone who works with—or intends to work with—at-risk families who have children in the schools. Independent parent and citizen organizations interested in involving parents and communities with the schools may also find it useful.

Commitment—the key to starting and running a successful parent involvement program for at-risk families—begins at the top. So school board members, superintendents, principals, and other administrative staff might be particularly interested in this report. Implications and specific guidelines for administrative action are found throughout the report, but especially in part 6, "Process."

If you're a project coordinator or have responsibility for parent involvement, or if you're a teacher who wonders why you've had trouble reaching at-risk families, you might pay special attention to chapters 6 and 7. Then check parts 4, "Special Ages," and 5, "Special Groups," for chapters on the particular kinds of at-risk families in your schools.

Nothing works for everyone, but educators concerned with at-risk families should find something in this report that is applicable to their own situation.

Good luck! What you do—or don't do—to involve at-risk families in the schools will have an important bearing on the future for all of us.

PART 1
BACKGROUND

Preview of Chapters in
Part 1: Background

Chapter 1. Who Is at Risk?

Who's at risk? To find out, a brief history of the term and how it's traditionally been used is provided, followed by an examination of how to identify children at risk and the two major risk factors: poverty and minority status. Outlined in this section is what has happened with our "bottom half" and what we can expect if nothing is done for them.

Chapter 2. Why At-Risk Children Especially Need Family Involvement

This chapter looks at the important connections and assets missing in an at-risk child's world. It also discusses how parent involvement can help by bridging the gap, changing attitudes and expectations, and making home and school settings more similar so that there is continuity in the child's world. The importance of the link to the child through his or her parents is emphasized.

Chapter 3. Benefits of Family Involvement

In this chapter, the benefits of parent involvement for children, parents, teachers, and schools are briefly noted, with a special emphasis on what at-risk parents themselves gain from it (which, in turn, positively affects their children).

Chapter 4. What Works: Forms of Parent Involvement

Generally, at-risk families have little contact with the schools. Why not? For one thing, traditional methods of involving parents do not work, and this is related to the history of poor and minority groups within the school system, along with other barriers. This chapter focuses on an adaptation of Joyce Epstein's forms of parent involvement, detailing each along with the goals for at-risk families. The chapter ends with two authorities proposing a variety of entry levels and activities for at-risk families.

Chapter 5. Schools Must Take the Initiative

This chapter shows why at-risk parents aren't usually able to reach out to schools—and therefore why schools must take not only that first step, but perhaps use aggressive outreach for ethnic and low-income families. The forms school initiative can take are explored and suggestions are proposed for what schools need to do. Most at-risk families *will* respond to schools' and teachers' initiatives.

Chapter 6. Barriers and Misunderstandings

Barriers and misunderstandings are examined in detail for both sides—parents and teachers. Answers are sought for why obstacles exist and where they come from. The chapter emphasizes that stereotypes are present for both groups and that at-risk parents and educators each play a part.

Chapter 7. Overcoming Barriers: New Beliefs and Principles

To help educators overcome the barriers and misunderstandings listed in chapter 6, this chapter looks at new beliefs and principles that can serve as a foundation for successful programs for at-risk families.

CHAPTER 1

WHO IS AT RISK?

*7*irst, a word about the term *family involvement.* I prefer it to "parent involvement" because with changing demographics, different cultures, and the many forms of family life today, a child is often under the care of the extended family. Sometimes stepparents, noncustodial parents, and grandparents have primary care for a child. However, since "parent involvement" is the term most often used, both will appear here.

Definition of 'At Risk'

The term *at risk* has become a cliché. As Walter Hathaway, research director for the Portland, Oregon, schools, notes, the term has virtually become "a verbal dumping ground" for a variety of ills, some of them educational, some of them personal or related to society (cited in Reeves 1988).

The history of the term is interesting. "High risk" has been in use only since 1980. But by 1987 ERIC was using "at risk" to refer, apparently, to school and academic failure, potential dropouts, the educationally disadvantaged, and underachievement.

The term itself appears to have been coined, says Reeves, by the Boston Coalition of Advocates for Students in their 1985 report *Barriers to Excellence: Our Children At Risk,* deliberately titled in reference to the report *A Nation At Risk.* Until the Boston Coalition's report, no one had suggested that it was the students—our children— who might be at risk, rather than the nation.

Actually, most of our children are "at risk" one time or another. "In our transitional society, with extremely high rates of family dissolution, mental health problems, substance abuse, and adolescent pregnancy, few children are risk free," says the report of the New York Education Commissioner's Task Force on the Education of Children and Youth At-Risk (New York State Department of Education 1988). Yet the report concludes that certain children are in critical need of social intervention.

At-risk children are not defined solely by low income or minority status. Even divorce, which is common today, can interfere with a child's academic and social success at school. James Comer comments that "given increasing divorce rates, the growing numbers of single-parent families and families in which both parents work, and the general complexity of modern life, even children of well-educated middle-class parents can come to school unprepared because of the stress their families are undergoing" (Olson 1990).

In spite of this broad use of the term *at risk*, this paper returns, for the most part, to the traditional definition, which applies the term to the poor, who are also often minorities, as well as to families of other cultures. The bottom line, then, for most at-risk families, is poverty.

Spotting At-Risk Children

How do you identify children at risk? They are those who show persistent patterns of underachievement and patterns of social maladjustment, says Kenneth Kamminger (1988):

> Not only are these children failing in schoolwork, they also frequently are behavior problems in the classroom or are passive and withdrawn in interactions. The behavior correlates of these underachievers have a common underlying theme, that is, the child is unmotivated or too distracted to succeed in school.

These signs can be seen alarmingly early. One study showed that patterns of underachievement identified in third grade were significantly correlated with dropping out in high school (Kamminger). In fact, many children are at risk even before they begin school, given their economic and family situations. "Growing up poor or in a single-parent family or with parents who themselves are high school dropouts increases the likelihood that children will have difficulties with schooling," states the Report of the New York Commissioner's Task Force.

The educational needs of children cannot be separated from their social needs. Both urban and rural families are often faced with multiple problems: lack of time, energy, and money; inadequate housing and schools; lack of community support; difficult family relations; innumerable social problems; and barriers related to race, class, culture, and language. "High risk" families are those contending with multiple problems.

Poverty: The Bottom Line

In a time of changing demographics and community needs, poverty is on the increase—and more children are at risk than ever. "Children are overrepresented among the poor," reports the U.S. Bureau of the Census (1991). In 1990, 20.6 percent of children under age eighteen were below the poverty level, compared with 19.6 percent in 1989. The poverty rate for children "remains higher than that for any other age group," the bureau reports. In 1990, children accounted for 40 percent of the nation's poor.

The National Policy Institute affirms the link between poverty and school failure, saying that socioeconomic level has a far greater bearing on dropout rates than race (Reeves).

Yet those at risk are more likely to be members of a minority racial group. The Census Bureau reports that in 1990 44.8 percent of all African-American children were poor, compared with 15.9 percent of white children. African-American families are nearly three times as likely to be poor as white families. Among Hispanics, 38.4 percent of children under eighteen are poor. Looked at in another way, one out of every five children lives in poverty, and the rate is twice as high among African-Americans and Hispanics.

The term *poverty* does not apply to a parent losing a job for a short time in a middle-class neighborhood. Martin Orland, a research specialist in the U.S. Education Department, defines "intense" poverty as (1) being poor over long periods of time and (2) attending school in areas with high concentrations of the poor (cited in Reeves 1988).

For each year that a child lives in poverty, the likelihood that he or she will perform below grade level increases by 2 percent, says Orland. Thus a child whose family has been mired in poverty for ten years is 20 percent more likely than the average child to do badly in school (cited in Reeves).

If that same child also attends a school with a high concentration of poor students, his statistical chances of school failure strikingly increase. In Orland's research, the percentage of low achievers in schools with relatively little poverty was 11.9

percent; it jumped to 23.9 percent in schools with moderate rates of poverty; and to 47.5 percent in schools with the highest poverty rates.

Another reason poor children are apt to be at risk is that they get a bad start early in life. Many poor mothers receive inadequate prenatal care, and their children tend to be low in birth weight and get inadequate nutrition and medical care. Undernourished children are less attentive and responsive in school. They get tired easily and are unable to sustain prolonged mental or physical activity.

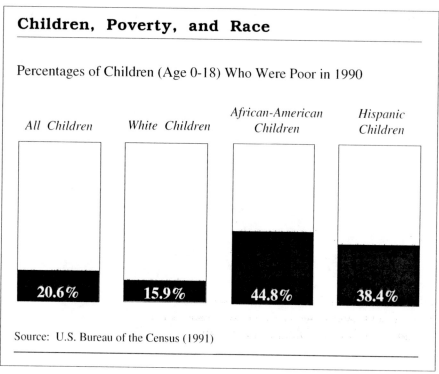

Children, Poverty, and Race

Percentages of Children (Age 0-18) Who Were Poor in 1990

All Children — 20.6%
White Children — 15.9%
African-American Children — 44.8%
Hispanic Children — 38.4%

Source: U.S. Bureau of the Census (1991)

Poverty is associated with health problems and restrictions in socialization that are likely to profoundly impair development in children. Children in poor families are more prone to illness in the early years and to sensory motor deficits. In addition, poverty breeds stress and depression, which are not conducive to healthy child development (Kurtz 1988).

Minorities: A Second Factor

It isn't just poverty that puts children at risk. As a University of California researcher observed, an important cause of the high incidence of academic failure is the fact that the preparation for learning that many children receive at home is inadequate or may differ fundamentally from what the schools expect (Jones 1989).

The U.S. is increasingly becoming multiethnic and multilingual. Whereas nonwhites and Hispanics made up 29 percent of the overall elementary-secondary school population in 1985, by 1995 their enrollments will increase to 34 percent, say the Western Interstate Commission for Higher Education and the College Board (1991). Enrollments of Asians and Pacific Islanders are increasing more rapidly than any other group (70 percent between 1985 and 1995), Hispanics next (54 percent), then African-Americans (13 percent).

Jones reports that forty languages, including dialects, are spoken in the Los Angeles school district. Too often we've ignored language and cultural differences. If language development is the key to learning, how can children who do not speak English—and who may have delayed language development in their own language—learn? And how can educators teach?

The national dropout rate among minority groups is 30 percent (Jones), with wide variation from one group to another and by region. In Texas, for example, the dropout rate is 45 percent for Hispanics and 14 percent for African-Americans.

"The paradox, of course," says Jones, "is that these minority groups, on whom this nation's future economy depends, are the groups that often experience the most difficult life circumstances and obtain the least educational preparation."

Public Elementary-Secondary Enrollments, High School Graduation, and Dropout Rates by Race and Ethnicity

	CHANGE IN ENROLLMENTS		COMPOSITION OF GRADUATING CLASS		DROPOUT RATES	
	Projected 1995-96 Enrollment	*Projected Increase in Enrollment from 1985-86 to 1995-96*	*Percent of 1988 High School Graduating Class*	*Percent of 1995 High School Graduating Class (Projected)*	*Status Dropout Rate* [1]	*Cohort Dropout Rate* [2]
American Indian/ Alaskan Natives	413,000	29%	0.7%	0.8%	Not available	27%
Asian/ Pacific Islanders	1.6 million	70%	3.0%	4.3%	Not available	2%
Latinos	5.1 million	54%	6.1%	9.2%	33.0%	18%
African-Americans	6.7 million	13%	13.0%	13.4%	13.9%	11%
White non-Latinos	27 million	5%	77.2%	72.3%	9.4%	8%

[1] Percent of 16- to 24-year-old population who had not completed high school and were not enrolled in high school or college in October 1989.
[2] Percent of tenth graders in 1980 who had not completed high school in 1986.

Source: Western Interstate Commission for Higher Education and The College Board (1991)

Parental Involvement and Our Bottom Half

The Japanese, says Reeves, claim to have the best bottom 50 percent in the world and thus achieve their extremely high average level of performance by seeing that their weakest students do well. American school reform, however, was launched with rhetoric on excellence that didn't take into account the bottom half. ✳

The phenomenon is called "the second achievement gap." According to Reeves, the gap is "between the bottom scorers and the top scorers, between minorities and nonminorities, and between the poor and nonpoor." The great danger, fears Davies (1989), is that of having a two-tiered

society: one affluent, well-educated, and optimistic; the other poor, increasingly isolated, badly educated, and despairing.

The high rates of failure of at-risk children and the gap between the advantaged and disadvantaged amount to a national crisis—socially, economically, and politically.

✳ Without substantial improvements in the way all children are taught—especially those at the "social margins"—we can expect a future that includes a lowered standard of living, fewer government services, intensified class divisions, a weakened democratic process, and lost human potential.

CHAPTER 2

WHY AT-RISK CHILDREN ESPECIALLY NEED FAMILY INVOLVEMENT

*P*arent involvement has been shown to be helpful in school achievement and behavior for all children. However, the ones in the bottom half—the ones doing poorest—need it most. Why? What is there about at-risk children that makes family involvement especially beneficial?

Bridging the Gap

The main reason why parent involvement with the schools is so important for at-risk children is that the cultures of home and school are markedly different for these children. This is unlike the experience of children from middle-class homes, for whom school is similar in values, expectations, and environment to their own homes and families.

When children live in two worlds, or when school and home are "worlds apart," as Sara Lawrence Lightfoot (1978) has put it,

> children cannot be expected to bridge the gaps and overcome the confusion of who to learn from. The predictable consequence in such situations is that children usually embrace the familiar home culture and reject the unfamiliar school culture, including its academic components and goals.

The Importance of Human and Social Capital

Some of us may not be able to imagine how distinct these two worlds really are for these children—how vast the difference is between home and school, particularly for low-income and minority children.

To help us understand this difference, let us consider the terms *human capital* and *social capital*—terms that are frequently used by educators today. If we take away the jargon, we can see how they apply to at-risk children's lives.

Resources

Capital is simply an asset or advantage. *Human capital*, then, as defined by Comer (1987-88), is "the development of skills and capabilities in individuals." Most commonly, though, it's used to refer to the parents' educational background. Or, more accurately, it is the resources that parents possess, primarily represented by their educational background, but also by their economic and social status.

...eraction

Social capital, on the other hand, is simply the relationships and interactions that take place among people. We might think of it as links and networks, as well as the kind of communication that occurs between parents and children, for instance.

In at-risk families, often both kinds of advantages are lacking. A child's parents may not have finished high school or may have little educational training. These deficits, however, may or may not contribute to the child's failure at school, depending on what happens in the relationships within the family, or even within the community that the family lives in. A family that has few educational advantages may compensate for this by the way the parents and children relate to each other.

FAMILY STUDY INSTITUTE

Chicago's Family Study Institute (FSI) is a division of the Academic Development Institute, a nonprofit corporation based in Chicago and supported by private grants and donations. FSI has developed two parent education courses, Studying at Home and Reading at Home, designed to be adopted by individual elementary schools and offered on a voluntary basis to parents. The courses focus on helping parents establish a home environment and encourage learning and academic achievement, such as setting up a regular time and place for studying, discussing school objectives and assignments at home in family meetings, and participating in family reading activities.

Each course consists of three weekly sixty- to ninety-minute group sessions at school supplemented by weekly activities that parents do at home. Volunteer parents lead the sessions, guiding small groups of parents through written curriculum materials and facilitating discussions of parents' experiences with home activities. The course materials are available in English and Spanish, and parent groups are offered in a variety of other languages with the help of parent translators.

Source: Goodson and others (1991)

One way to help restore the social capital for these families is for the parents to become involved with their children's schools and teachers. For one thing, such involvement is important because it helps bridge the gap between home and school for the child. It also helps children function in a school setting where shared goals and values develop—that is, where the children's teachers are not expecting something from them that conflicts with family expectations.

Attitudes and Expectations

Suzanne Ziegler (1987) draws on research from Joyce Epstein and Anne Henderson to explain the gap in school achievement so often found between working-class and middle-class children. She attributes this to substantial differences in attitudes and expectations in child-parent patterns and in parent-school interactions.

For instance, Epstein (1986) says that students gain in personal and academic development "if their families emphasize schools, let the children know they do, and do so continually over the school years." Henderson (1981) also says that when parents show a strong interest in their children's schooling, "they promote the development of attitudes and expectations that are a key to achievement, attitudes that are more a product of how the family interacts than of its social class or income."

But what happens when schools discourage parents from taking an interest, or treat them as powerless or unimportant? Obviously, by doing this, schools promote the development of attitudes in the parents that are passed on to their children—and that inhibit achievement. What usually is communicated is that school isn't important. And if school isn't important, why bother trying to do well?

What Schools Can Do

Lily Wong Fillmore's work with children whose first language is not English attributes the scholastic failure of many working-class white and minority background children to "a poor match between the experiences of the home and those of

Part 1: *Background*

the school" (Council of Chief State School Officers 1989). She calls for:

1. Better communication between home and school regarding children's preparation for school

2. Greater accommodation to the cultural patterns of students and how lessons are presented

3. More attention paid to the social environment of the classroom and student/teacher relationships

All of the above can be facilitated by involving at-risk families with the schools.

Over and over, experts who work with these children emphasize that the connections between schools and at-risk families must be increased. They also recommend that schools become more decentralized and caring. But there's a desperate need to reduce the disparity between home and school for these children and their families.

Settings

Another way of conceptualizing this problem is to think of it in terms of *settings*. Ziegler suggests that it may be particularly important for teachers to communicate with the parents of at-risk children so that parents and teachers understand each other's settings and expectations "and learn how to be mutually supportive of the student, which may include some modification of both settings."

Both settings *can* be changed or altered: school can become more home-like and home can have a school-like component, so that the two worlds become more similar. Bringing parent volunteers into the schools, for example, is one way to make schools more home-like. Home learning, on the other hand, is a way to bring school into the home. "When it is successful," says Ziegler, "changes occur at home and at school, so that the two environments become more similar and familiar to the children."

Parents Are the Link to the Child

Yet another way to describe this desired state is to speak of school settings that are family-like and family settings that are school-like. The latter happens when parents encourage intellectual de-

velopment, such as through reading, discussions, approval of school work, respect for children's efforts, and provision of a quiet space to study.

At-risk parents can become more sensitive to the importance of all these things. Likewise, schools that value the uniqueness of children make them feel part of the school, as a family would do. A sense of belonging, especially for African-American children, has been found to be important for these students.

The ideal link to the child is through his or her parents, Ziegler points out, as they are the persons with whom she has a primary relationship:

> When the child sees her parent visit the class, talk to the teacher, or receive a personal note from the teacher which is read to the child, the likelihood increases that the child will feel that her two worlds overlap and that she is at home in both. The positive impact of this kind of relationship, it is posited, is strongest for those with the least experience of it—the young and minorities, for example. (Ziegler 1987)

Providing Support

When schools are involved in providing support to at-risk families, they often are able to foster values and behaviors in at-risk youth and their parents that society takes for granted. By incorporating family support and education activities into the school site as part of parent involvement programs, schools are contributing to the reservoir of knowledge and attitudes these parents impart to their children (human capital).

"Researchers suggest that human capital is potentially more important for educational success than material capital," says the Council of Chief State School Officers (1989). "Hence, educators must work to assure that all children have both schools and parents who are able to instruct them well."

However, when families are weak and the human capital scarce, James S. Coleman (1987) suggests that schools are more effective if they can draw on the social resources of the surrounding community—which requires collaboration with other agencies in the neighborhood and larger community. But it can pay off with benefits for everyone: children, families, schools, and the community.

CHAPTER 3

BENEFITS OF FAMILY INVOLVEMENT

*E*veryone benefits from parent and family involvement in the schools: kids, parents, teachers, schools, and the community. For at-risk children and families, there's a lot to gain.

The benefits of parent involvement have been widely reported, and some are briefly listed here. An important result of family involvement with the schools is the benefits that *parents* of at-risk children receive (which in turn affect their children).

For Children

Research has pointed out the negative effects of the lack of parents' and families' involvement with the schools—the skills deficit that at-risk children experience, for instance, and poor performance of many of these children at school.

Substantial research links parent involvement to child development and to both academic and social success of children in school. This applies to all grade levels and to programs that involve parents as tutors, as well as those in which parents play a generally supportive role. Pro-

grams need not be extensive or costly to be successful.

In short, the results of parent involvement include:

- Improved academic achievement
- Improved student behavior
- Greater student motivation
- More regular attendance
- Lower student dropout rates
- A more positive attitude toward homework.
- Increased parent and community support (Hester 1989)

New studies also indicate that:

1. If there's a strong component of parent involvement, it produces students who perform better than those in programs with less parent involvement.

2. Children whose parents are in touch with schools score higher than those children of similar aptitude and background whose parents aren't involved.

3. Parents who help their kids learn at home nurture in themselves and their children attitudes that are crucial to achievement.

4. Children who are failing in school improve dramatically when parents step in to help. (Henderson 1988)

An example of one simple program took place in Chicago, where 99 percent of the parents in forty-one classes signed a contract to provide work space at home for their child, to encourage and praise schoolwork, and to cooperate with the teacher to provide items needed for schoolwork. The result? Students in the program achieved twice the grade-level gain of nonparticipants (Krasnow 1990).

Many research studies are based on innercity schools with large populations of low-income and minority students. In Anne Henderson's update of *The Evidence Grows* (1987), the eighteen new studies, along with the thirty-five original ones, support the conclusion that parent involvement in any form appears to produce measurable gains in student achievement. "If school improvement effects are judged successful when they raise student achievement," Henderson (1988) says, "the research strongly suggests that involving parents can make a critical difference."

In addition, it's also important to note that the effects seem to be permanent. For example, Henderson (1988) says studies show that low-income and minority graduates of preschool programs with high levels of parent involvement are still outperforming their peers when they reach senior high school—and at least one study shows that positive differences are maintained into college years.

For Parents

Through being involved in schools, parents develop a greater appreciation of the important role they play in their children's education, a sense of adequacy and self-worth, strengthened social networks, and motivation to resume their own education, says Davies (1988).

Specifically parents:

1. Receive ideas from the teacher or project coordinator on how to help their children

2. Learn more about the educational program and school system

3. Change their behavior at home to be more supportive of the child (Hester)

But that's not all. States researcher Urie Bronfenbrenner:

Not only do parents become more effective as parents, but they become more effective as people. It's a matter of higher self-esteem. Once they saw they could do something about their child's education, they saw they could do something about their housing, their community and their jobs. (Amundson 1988)

For Teachers and Schools

Epstein (1986) has shown that teachers discover that their lives are made easier if they get help from parents, and that parents who are involved tend to have more positive views of teachers. For instance, parents tend to rate teachers' interpersonal skills higher, appreciate teachers' efforts more, and rate teachers' abilities higher, says Hester.

According to a parent survey reported in the newsletter of the Center for Research on Elementary and Middle Schools (1989), "parents who are involved at home and at school say that the school has a more positive climate. Even more so, parents who perceive that the school is actively working to involve them say that the school is a good one."

Finally, involvement can also lead to feelings of ownership, which lead to increased support of schools. This may manifest itself through greater political support and willingness to pay taxes to fund schools, which, as Davies (1988) suggests, are important byproducts.

CHAPTER 4

WHAT WORKS: FORMS OF FAMILY INVOLVEMENT

*A*t present, relatively few low-income and minority parents are involved in their children's schools. In 1988, a federally sponsored poll of 25,000 parents found that about half of all respondents had initiated contact with schools regarding their children's academic performance (Rothman 1990). One-third reported having contacted their schools on academic progress. Not surprisingly, parents with higher incomes and more years of schooling were more likely to have initiated contact.

In the majority of schools in the three locales studied by Davies (1988)—Boston, Liverpool, and Portugal (all with low-income students)—little involvement from parents was found, regardless of social class. Most parents of low socioeconomic status, though, have little or no contact with the schools, Davies reported. What little contact they do have is usually negative: they only hear from the school when their child is in trouble.

The Hispanic Policy Development Project (Nicolau and Ramos 1990) spent three years conducting research that led to two sobering findings:

1. Successful education requires schools and families to function as full partners in children's education.

2. The interaction between poor Hispanic parents and the schools their children attended ranged from low to nonexistent.

They set out to discover why this crucial connection was so seldom made, resulting in the publication *Together Is Better: Building Strong Relationships Between Schools and Hispanic Parents.*

Traditional Methods Don't Work

There are reasons why at-risk parents have so little involvement with their children's schools. For one thing, there are many barriers, misperceptions, and misunderstandings on both sides. A later chapter will deal with these barriers in more detail.

Another important reason, tied in with the one above, is that traditional methods of involving parents do not work with many at-risk parents. Yet schools continue to rely upon traditional avenues of involvement such as open houses, parent-teacher conferences, the PTA, and volunteer programs even though these forms of involvement may be more effective with middle-class parents. This is not to say that the types of involvement mentioned above won't work with at-risk parents, but they may have to be modified for use with various populations.

Of course, part of this problem involves the history of American public schools and low-income or minority families. Traditionally, American public schools and middle-class parents have taken it for granted that there was continuity between home and school. Middle-class parents have assumed that schools will educate their children for successful roles in mainstream society, and educators have relied on middle-class parents to take an active role in socializing their children for school, as well as supporting the schools.

Socializing children for school has meant, according to Carol Ascher (1987):

1. Conveying the importance of education

2. Backing up teachers by making attendance, homework, and good grades a priority

3. Being willing to participate in school activities, such as the PTA

Not so with poor and minority parents. Their history with the school system has been quite different. Generally, there has been suspicion and mistrust on both sides. What's happened is that

> at the same time as poor and minority parents have complained that the schools are not run to benefit their children, and that teachers do not welcome them, educators have lamented that exactly those parents, whose children tend to be low achievers and who most need extra help to achieve, have tended to be so burdened by their own lives that they are the hardest to reach. (Ascher)

Forms of Parent Involvement

There are several ways to look at different forms of parent involvement, but mainly they're simply different phrases for different kinds of activities or roles. The question is: What works for at-risk families?

Joyce Epstein's model is often used, and it has been adopted by Davies (1989) in his Schools Reaching Out (SRO) projects. So her model, slightly modified, will be used here to include both the roles of each form of involvement and the goals for at-risk parents.

School Support for Families

Parents have basic obligations for their children's safety and health. These obligations include preparing their children for school, administering effective discipline, and providing positive conditions for learning and behavior.

The goal for at-risk families is to help them establish home environments that do all these things, including supporting learning.

However, at-risk parents often need help even with the basics, such as providing for their children's physical needs. This is where human service agencies can link up with schools to offer family support services.

Parents as Learners

Being a parent is a huge responsibility; there is much that parents must learn if they are to effectively help with their children's education. So at-risk parents must also become learners.

This form of parent involvement includes participation in workshops that train and educate parents in areas such as child development, parenting skills, or helping their children at home. The most effective parent education programs are those planned cooperatively by parents and school staff members.

The goal is to provide education that meets parents' needs and concerns, as well as the school's.

School-Family Communication

This represents communication from school to home about school programs and the child's progress (memos, conferences, home visits). For at-risk families, two-way communication—that is, communication from home to school—is also important.

The goal for schools is to make sure that all communication or information can be understood by all parents and also to design more effective ways of reaching these parents. Schools might bring home into school through using parents in the classroom to share songs and stories from their own culture, for instance.

Family Support of Schools and Teachers

This takes place at school, generally, and includes parents who assist teachers, administrators, or children in the classroom. It also includes parents who support the school's activities and attend performances, sports events, and other activities.

WAYS PARENTS CAN BE INVOLVED

- Assist with homework and review assignments
- Consult with the teacher
- Assist with schedule planning
- Serve as a resource person
- Assist in the classroom
- Initiate conferences
- Provide study time and a good study environment
- Promote writing at home
- Provide educational resources
- Model appropriate skills and behaviors
- Blend education and family activities
- Talk about goals
- Post examples of good work
- Visit classes
- Reinforce skills
- Encourage improvement
- Praise good performance

Parents who volunteer or who come to school events help further communication between parents and teachers. The act of attending school-related functions reinforces the importance of education to their children. This category could also include parents working with teachers in helping their children at home.

For at-risk parents, educators' goal is to make such activities nonthreatening and meaningful, so that parents will want to participate.

Helping Their Children at Home— Parents as Teachers

Former U.S. Secretary of Education William Bennett states, "Not every teacher is a parent, but every parent is a teacher" (Hester 1989). We have seen that the power of parents to affect student achievement is considerable. If parents are involved in the education of their children, they once again give their children that all-important message, along with a positive example, that education is important.

This form of parent involvement has parents working at home with their children in learning activities. Can parents of at-risk students do this? Yes, Dorothy Rich (1985) says, a resounding yes. Head of the Home and School Institute, Rich has been devising "recipes" for home learning for over twenty-five years. In recent data, for example, 94 percent of the thirty-three migrant families in Tampa reported changes in their children's school performance as a result of parents' being taught to work with their children at home (Rich, personal communication, May 27, 1990).

However, parents of at-risk students need ideas and instructions from teachers on how to monitor and assist children at home with learning activities that are coordinated with their homework. Including materials is also helpful. Most at-risk parents, when shown how, are anxious to help.

The goal, then, is to design, develop, and provide effective ideas on how parents can help their children at home and to train parents to use instructional materials as needed.

Parent Participation in Decision-

Making—Parents as Advocates

In this form of involvement, parents assume decision-making roles regarding school issues, problems, and programs. Parents might be part of the PTA, School Advisory Council, and other steering or decision-making groups, or they might be involved in planning events.

Empowerment is an important component to consider when designing parent involvement programs for at-risk parents. Family Matters at Cornell University stresses the importance of empowerment as one of the keys to overcoming social class and cultural barriers related to parent involvement in schools.

Low-income parents, who so often feel a sense of exclusion and powerlessness, responded well, for instance, to decision-making participation in the Head Start program during its early years. Comer's SDP model, which has been replicated in over 100 schools throughout the country, maximizes parent involvement at the school level. In fact, parent participation in decision-making and governance is an integral part of the program and a key to its success.

Of course, parent involvement is a process that usually occurs gradually. However, when parents are ready for greater involvement, the ability to participate in decision-making can be important. It's not true that socially marginal parents aren't interested in having their voices heard in some way.

Which Forms of Involvement Are Best?

Any way you look at it, parents have a number of roles to fulfill. There is debate, however, about the best ways to involve parents. The goal here is to decide how and when to recruit and train potential at-risk parent leaders.

According to Epstein, different types of parent involvement seem to produce different results:

> For example, several studies show that when parents help their child at home in a particular subject, it's likely to increase the student's achievement in that subject. By contrast, involving a few parents in decision-making on school committees

---

PROJECT AHEAD (ACCELERATING HOME EDUCATION AND DEVELOPMENT)

Project AHEAD is a parent-to-parent program serving disadvantaged families of children attending schools in the Ten Schools Program of the Los Angeles Unified School District. These schools have only minority students enrolled and are under court order to receive supplemental services to offset the effects of racial isolation.

AHEAD was developed in 1977 by the Martin Luther King Legacy Association (MLKLA) of the Southern Christian Leadership Conference in Los Angeles and currently is operated and funded jointly by the MLKLA and the Los Angeles Unified School District. Project AHEAD's parent educators are indigenous to the community and parents of successful school children. They make biweekly home visits and facilitate monthly meetings of parents in the schools.

The curriculum is based on the work of Dorothy Rich, who subsequently incorporated the ideas into a book entitled *Megaskills.* Parent educators introduce home activities that guide parents in helping their children develop critical skills for success ("megaskills"), such as responsibility and self-esteem. In addition, the program works with parents on school-related topics such as reviewing report cards and preparing for parent-teacher conferences.

Source: Goodson and others (1991)

---

probably won't increase student achievement, at least in the short term...a few volunteers at school won't help other parents know how to help their children at home. (Cited in Brandt 1989)

Comer and Davies would both likely challenge the assertion that volunteers do not help student achievement, though they might concur that it's not in a direct, straightforward way. Nevertheless, educators will want to be familiar with the different forms of parent involvement and decide what their goals are, what kinds of at-risk groups their school includes, and where they want to start.

Research doesn't show with any clarity what outcomes are associated with different forms of involvement. Ascher (1987), for example, reports that there is little research on direct involvement of parents in the schools. Yet there is a strong positive relationship between parent involvement in home and community affairs and student achievement.

Agreeing with Epstein, Ascher, reporting on a survey of 185 midwestern elementary principals, claims that not all types of parent involvement have an impact on student achievement: "While community support, fundraising, and attendance at school meetings were all highly correlated with achievement, citizen participation in policy decision-making was not."

On the other hand, having children score higher—that is, improving test and I.Q. scores—is not the sole reason for encouraging parent involvement.

Davies (1989) comments on James Comer's work with the SDP (School Development Program) schools:

> Comer has demonstrated that to improve urban schools, it is not enough to aim only at the intellectual and academic development of children—that their social, emotional, and physical development are inescapably linked to the intellectual.

Therefore, Comer's mental health team approach involves not only teachers, but also various specialists, parents, and community agencies. By improving "school climate," as well as by adding a new curriculum, SDP schools have helped at-risk children to perform at much higher social and academic levels (Daviesmm 1989).

Volunteering and Decision-Making

The areas of volunteering and decision-making or governance are the areas most fraught with controversy. As noted earlier, parents of at-risk children aren't likely to be found serving as volunteers in schools.

A recent study published by the National Research Council found that public schools with high minority enrollments are less likely to use volunteers than suburban schools. When volunteers are used, there are usually fewer of them. Volunteers in most schools are more likely to be white, well educated, and middle class (Olson 1990). The same is true for those parents who are involved in decision-making and governance.

In thinking about forms of family involvement, consider first the comment made by Nicolau and Ramos: you simply need to get them involved in some way, *any* way.

Using a Number of Entry Points

Perhaps Owen Heleen's model (1988) is most appropriate for at-risk parents. He proposes nondirectional participation—that is, using a number of entry points that are appropriate to the family's level of skill, need, time, and energy. For example, parental choice of schools, though initially involving little participation, may lead to increased involvement. Or a contact through a mediating agency, such as a church group working for school support or a home visit program, may stimulate parent involvement for some families.

Heleen believes that family involvement can become a reality even with the hardest-to-reach families, but only if

> school systems develop a broad range of participatory opportunities that work cooperatively with parents and the community, allow parents to determine their own needs, provide initially low-investment opportunities, and work with other community structures.

Davies' advice echoes Heleen's. The Schools Reaching Out (SRO) program offers a wide variety of styles and timing for both parent and community involvement and focuses on programs both inside and outside the school. When the school provides many different types of activities, it is easier for parents to participate in the school culture in the way that is most comfortable or interesting to them.

CHAPTER 5

SCHOOLS MUST TAKE
THE INITIATIVE

*W*hat's more important: A parent's socio-economic status or the parent involvement practices of the school? That the parent is a single mother and a high school dropout or school involvement practices? Says Kenneth Kamminger (1988):

> The data are clear that the school's practices to inform and to involve parents are more important than parent education, family size, marital status, and each grade level in determining whether inner-city parents get involved with their children's education in elementary school and stay involved through middle school.

That is, parents' level of involvement is directly linked to specific school practices. Parents are more involved at school and at home when they see their schools having strong parent involvement programs.

Many parents will never realize their potential (and hence neither will their children) unless schools and teachers reach out to them (Ziegler 1987).

At-Risk Families Cannot Reach Out

As has been pointed out, many parents view schools as places where they are called to discuss problems, or places where they themselves failed, or institutions they fear or are in awe of. Also, the daily struggle to survive may make it impossible for some families to reach out to a place that doesn't provide relief for their immediate needs.

Parent attitudes can change, but aren't likely to without intervention. So it is clear that the initiative *must* come from the schools. At-risk families can't usually do it.

An Example of Teacher Initiative

To emphasize the difference teacher initiative can make, Ziegler shares an anecdote. She tells of two students, Jessica and Derek, who had problems with reading. Neither of the children's parents initiated contact with the school. As Derek's mother said, "Teachers should take all the initiative." During both years of the study, Derek's teachers phoned and sent notes home to his mother about his academic problems.

Jessica's mother, however, heard nothing from the school about Jessica's continuing problems—even when she was assigned to special education in third grade.

At the end of two years, Derek was reading well beyond grade level, while Jessica was still several years behind. Even though the authors acknowledge there were other factors at work, Derek's teacher's communication with his mother seems to have played a key role in his dramatically improved reading ability.

At-Risk Families Are Interested

But will parents respond to a school's or teacher's initiative? Generally the answer is yes, but, of course, it depends on how the message is communicated.

Although some parents expect the school to make the first move, says Ziegler, most parents are very responsive to positive expressions of interest and concern by teachers and will implement their suggestions. They may simply be waiting for direction and guidance. Many parents receive little communication, she adds, and may be apprehensive about asking for more: "But when teachers do reach out to involve parents, the response is great." She also notes that many surveys show that parents are eager for more information and teacher-initiated contact.

Parents with limited educational backgrounds do not necessarily lack interest in the school their children attend. What's lacking in most schools and districts are appropriate strategies or structures for helping low-income parents to become involved.

What Should Schools Do?

"All parents, but particularly those who feel isolated and alienated, must be made to feel welcome in the schools if they are to assume greater responsibility for their children's educational outcomes," says Judith E. Jones (1989). "In many

SCHOOLS REACHING OUT (SRO)

When developing a national project called Schools Reaching Out (SRO), the Institute for Responsive Education (IRE) in Boston focused on three themes:

1 *Providing success for all children.* All children can learn and achieve school success and none should be labeled likely failures because of the social, economic, or racial characteristics of their families or communities.

2. *Serving the whole child.* Social, emotional, physical, and academic growth are inextricably linked. In order to foster academic development, all other facets of development must also be addressed by schools and families.

3. *Sharing responsibility.* The social, emotional, physical, and academic development of children is a shared and overlapping responsibility of the school, the family, and other community agencies.

The SRO project set as its purpose to redefine and expand parent involvement as a part of urban school reform. The project began in 1988 with two demonstration schools: the David A. Ellis Elementary School in Roxbury, Massachusetts, and P.S. 111 on the west side of Manhattan.

The project has now expanded into the League of Schools Reaching Out, with a current membership of forty-one elementary and middle schools in thirteen states and Puerto Rico. The league members subscribe to no single orthodoxy, but share a commitment to the above three themes.

The schools in the league will be considering issues raised in seven reports written on the SRO project by researchers who gathered data not only in the two demonstration schools but also in other member schools. The schools are also starting to put together new and broader definitions of parent involvement.

Source: Adapted from Don Davies (1991)

Part 1: *Background*

cases," she adds, "the parents of at-risk children need as much support as their children do. Schools have important roles to play here."

Some schools are reaching out in creative ways. For example, they may sponsor events at the beginning of the school year rather than at the end, plan social events and use school buses to get the parents there, and increase the literacy of parents and children in joint programs.

Examples of School Initiative

Davies (1987) suggests several ways schools can reach out:

1. Have adequately prepared and sensitive school representatives go into homes to meet with families

2. Have some meetings outside the school in settings less intimidating and more accessible to parents

3. Use natural and informal settings to reach and talk with parents (such as churches, markets, social centers)

4. Prepare materials in other languages for parents whose English proficiency is weak

5. Schedule activities that are attuned to at-risk parents' needs

However, Derek Toomey (1986) cautions that "the more parent participation is accepted and encouraged, the more *inequity* may result as enthusiastic parents come forward and the 'silent majority' remains silent." That's why he suggests that aggressive school outreach, including home visits, may be especially important to ethnic and language-minority families.

All Summed Up

In short, says James A. Sandfort (1987), schools need to:

- Change their belief systems about at-risk families.

- Admit that help is needed.

- Ask parents to become involved and take responsibility for their children's education.

- View an interested parent as a potential partner, not a problem.

- Communicate with parents, letting them know specifically what it is they must do.

- Begin at the top: the principal must be a catalyst.

- Develop and promote strong programs of parent involvement that involve administration and colleagues as well as individual teachers.

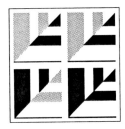

CHAPTER 6

BARRIERS AND MISUNDERSTANDINGS

"*I*t is the parents of at-risk students who are often least likely to be involved with the school," states the New York State Department of Education (1988). However, educators as well as parents must assume responsibility for this lack of involvement.

Some obstacles to involvement are due to benign neglect, others to political or professional barriers that keep parents out of the way, still others to emotional barriers felt by parents themselves. Finally, some are simply due to ignorance, lack of awareness, and misunderstandings.

Barriers for Parents

Feelings of inadequacy, failure, and poor self-worth

Many low-income parents have low self-esteem and, consequently, feel insecure about their ability to be involved in their child's education—either at home or at school. "They often see themselves as not being very smart, and many talk about how they did not do well at school, did not learn much, and were academic failures," says

Davies (1988) in his report on low-income families in three locales.

Davies states that many of these parents have low expectations for themselves and their children, though they almost uniformly express strong interest in their children's education. Michelle Sarkees (1989) says some may feel they are unsuccessful parents and thus feel discouraged by what they consider to be personal failures.

Although most doubt their ability to become involved in their child's schooling, many participants in Davies' (1989) study said they would like to learn more about how to help.

Negative attitudes or bad experiences with schools

Low-income parents, says Davies (1989), do not consider themselves hard to reach:

> They will come to school when asked for a good reason, but by and large they don't like to come on their own, and many—perhaps most—carry bad memories of schools and being intimidated by teachers and administrators. Most say they simply don't like to go to a school.

Nicolau and Ramos (1990) add that many Hispanic parents may fear appearing ignorant ("I am called by the school when there is a problem with my son, then the teachers make me feel embarrassed and hurt about his behavior"). Or they may feel overwhelmed by educators ("I went to the third grade; how can I question my son's teacher?"), or intimidated by their own lack of success in school ("Teachers don't like me. I flunked school. Better for my kids if I stay away as much as possible").

Suspicion or anger that schools are not treating them equally

Many parents harbor negative feelings toward school, seeing themselves as pawns, not partners, in public education. Sarkees says that some parents have developed a resistance to authority, often as the result of frustrations or concerns about previous educational experiences provided to their child. Thus they may be suspicious of parent education programs.

African-Americans have a deep distrust of public schools, based on past discrimination. "Blacks may say they believe schools help people get ahead, but actually they do not buy the white middle-class folk theory of achievement through education," says John Ogbu, researcher at the University of California (cited in Reeves 1988).

James Comer illustrates this mistrust by relating the experience of one first-grade teacher in New Haven on the first day of school: "A six-year-old raised his hand, as instructed by his teacher, and said, 'Teacher, my mama said I don't have to do anything you say'" (Reeves).

Ascher (1987) says that parents of poor and minority kids often are suspicious of school for teaching subjects whose importance they don't understand, or, more commonly, for "cheating their children of the same quality of education that they believe middle-class children receive."

Leave it to the schools

Many low-income parents, as well as those from other cultures, see teachers as authority figures and leave it to the school to educate their children. Annette Lareau (1987) found that par-

ents with low socioeconomic status, who also lack educational skills, separated themselves from their children's education. These parents perceived education as the teacher's job, not the parents'.

Cultural and language barriers

Nicolau and Ramos list reasons why barriers exist between Hispanics and schools, including a lack of understanding of U.S. education and a tradition of not questioning schools or teachers. Parents said things like, "They know what is best for my children," or "I want to be correct but nobody tells me what is correct here," or "They say if we cannot speak English, there is no point in wanting to see the principal or counselors." Southeast Asian parents, as well as Hispanic parents, believe they are being helpful by maintaining a respectful distance from the schools.

Economic, emotional, or time constraints

Economic hardship and unemployment can profoundly affect both adults and children. Many chronically poor parents or parents who suddenly find themselves unemployed suffer from depression. The effect of parent job loss on children is not certain and seems to depend on the degree of parental depression and duration of problems in the family.

"Depressed parents," says P. David Kurtz (1988), "tend to be harsh and intolerant of their children, demand independence before their children are ready and are emotionally withdrawn from their children." Children whose parents are emotionally unavailable experience rejection, insecurity, and possible social development lags that may influence their adjustment to school.

There is also growing evidence about how children are affected by having a parent who is mentally ill. "Children of mentally ill parents have significantly increased risk of developing psychosocial problems during the school-age years than do children of mentally stable parents," says Kurtz.

Family discord and hostility seem to be the chief disruptions. The primary effect is the occurrence of conduct disorders in children. Their antisocial behavior makes these children, especially boys, high risks for inappropriate adjustment to school.

Often excessive energy is required to meet the family's basic needs. Many are struggling simply to survive.

> It is not reasonable to expect that individuals who are barely surviving will have the time, the inclination, or the psychic energy to get themselves together for a school meeting or a workshop. It is clear that most cannot help their children until they have gotten help for their own all-consuming problems. (Nicolau and Ramos 1990)

Or as Ascher puts it, "A welfare client may have the time to come to school, but may not have the emotional or spiritual resources to do so."

Logistical problems: child care, transportation, scheduling

There are logistical problems, too. Often both parents work, sometimes at more than one job. Mothers may be single and on welfare and have a number of children to care for. As one Hispanic parent put it, "My husband, he works two jobs and I have two babies. We got no time to go to school" (Nicolau and Ramos).

Child care may be nonexistent or too expensive—and the same goes for transportation. Working parents can't attend meetings in the day, and single parents often choose to spend time with their children in the evening rather than go to a school event.

"Unless this mismatch in schedules can be overcome," the 1987 Metropolitan Life survey noted, "there remains a need for working parents to occasionally take time off from work, or else forego direct contact with teachers" (Harris 1987).

Barriers for Schools and Teachers

Commitment to parent involvement

A number of school practices have discouraged or completely blocked parent participation, says the National School Boards Association (Amundson 1988): "First, although most school

officials say they want parent participation, in practice they offer parents only limited opportunities for involvement."

Parents can't be effectively involved with schools if educators continue to view their participation as desirable but not necessary. It is the difference between looking at parents as extras and looking at them as partners.

> Teachers frequently ask, "How do I get involved? How do I get them to attend meetings?" But the real question that each teacher needs to ask is, "Do I really want to involve the parents?" Only when the answer is an unqualified "yes" will the means to do this become feasible. (Smith 1970)

Confusion about the role of teachers

Both teachers and parents have stereotyped images of each other, says Ziegler (1987), that stem from childhood experiences and guide their views about schooling. Teachers, for instance, report that they feel uncertain about how to involve parents and still maintain their role as experts.

At the root of conflict between teachers and parents is their often differing views on parent involvement. A 1985 survey by the National PTA, cited in the National School Boards Association report (Amundson 1988), found that about three-fourths of the parents surveyed said they were interested in attending classes and workshops with teachers and principals, as well as serving as advocates for their school in meetings with the school board or on advisory committees. School administrators, on the other hand, said they did not want parents participating as advocates.

In other words, teachers seem to see parents' role as minimally supportive, traditional, and perhaps passive, say Diana T. Slaughter and Valerie Shahariw Kuehne (1988). The proper role for parents, according to teachers, is home-based.

However, add Slaughter and Kuehne, parents express interest in more active roles—in being colearners with their children, functioning as advocates, and participating in decision-making.

Not too many years ago, says Dorothy Rich (1987), parents were told "hands off, you don't know what you're doing" in regard to their children's education. But today, she stresses, the message must be "hands on."

Concerns about turf and territory

Some teachers are worried that parents will undermine their authority and disrupt their classrooms. Rhoda Becher (1984) points to a report by the National Education Association stating that teachers express concern that parents will try to take over their teaching responsibilities and won't follow the teacher's instructions and school regulations.

"There has always been the question of who controls the child's life in school," acknowledges Sandra Feldman, president of the United Federation of Teachers in New York City. "Teachers are always concerned that parents will interfere" (Jennings, May 2, 1990).

They are also concerned that parents will cause confusion and disrupt the classroom because they do not know how to work productively with children. And they're worried that parents may use nonstandard English or demonstrate other characteristics that teachers do not want in the classroom.

Doubts about their abilities to work with at-risk parents

Many teachers harbor doubts about whether certain parents are willing or able to be involved in helping their children. Working-class parents, non-English speaking parents, immigrant parents, and single parents are among those groups about which teachers have reservations.

But it's been found that teachers learn by doing, says Ziegler. Those who take the initiative in reaching out don't seem to be defeated by barriers, but instead have been able to work successfully with parents of all educational backgrounds.

Epstein (1983) confirms this. While some teachers she studied had worked out successful practices to use with parents who had less than a high school diploma, other teachers did not know how to involve less-educated parents and thus claimed these parents lacked the ability or willingness to help.

Unfortunately, teachers receive little or no training in working with parents. Preservice training for teachers and administrators devotes minimal, if any, time to relationships between families and schools. Therefore, says Jane C. Lindle (1990), many teachers find they're ill-prepared for meeting parent expectations or ascertaining the needs of parents.

KENAN TRUST FAMILY LITERACY PROJECT

The Kenan Trust Family Literacy Project is a full-day, center-based program for parents and their preschool children in Louisville, Kentucky. The program is funded primarily through grants from the William R. Kenan, Jr. Charitable Trust of Chapel Hill, North Carolina, and is an adaptation of the PACE (Parent and Child Education) Program developed by the Kentucky Department of Education.

The Kenan model builds on four activities: preschool for children; adult basic education for parents; Parents and Children Together (PACT); and Parent Time (PT). Parents and children attend the program together three days a week for a full school day (9 a.m. to 2 p.m.).

For three hours in the morning, the children attend a cognitively oriented preschool program based on the High/Scope model, while their parents receive instruction in adult basic education and literacy. For at least forty-five minutes a day, the parents and children play together during PACT time, with the adult education and early childhood teachers present to facilitate interaction and learning. While the children nap, parents meet for Parent Time to discuss issues such as parenting, child development, home activities, and personal care and growth.

Source: Goodson and others (1991)

Teachers not only have reservations about whether they can motivate at-risk parents, but they also report they are uncertain about how to implement such a program.

A belief that at-risk parents do not care and will not keep commitments

Perceiving "the other side" as being uncaring only heightens the distance between parents and teachers. Adopting this kind of attitude can lead to an unproductive, escalating cycle of mutual blame.

Many teachers tend to ignore poor and minority parents, assuming that less-educated parents don't want to become involved in their children's education. But recent research refutes this assumption. Studies of poor and minority parents in Maryland, New England, and the Southwest have found that these parents care deeply about their children's education, but may not know how to help (Reeves). "We poor parents have dreams for our children's future," says Susie Smith, a resident in a Chicago public housing project. "Education is crucial to us; it is our kids' only legal ticket to a better life" (Reeves).

In a survey reported by the Center for Research on Elementary and Middle Schools (CREMS), 171 teachers in eight urban innercity elementary and middle schools generally agreed that most parents of students in their schools are not involved with the school and don't want to be. But when the approximately 2,300 parents of those students were surveyed, they agreed only in part. Although many acknowledged that they were not involved because they worked full-time or had other reasons why they could not come to the building during the day, this did not mean they lacked the desire to become involved. Many said they had not been asked and weren't sure how to proceed. The parents in these schools were "emphatic about wanting the schools and teachers to advise them about how to help their children at home."

Henry Becker and Joyce Epstein (1982) found that a great deal has to do with teacher attitudes. They say that general guidance and modest efforts directed to parents had significant results:

Thus, whether parents with little schooling are viewed by the teachers as capable of assisting their children in reading at home may depend on whether the teacher has worked out procedures and communication patterns that would enable parents with little schooling to assist.

Low teacher expectations for at-risk children

Teachers' ideas about what constitutes a "good" family and proper childrearing also affect how they relate to at-risk children and their families. "Children from families who deviate from these middle-class norms," says Davies (1988), "are expected by many educators to have trouble in school—to be behavior problems and low achievers."

For example, one teacher said, "As soon as I saw and talked to the mother, I knew that boy would fail." Another teacher said, "Well, what can you expect of these children. We do the best we can, but look at the homes they come from" (Davies 1988).

In their study of urban schools, the Carnegie Foundation found that more than one out of five teachers simply do not believe that all students can learn. These teachers' low expectations, they concluded, became a self-fulfilling prophecy (Reeves).

Schools assume a passive role or fail to help parents feel welcome

Epstein asserts:

> If schools don't work to involve parents, then parent education and family social class are very important for deciding who becomes involved. But if schools take parent involvement seriously, and want to involve all parents, then social class and parents' level of education decrease or disappear as important factors. (Interviewed by Brandt 1989)

Based on her research, Epstein speculates that only a relatively small percentage of parents have personal problems so severe that they cannot work cooperatively with teachers, given the proper assistance.

In the CREMS survey, many of the 2,300 parents reported that they had not been asked by the school to become volunteers or to help. Nor have many parents been given specific directions.

In a speech to school administrators, a Hispanic parent "explained that it was not so much that everyone in her daughter's school needed to speak Spanish, but rather that when she entered the building there was a welcoming attitude" (Krasnow 1990).

Locked doors and notices to check in immediately at the office can be forbidding and interpreted as signs of mistrust. For too long, says Bob Chase, vice-president of the National Education Association, some schools have made parents feel like intruders: "We restricted conferences to certain days, and we didn't welcome parents into classes. The barriers were unspoken, but they suggested we were the professionals" (McCormick 1990).

Working parents and single parents need activities that are scheduled at times they can come, rather than at times that are most convenient for school personnel. As indicated earlier, at-risk families may need such extras as child care, transportation, and possibly meals. A lack of child care or transportation can contribute to parents' inability to participate in school events.

Communication from schools focuses on the negative

Communication between schools and parents with low socioeconomic status is primarily negative, focused largely on academic and behavioral problems of children, says Davies (1988).

Research shows that most teachers don't contact parents unless there is a problem:

> In this situation, parents find themselves dealing with a stranger, the teacher.... Furthermore, because they probably have had no contact with the teacher until this point, parents feel no desire to

support the teacher, a stranger, over the interests of their child. (Lindle 1990)

Many teachers also overestimate the number of contacts they have with parents, whether negative or positive. Surprisingly, large numbers of parents are excluded from some of the most common communications from school. Epstein noted in one survey that over one-third of the parents reported that they had no conference with the teacher during the year, and almost two-thirds never talked with a teacher by phone (Amundson 1988).

Dwelling on the hard-to-reach concept

Davies (1988) says many teachers dwell on family problems and conditions, such as crime and poor living conditions, and talk little about the strengths all families have. They label these parents "hard-to-reach" because of their home and neighborhood environment and the parents' characteristics; "parent apathy is a recurring theme."

Unfortunately, Davies says, only a minority of educators acknowledge that school policies or educator attitudes may be part of the problem.

Davies (1988) says there is something flawed about the hard-to-reach concept: "Most of the parents in our study were 'reachable,' but the schools were either not trying to involve them or were not knowledgeable about, or sensitive to ways to overcome barriers of culture, class, or language."

Lack of time and funding

Many demands compete for teachers' and principals' time. Teachers who are also parents have some of the same time problems that other working parents do. Schools may give lip service to reaching at-risk families, but to actually do so may require released time for teachers as well as employing parent coordinators. In addition, there may be a lack of access to appropriate family involvement materials. Finally, lack of sufficient funding for family involvement programs is an ongoing problem at all levels of the educational system.

CHAPTER 7

OVERCOMING BARRIERS:
NEW BELIEFS AND PRINCIPLES

*S*everal programs that involve the families of at-risk students have achieved success by replacing old beliefs and assumptions with new ones. There are also certain principles on which effective at-risk family involvement programs are based. The following "new beliefs" result from the work of Rhoda Becher, Don Davies, and the Family Matters program at Cornell University.

New Beliefs about Parents and Families

All families have strengths

Parents, says Becher (1984), already make contributions to their children's education. Successful programs emphasize the strengths of parents and let them know these strengths are valued.

They also build on the particular assets that many poor and minority families have. For instance, these families are usually more group-oriented and interactive than the white middle class (which stresses individualism and competition)—and it's exactly these collaborative skills that the labor market needs today.

Sue Berryman, director of the National Center on Education and Employment at Teachers College, Columbia University, says there is another school reform waiting in the wings, one that "will be organized in some way around a much fuller definition of human talent than narrowly defined academic achievement skills" (Reeves 1988). This will be so, she says, not only because the economy needs a wider range of skills, but also because at-risk families may bring a greater diversity of talents to us. Some of the talents these groups have are in spatial relationships, physical coordination, music, interpersonal perceptiveness, and inner attunement.

Parents can learn new techniques

Successful programs help parents identify new things they're capable of doing, says Becher. This perspective also suggests that parents have both the ability and interest to expand and enhance their parenting skills. An aim of successful programs is to help families overcome obstacles to effective functioning—and one way to do this is by teaching them new skills and behaviors.

Parents have important perspectives about their children

Successful programs recognize and draw on parents' perspective and knowledge about their children. Teachers realize that parents can be important and useful in helping them improve children's education. "Valuable information on child rearing and family functioning has been gleaned even from disadvantaged parents and passed on to benefit other parents," reports Moles (1990).

Most parents really care about their children

Successful programs acknowledge and rest on a sincere belief that most parents really care about their kids. This has been demonstrated over and over by parents' comments.

Of course, there are families struggling with multiple problems. As Slaughter and Kuehne (1988) point out, "Generally, under impoverished conditions, many families are considerably more survival-oriented than child-oriented, although for many adults their children are their most precious possessions."

Cultural differences are both valid and valuable

"Diversity is not a disease to be cured or an aberration to be stamped out by the experts," says Davies (1988). Successful programs learn about other cultures and respect their beliefs. They find ways of building on the loyalty and obedience, for example, that Hispanic parents instill in their children. Or they find ways to bring other cultures' traditions and values into the classroom.

Many family forms exist and are legitimate

There is no single pattern, says Davies (1988), that determines healthy child and family development. Yet the number and types of resources that parents can marshal can be a key factor. In cases where children are cared for by grandparents, stepparents, or other members of an extended family, successful programs are prepared to reach

---

THREE INNOVATIVE PROGRAMS

SAN DIEGO, CALIFORNIA. Oak Park Elementary School found that an effective way to involve parents from diverse cultural backgrounds was to train representative parent and teacher facilitators who could meet with each ethnic and racial group separately to brainstorm, solve problems, and discuss issues and concerns. As a result, each group felt for the first time that it was important and that its views counted. After the separate meetings, the school held a joint session to develop a parent involvement plan. Parents and teachers were surprised to see that all groups shared common concerns and needs (Chrispeels 1991).

BROOKLYN, NEW YORK. Developing Multicultural Awareness Through Literature is federally funded under family-school partnership grants. Seeking to empower parents and children by recognizing their cultural differences as assets, this program introduces children, parents, and teachers to some of the world's best children's literature. Teachers receive training in family involvement activities and parents and students are given educational materials for learning at home (Cross and others 1991).

FRESNO, CALIFORNIA. Early intervention is the central priority for this family-school partnership program called Project MIRROR (Managing Integrated Resources—Reaching Out Remediation). Community role models work with families and students. Successful individuals from disadvantaged backgrounds share their own experiences with the disadvantaged students of West Fresno to create a "mirror" effect. The program is designed to improve the level of participation and involvement of families in the education of their own children. Activities include teacher and family training; a family-school retreat; a strategic planning session to establish dialogue between school and families; and a prescriptive learning and family tutorial component, which features an automated homework information system (Cross and others).

---

out and provide family support where resources are limited.

New Principles for Programs

The following principles for involving parents of at-risk students come mainly from the work of Davies (based also on the Family Matters program at Cornell University), as well as from various other experts.

The No-Fault Model

As we've seen, there are misunderstandings and obstacles on both sides, and blaming each other—parents or teachers—only stands in the way of developing genuine partnerships. Teachers as well as parents have new things to learn. But then teachers, like parents, also need support. When you're beginning a program for at-risk families, proceed from the premise that a child's learning difficulties are not caused by any single source; in other words, don't place all the blame on either the family or the school. We are all responsible and we all must work together.

A Nondeficit Approach

It is not helpful or accurate to view at-risk families as deficient or failures. Nor is it useful to look down on any family, talk down to them or "at" them, or regard them in a patronizing way. Respect families for who they are—and look for assets and strengths.

The Importance of Empowerment

All individuals and families need to feel empowered, especially at-risk families, who so often feel powerless. *Empowerment* has been defined by V. Vanderslice (1984) as a process through which people become more able to influence those individuals and organizations that affect their lives and the lives of those they care about. Moncrieff Cochran and Charles R. Henderson, Jr. (1986) link empowerment to helping individuals remove obstacles that impede their efforts to achieve equal status in society.

Anything that can be done to give at-risk families more control over their lives—and their children's education—will be helpful.

An Ecological Approach

We live in an interdependent world today, one in which a child's world is linked to the family, which is linked to the neighborhood or community, plus to the child's school. And each realm influences others. Family involvement in the school can have an impact both within the family and on the community in which the family lives. For example, if parent involvement results in an unemployed mother gaining the self-confidence to get a job, that job will then affect her need for child care. Further, her employment may affect her ability to be as involved as she was before in school activities. We need to see all the connections in a child's world.

Collaboration: The Only Way

Partnership with at-risk families is impossible without collaboration, both within the school and outside it. Schools alone can't provide all the services that at-risk families need, such as parenting education, counseling, health care, housing, and so forth.

The school staff also need to function in a collaborative way with one another in order for real change to occur, believes Krasnow (1990). It's too much to ask a single teacher to do it alone, just as it's asking too much for schools to provide all the help and resources that at-risk students and families need.

We know now that the community and schools *must* work together to achieve successful parent involvement programs for at-risk families.

PART 2
COMPONENTS

Preview of Chapters in Part 2: Components

Chapter 8. Communication: The Importance of Personal Contact

Good communication lies at the heart of every effective family involvement program. Without a doubt, the most effective way to communicate with at-risk families is personal contact, especially home visits. After a brief look at parent-teacher conferences and school-parent contracts, this chapter details the benefits of and effective procedures for conducting home visits. The chapter also tells how to make communication a two-way street by bringing the home into the classroom as well as reaching out to homes.

Chapter 9. Home Atmosphere: Attitudes and Expectations

The values parents hold about education shape their children's view of learning. Children of parents who believe in hard work and discipline, emphasize high aspirations, and provide stimulating learning materials in the home are far more likely to succeed in school than children whose parents prefer leisure to work, have no rules about TV, and are indifferent to learning. This chapter suggests some ways schools can encourage families to reinforce the values and activities of the school.

Chapter 10. Preparation: Getting Children Ready for School

Low-income families and those from minority cultures may not prepare their children for school by teaching them skills (such as how to hold a pencil) that are essential for their successful progress in school. Making matters worse, many teachers don't know how to deal with children who have been socialized differently than middle-class children.

Chapter 11. Home Learning: The Wave of the Future

When learning in the home reinforces what is learned at school, children excel. This chapter explores various approaches to and benefits of home learning, drawing on the research of Dorothy Rich and Joyce Epstein. Activities for parents with low literacy skills are suggested, and examples of home reading programs are given.

Chapter 12. Decision-Making and Advocacy: The Importance of Empowerment

Many low-income and minority parents feel a sense of exclusion, powerlessness, and hopelessness—attitudes they pass on to their children. To deal with this problem, family involvement programs must incorporate ways to empower parents by involving them in decision-making about the schools their children attend. Programs that have sought to give poor and minority families a greater role in school decision-making include Head Start, The Early Childhood and Family Education Program, and James Comer's School Development Program.

Chapter 8

COMMUNICATION: THE IMPORTANCE OF PERSONAL CONTACT

*C*ommunication is so important that experts assert that the lack of information flowing between home and school may lie at the root of the dissonance between teachers and parents. Whenever human beings communicate, natural barriers exist. In the case of schools, these barriers must be broken down if parents are to become involved in their children's education. This is doubly true with at-risk families.

Diane D'Angelo and C. Ralph Adler (1991) give an example. Imagine, they say, you are playing the game where you pass a message around a circle, one person whispering it to the next. By the time it gets to the end, the message usually bears little resemblance to the original one. Now imagine that the first child has a hearing problem, the second child can barely speak English, and the third child does not want to believe the message. By the time the message completes its route, neither the language nor the content of the message would be intelligible.

D'Angelo and Adler say schools are beginning to realize that the initial contacts between school and home can make or break relationships and that first contacts often set the tone for subsequent communication. "Communication is like a magnet," they say, "that draws together the 'spheres of influence' that affect children's lives—school, home, community, and the peer group."

Evidence is growing, they add, that extra care in fashioning and maintaining communication between schools and families is paying off. Underlying these new approaches is the recognition that any parent may be "hard to reach" at times. They list many variables such as the parents' literacy level; language preferred for reading, writing, and speaking; daily commitments and responsibilities; parents' comfort in becoming involved with the schools; and cultural beliefs. Therefore, it's not possible to design a single method of communication that will always reach all parents.

Communication strategies, D'Angelo and Adler explain, should be adapted to the needs of particular families. For instance, some material will need to be translated into other languages or put in alternative formats (see "Tapping Technology" on page 38) to meet the needs of parents who do not speak English or who cannot read.

The Most Effective Form of Communication: Personal Contact

The best way to begin is to try to understand why some parents are hard to reach. Typically, teachers have communicated with parents in writing, by sending messages through the mail or sending them home with the students. However, these communications are often ignored or they may be unintelligible to poorly educated or non-English-speaking parents.

Nicolau and Ramos (1990) found the same problem in parent involvement projects that were attempted with Hispanic parents. For reasons mentioned earlier, most low-income Hispanic parents resist entering into parent/school partnerships. Therefore, project coordinators found that their first challenge was finding a way to stimulate parent interest and attendance at the first event.

A number of ideas were tried, including telephone calls, flyers, handwritten notes from teachers, notices posted in local neighborhood places, articles in local newspapers, distribution of Spanish-language posters, announcements at Sunday Spanish-language church services and on local radio and television programs, and home visits.

With the exception of home visits, most of the methods proved inadequate. They did not convince parents to participate in any activity, although in conjunction with more effective techniques, some may have helped.

Most Effective Method: Home Visits

What's most effective? Over and over, project coordinators gave one answer: home visits or other personal contact with parents.

"The personal approach," Nicolau and Ramos stress, "which means talking face to face with the parents, in their primary language, at their homes, or at the school, or wherever a parent could be 'engaged' was the strategy deemed most effective by 98 percent of the project coordinators."

Passive forms of communication, such as flyers and letters, were listed as least effective. Home visits, project coordinators concluded, are a must. Home visits helped to personalize invita-

NEWSLETTERS

Some schools, including many with Chapter 1 programs (see D'Angelo and Adler), have had success publishing newsletters to keep parents informed about school happenings or to involve them further in their child's education. For example:

• The Chapter 1 program in Omaha publishes a monthly newsletter that highlights home activities coordinated with classroom activities. Each issue focuses on a classroom theme. The newsletter also reports on the meeting of the parent advisory council and gives information about the Chapter 1 program and how parents can get involved.

• In Cahokia, Illinois, the Chapter 1 schools distribute a newsletter that includes student writing, notices of parent meetings, and activities that parents and children can do together.

• Similarly, the Chapter 1 program in Palatine, Illinois, distributes a quarterly newsletter to parents that is available in Spanish for bilingual families. It highlights Chapter 1 student writing, which parents eagerly read. It also has news of upcoming events of interest to parents.

• The Seattle School District No. 1 also publishes a newsletter, entitled "Helping at Home," that gives suggestions to parents for boosting their children's academic success.

If you want to subscribe to a newsletter that answers the question, "How can I help my child?," *Parents Make the Difference* is an excellent choice. Its articles are short, readable, up-to-date, and appealing. The newsletter is published monthly from September through May. For more information contact The Parent Institute, P. O. Box 7474, Fairfax Station, VA 22039; (703) 569-9842.

tions, which is an element many Hispanics find important. Coordinators emphasized, though, that a single home visit or conversation may not do the job—that it may be necessary to make personal contact two or three times to convince parents to attend an activity.

Why Personal Contact Works

Suzanne Ziegler (1987) explains that the effectiveness of parent involvement may be due to the message children receive when they see their teachers and parents in direct, personal contact. Children sense consistency and caring in both home and school environments. Ziegler hypothesizes that the more direct, frequent, and personal the parent-teacher contact, and the more visible the contact is to the child, the greater its potential.

Urie Bronfenbrenner (1972) also suggests that the more personal the modes of communication—face-to-face versus the telephone, for instance—the more powerful. He believes that the more direct the links are between settings, the more they enhance the potential of each setting. Thus a child whose parents have formed a relationship with the teacher is more likely to learn than is a child from a family that has no connection with the teacher.

Parent-Teacher Conferences

There are two basic formal ways to achieve face-to-face contact—through home visits or, more traditionally, through the parent-teacher conference. (More will be said about home visits later in this chapter.) For conferences, parents are usually expected to come to the school. Because of past negative associations with school, some low-income parents find this uncomfortable. Parent-teacher conferences, however, do allow for interaction, but often are held infrequently and are difficult to schedule. As a result, many parents only see teachers when their children are having academic or disciplinary problems.

Some schools are experimenting with parent-teacher conferences. At an initial parent-teacher conference in Lima, Ohio, parents are given a packet designed to help them engage in learning activities with their children at home (D'Angelo

TIPS FOR WRITTEN COMMUNICATION

The key to creating effective written materials is the presentation and the reading level of the materials, say D'Angelo and Adler. They suggest the following tips, from Push Literacy Action Now of Washington, D.C., to help educators develop better written information for parents:

1. Keep sentences short (never more than twenty words).

2. Keep paragraphs short (an average of six lines).

3. Use easy, short, familiar words.

4. Get to the point; omit irrelevant information.

5. Write things in logical order (who, what, where, when, why, and how).

6. Be definite; give a clear picture of what you want to say.

7. Be direct. Speak to each reader. Say "you should" instead of "parents should."

8. Use the active voice more than the passive. Put the subject at the beginning of the sentence ("Please sign the consent slip" rather than "A consent slip must be signed").

9. Use pictures and subheads. Readers tend to drown in a sea of solid text. Bold print emphasizes important words or phrases.

10. Watch type size and use of capital letters. Don't overuse capitals; they are hard to read. For easy reading use at least 12-point type.

11. Know your audience. How well do they read? If you aren't sure, test your materials on a few representative people.

12. Be yourself. Write as you would talk. Write to express, not to impress.

13. Write and rewrite. Read a draft over. Can you say something more succinctly or in a more interesting way? Have you used jargon or abbreviations that your audience may not know? Ask someone else to read what you've written. Then rewrite it.

Source: Adapted from D'Angelo and Adler (1991)

TAPPING TECHNOLOGY

Many schools and Chapter 1 programs are finding new ways to make contact with a wider range of parents through the use of electronic communications. "In the 1990's," Epstein (1991) states, "technology can help improve many types of involvement. This includes radio, television, video and audiotapes, computers, and other electronic connections between home and school, some of which offer the possibility of two-way communication."

RADIO

• In McAllen, Texas, the school district has created a community partnership with local radio stations. It sponsors "Discussions Escolares," a weekly program in Spanish that encourages parents to become more involved in their children's education.

Some of the topics the program has addressed include communicating with teenagers, parent involvement at school, creating a learning atmosphere in the home, preventing school dropouts, and family and school relationships. Parents may check out copies of the script or a cassette tape from the parent coordinators at their schools (D'Angelo and Adler).

VIDEO

• Videotapes have been used to tape workshops, meetings, or other events of interest to parents who cannot come to school for these events. Parents who own VCRs can check out the videotapes and view them at home.

• Poudre School District in Fort Collins, Colorado, produced a videotape titled "Reading Aloud to Children," which demonstrates practical techniques for improving and enjoying family reading. The tape was designed to stimulate discussion in parent groups or to help parents as a resource at home. The tape is available in both English and Spanish (D'Angelo and Adler).

• At Park Elementary School in Dolton, Illinois, two teachers have used video as a means for parents to view their children at work. A grant enabled them to rent a video camera and film students in the classroom. The videotapes are sent home regularly to help parents develop a better understanding of their children's activities and behaviors. "After seeing the tapes," commented Diana Brown, one of the teachers involved in the project, "the parents were much less threatened by the school setting." As a result, parent involvement increased tremendously (Jennings, August 1, 1990).

• Since 90 percent of the families in one school owned VCRs, an Illinois school produced instructional videotapes in cooperation with the local cable company. This joint venture resulted in two series of tapes: a video bank of "critical lessons" and a parent education series. The parent education tapes showed parents effective ways to motivate their children to learn. For example, one tape concentrated on teaching parents to observe their children's study habits and organizational skills.

The "critical lessons" were taped class sessions that students could use as instructional supplements. Each tape allowed students and their parents a chance to view the class and study the important points of the lesson. This enabled parents to discuss ideas with their children and become actively involved in their children's learning. This innovative use of technology acknowledged the fact that many parents cannot come to school to see what their children are doing. Thus the project brought the school to the parents (Chapman 1991).

and Adler). Other schools hold regular conferences with parents to discuss student progress as a way of distributing report cards or in place of them. Some schools schedule evening conferences for working parents.

School-Parent Contracts

A number of schools are experimenting with school-parent contracts as part of parent conferences. Such contracts are an important part of the Quality Education Project, which was started in 1982 by Nancy Honig, wife of California's Superintendent of Public Instruction Bill Honig (Jennings, August 1, 1990). As part of their "pledge," parents sign a document promising they will provide a quiet place for their children to study, encourage them to complete their homework, get them to bed by 9 p.m., send them to school on time, spend at least fifteen minutes a day reading to or with them, and attend back-to-school nights, parent-teacher conferences, and other school events.

In exchange, teachers promise to provide a safe place for children to learn, teach all the concepts necessary for academic achievement, strive to be aware of children's individual needs, and communicate with parents about their children's progress (Jennings).

Contracts are also an important part of the Accelerated Schools program, which aims to bring the achievement of disadvantaged children up to grade level by the end of sixth grade. Parents sign a written agreement that includes ensuring that children go to bed at a reasonable hour and attend school regularly and punctually. Teachers' obligations include keeping parents informed about students' performance. "The purpose," says Accelerated Schools founder Henry Levin, "is to emphasize the importance of the parental role through the dignity of a written agreement that is affirmed by all parties" (Jennings).

Home Visits

Carol Ascher (1987) states that only one study has tried to directly compare school-based parent involvement with home-based parent involvement among low-income families. "In this study," she reports, "programs offering home visits were more successful in involving disadvantaged parents than were programs requiring parents to visit the school."

Since most families want to help their children learn, schools should reach out to families in their homes and neighborhoods to provide information, materials, and guidance to the large constituency that does not come to school, say D'Angelo and Adler.

Home visits say, "We care about you." If teachers make visits before school starts, a child has the chance to become acquainted with his or her teacher before school begins. A sense of belonging is especially important to an at-risk child. Home visits set a tone of mutual understanding that makes subsequent school/home communication more successful. For example, family crises that occur during the year can be dealt with more successfully if a home visit has been made prior to the beginning of the school year (Wolf and Stephens 1989).

Benefits of Home Visits

SCHOOLS

The benefits of home visits are that the school can:

1. Gain insight into parent/child relationships

2. Obtain specific information about the student that is of value in providing motivation

3. Observe situations that might forecast potential changes or account for problems that have already taken place

4. Provide information and support to the parents

5. Learn more about the home environment and how the school and personnel are perceived by the family (Decker and Decker 1988)

"Principals who encourage and even require the making of home visits," say Wolf and Stephens, "find that the parents are more likely to become allies with the teacher and administrative staff on behalf of the child's learning experience. Parents who welcome a teacher into the home gain a more positive attitude and are more supportive of the school."

PARENTS

The benefits of home visits are that parents can:

1. Meet on a more relaxed basis and communicate in the security and comfort of their own home

2. Have the opportunity to ask questions of an educator, social worker, or other parent volunteer

3. Talk about problems or frustrations that require direct observation

4. Ask how to help the student at home

5. Learn more about the American public school system (Decker and Decker)

Both parents and schools, then, benefit from home visits. Project or parent coordinators can learn a great deal about the home setting and interaction of parents and children. Brice Heath argues that "just as parents can be helped in their parenting functions, teachers' effectiveness can be enhanced by learning from parents how they teach. This can help make teachers' instructional styles more harmonious with those the children have grown up with" (cited in Ascher).

How To Conduct a Home Visit

Home visits can cause anxiety for both parents and teachers or coordinators. Most parents have little or no experience with school personnel coming into their homes and are uncertain about what to expect. Likewise, many school personnel have no training or experience in making home visits and are often apprehensive about how they will be received.

"No single format is appropriate for every home visitation," say Decker and Decker. "However, for the visit to have a successful outcome, the liaisons must go into the homes with open minds, positive attitudes, and the belief that parents have something of value to contribute."

Nicolau and Ramos offer more specific advice. For instance, home visits are essential with high-risk families who have multiple problems. The first visit, they say, is crucial in setting the tone and establishing rapport: "No lectures, no teaching. Just a friendly chat. Be a good listener and

TELEPHONES

The telephone is being used to reach out to parents. School districts such as San Diego and Indianapolis have established homework hotlines for students and parents.

• In Casey County, Kentucky, some classrooms have been outfitted with portable phones to make it easier for parents and teachers to contact one another.

• The Chapter 1 program in Omaha, Nebraska, has established a telephone service called the Chapter 1 Talk Box. Callers hear a three-minute message about books and reading. Messages are changed twice a week and correspond with lessons in the classroom (D'Angelo and Adler).

• At Lincoln Prep High School in San Diego, the school helps students and their families find needed community services through a school-sponsored telephone referral system (Chrispeels).

• In Connecticut, ten schools have been using the telephone as a constant link between schools and families. As part of a pilot program offered by the Southern New England Telecommunications Corporation, several classrooms have been equipped with a phone-message service that can send recorded messages of any length simultaneously to all students, or to any parent individually. Parents can also leave messages to which the teacher responds. Teacher Madeline Mongillo uses the system to send messages to parents about each day's assignments and activities. It replaces the old paper messages, she says, that often would get lost in students' book bags.

draw out dialog from the parents. This will help you to learn more about them, and about their needs. Acknowledge the difficulty of being a parent in today's world. Share a personal example with the family to help the process."

When the parents begin to open up, that's the time to let them know that help is available (such as child care, interpreting, family counseling referrals, ESL classes, transportation, and parenting help). However, keep in mind that it may take time for some high-risk families to feel at ease and ask for help. For these families, they suggest many visits, keeping in touch by telephone on a weekly basis, and leaving a telephone number and stating when you can be reached.

Requirements for a Home Visitor Program

Davies (1991), who has experience with home visits through his Schools Reaching Out project, suggests the following requirements for a home visitor program:

1. A definition of parent involvement that isn't limited to the school building, plus viewing families as sources of strength.

2. Funds to pay the home visitors. He suggests using Chapter 1 funds or funds for bilingual education.

3. Training must be provided to the home visitors. Colleges, universities, and social service agencies are likely sources to help home visitors see their responsibilities and the skills they will need.

4. A modest amount of supervision and support is needed. The principal or parent coordinator, for example, must oversee the program and supervise the home visitors.

5. Administrators and teachers must be willing to communicate with home visitors so that their work in students' homes will be closely linked to classroom and school objectives.

For examples of home visits and how they helped children and families, compared to families who did not receive them, see chapter 16, which discusses preschool programs. Home visits are often an integral part of school programs at this level.

A HOME VISITOR PROGRAM

At the David A. Ellis School in Roxbury, Massachusetts, a home visitor program has been established under the Schools Reaching Out (SRO) project. Personnel recently reached seventy-five families who had had little contact with the school but said they would welcome such visitors.

The school recruited four women from the community to serve as the home visitors. They all had experience in community work, were paid $10 an hour, and visited four to five families a week. What did these home visitors do?

• They provided information to families about school expectations, curriculum, rules, and requirements.

• They dispensed advice and materials on how family members could help children with schoolwork.

• They reinforced the school's "Raise a Reader" program, in which parents were encouraged to read regularly to their children at home.

• They provided information and referrals on topics ranging from housing and health services to summer camps and childrearing.

• They listened to family members' concerns and discovered family needs and interests, which they in turn conveyed to the teachers.

• They met with groups of teachers and discussed strategies with them for helping with homework, dealing with parents' questions about schoolwork, and fostering children's language development.

The home visitor program in the demonstration Ellis school was one component of a three-part strategy for schools that want to move toward partnership with at-risk families. It can be easily adapted by almost any school.

Source: Adapted from Davies (1991)

Other Forms of Communication

Joyce Epstein (interviewed by Brandt 1989) emphasizes that communication must be in a language that parents can understand. If at all possible, home visits or personal contact with a family of another culture should be made by a person who speaks the language of the family that is being visited. If this is not possible, using interpreters is the next best option.

"We need to know not only whether messages are going home," Epstein says, "but who understands them and who does not, and who we are reaching and who we are not reaching, and why."

She suggests other ways of reaching parents who can't come to workshops or meetings: audio recordings, videotapes, newsletters, and cable TV shows. According to Nicolau and Ramos, these methods may have an impact, but probably only after an initial personal contact has been made.

Good communication also involves keeping parents informed about student performance. Schools working to involve parents notify them as soon as a student's performance begins to slip or whenever a student has done something well. Some schools regularly send home personal letters about students' problems and accomplishments. Some programs also provide students with a special folder in which to carry home schoolwork and notes from the teacher at the end of each week.

Two-Way Communication

With at-risk families, communication usually begins with the school as initiator—that is, from school to home. But in keeping with the premise that all families have strengths and that we must build on those strengths, communication needs to be a two-way street. Thus communication must also flow from home to school; home must somehow be brought into the school.

Ascher says that "70 percent of the research on programs in which school-to-home influence predominated showed positive effects on student achievement. On the other hand, all of the programs stressing mutual influence had positive results."

COMPUTERS

• Some schools are offering take-home computers to assist students in learning at home. Sometimes these are used in literacy programs or ESL training. Computers are often checked out on a revolving basis from the schools. A take-home computer program assists Appalachian students and their parents in improving students' skill levels in reading and mathematics.

• Fort Lupton, Colorado, has a project titled "United Partners" that features a computerized database of community resources. Training in the use of the database is offered to parents, as well as to students and school personnel. The program has also installed a model technological system that links selected homes of special populations with the schools to give them more access to information and to ensure equal opportunities for high-quality education.

Source: Adapted from Christopher T. Cross and others (1991)

Bringing the home into the classroom is part of the Schools Reaching Out (SRO) program. It encourages activities that incorporate family issues, experiences, and cultural traditions into the school curriculum. "One-way transmission of information from the school to the home runs the risk of continuing a deficit attitude toward families," states Krasnow (1990). "The cultural norms, traditions, and issues within the home have a place in the classroom." In Washington, D.C., for example, a summer day camp project recruits Hispanic parents to share their cultural resources—languages, songs, stories, and crafts—with the children (Nicolau and Ramos).

Volunteers and the Culture of the School

Lily Wong Fillmore attributes the failure of many working-class white and minority background children to a poor match between experiences at home and those at school. She recommends greater accommodation by the school to the cultural patterns of students in the way in which instruction is presented and organized, the models of teaching used, the structure of the learning and social environments of the classroom, and the roles and relationships of students and teachers (Council of Chief State School Officers 1989).

Another way of bringing home into school is to have parents volunteer in the classroom. "It is important to recognize that the presence of parents in the school not only provides more adults to teach reading or offer help and support to the children but also transforms the *culture* of the school," says Ziegler.

Lightfoot (1978) points out that with mothers present, for instance, there is no way that the curriculum and environment can remain unchanged:

> Even if the content of the lesson appears the same on paper, the transmission of the lesson takes on a different quality and character when presented by mothers. Even if the concepts are unfamiliar and alien to the child's experience, the mother-teacher style of interaction, her face, and her character are not strange. It feels like home. (Cited by Ziegler)

In effective school-home contact, both settings are changed. When a parent involvement program is successful, says Ziegler, "changes occur at home and at school, so that the two environments become more similar and familiar to children." Besides using parents as volunteers to make schools more home-like, Ziegler also suggests parent rooms or parent centers in the school, which also makes schools more inviting to parents. To learn more about parent centers, see chapter 14.

How parent involvement develops depends both on the ease and extent of two-way communication between parents and schools, Bronfenbrenner stresses. While he acknowledges that schools must often serve as the initiators, parents must not be merely passive recipients: for parent involvement to really work, they must be cocommunicators.

Chapter 9

HOME ATMOSPHERE: ATTITUDES AND EXPECTATIONS

"*C*learly, all parents communicate important values about school and learning to their children," says Krasnow (1990). "These determine and shape a child's view of learning. Closer family-school connections, shared values, and mutual respect can positively influence school success."

A positive atmosphere in the home—characterized by such things as parents' high aspirations for their children, a belief in hard work and discipline, and the availability of good reading materials—is the strongest predictor of high student achievement. According to Martin Orland, home atmosphere explains more of the variation in student achievement than do parental income levels or socioeconomic status. But, of course, home atmosphere and family income levels are themselves linked; in the homes of far too many poor people, little value is placed on education.

Orland says that home atmosphere may vary dramatically, depending on the length and depth of a family's poverty. "That is why," he says, "the entrenched nature of poverty in some portions of the population—and mounting evidence that certain behavior trends, such as teenage motherhood,

may be accelerating the intergenerational transfer of that poverty—are of such concern to educators" (cited in Reeves 1988).

Home environment is one of the most powerful predictors of school achievement. The continuing low scores of many urban children in both reading and math suggests the need for richer home experiences. Hence the growing interest today in learning that takes place in the home.

Parent Attitudes

"Throughout their children's growing years," says Joan A. Newman (1989), "parents of the most successful children model behaviors most likely to help them do well." Some characteristics of parents whose children succeed include taking an interest in their children's interests, listening to their children and being responsive to them, and respecting them even when they make mistakes.

In addition, Benjamin Bloom's (1985) landmark study of people who had attained a world-class level of achievement throws light on other important beliefs and attitudes. He consistently found that home environment was critical for excellence. These "successful" families shared a number of characteristics:

1. They were hard-working.
2. They believed in doing one's best, whatever the task.
3. They believed that everyone, including the children, should use time productively and set goals.
4. They emphasized self-discipline and that work comes before play.

Effort Versus Ability

Bloom found that achievement of these people was due less to superior talent than to hard work and encouragement from families and teachers. This may also be part of the reason that some cultures or groups of at-risk families do better than others. Both effort and ability can affect school performance.

Japanese children spend more time in school than American children and have more hours of homework. But parent attitudes may be the primary reason they are more successful.

Working Mothers magazine asked mothers in Minneapolis/St. Paul, Minnesota, and mothers in Taiwan and Japan what accounts for a child's success in school—luck, natural ability, or effort? Chinese and Japanese mothers said effort was the most important element, whereas American mothers responded that ability was the key (Amundson 1988).

"That's enormously important," said Marc Tucker of the Carnegie Forum on Education and the Economy. "If you think natural ability is the source of achievement, you don't have to do much." For example, he suggested that "you don't have to pay attention to curriculum content, or how much TV children watch, or what demands you make on them, or how much support you give." In contrast, Tucker noted, if you think effort is most important, you emphasize all of those things (Amundson).

Why Asian Children May Do Well

Parents who think that effort is the key to success expect their children to learn. That may be why so many Asian immigrant children do so well. Amy Tan's novel, *The Joy Luck Club*, gives examples in the Chinese-American community that address this question. The mothers in this novel stress the importance of effort with their daughters. One mother thought that her daughter could do or be anything in America if she just tried. When her daughter didn't become the concert pianist that the mother had hoped for, the mother said, in effect, "You could be genius. You just not try."

For at-risk kids, belief in the importance of effort may be central to success. When parents believe in effort—or can be taught to raise their expectations for their children—then children expect more of themselves and are more self-confident. These changes lead to more successful experiences in school, as well as in the community.

(Of course, there is a dark side to the emphasis many Asian parents place on their children's achievement. Some Asian youth experience inordinate psychological stress because they feel they cannot meet their parents' expectations. In motivating children to excel in school, as in all areas of life, moderation is a virtue.)

The Power of Reinforcement and Modeling

When the community and family reinforce what is presented in school, students are more likely to see the two environments of home and school as related. When there is an obvious link between school and community, the impact is even greater.

Reinforcement of what the school is teaching happens when parents become involved in their child's school and what he or she is studying and learning. When at-risk parents are taught how to help their children at home and how to make modifications in their home environment, they are reinforcing not only what their children are learning, but also conveying the attitude that learning and school are important.

Suzanne Ziegler (1987) examines why parental reinforcement has such a powerful effect on children's achievement. Since children spend so much time at home, the people there (parents, siblings, grandparents) are powerful models who may or may not reinforce messages like "reading is a desirable way to spend time" or "talking about things helps you to understand them better" or "being observant is a good thing." When they do, and when these messages are consistent with those given by teachers, children are far more likely to absorb them. When learning isn't reinforced it is extinguished, and home reinforcement may be essential, especially for young children.

There is the story of the Asian immigrant families who would buy two sets of textbooks, one for their child and one for themselves, so that the mother could study to help her child do well in school. These families were modeling that school was important and reinforcing it by working with their children.

Family Activities: The Curriculum of the Home

R. M. Clark's research (1983 and 1987) illustrates that family activity patterns of successful students are consistent. High achievers tend to be involved in a number of enrichment activities. In contrast, the family activities of underachievers focus on passivity and leisure; learning activities are lacking. In addition, students who are unsupervised or primarily involved in home activities such as play or viewing television are more likely to be underachievers.

However, what H. J. Walberg (1984) calls "the curriculum of the home"—such things as leisure activities, reading, and family conversations on everyday events—is alterable. According to Oliver C. Moles (1990), several programs and practices to help parents strengthen the home environment have been shown to be successful in raising achievement levels among children from low-income and minority families.

Parenting Styles

Sanford Dornbusch and others (1987) have found that parenting styles produce significant variations in student achievement. Across ethnic groups, educational levels, and family structures, he consistently found that authoritarian styles and switching from one style to the other are associated with the lowest grades. Permissive parents are

HOW CAN SCHOOLS ASSIST IN ENRICHING HOME ATMOSPHERE?

• *Volunteering.* When parents assist in a classroom, even if it isn't their own child's, it is probable that "by training the parent to teach in the school setting, the teacher can anticipate that the parent will transfer to the home environment some of his knowledge about stimulating the growth of the...child" (Ziegler).

• *Parent Education and Home Learning.* See chapter 13 for the ways in which parent education can alter the home environment. Home learning is a wonderful way to enrich the curriculum of the home. The Committee for Economic Development states that programs should teach parents how to provide a home environment that encourages learning.

• *Home Visits.* Home visits, as seen in Project Hope (see chapter 15), can produce a dramatic change in home atmosphere. Children of parents who participated in the Perry Preschool Program had better grades, fewer absences, and fewer special education placements during their public school years than did a control group of children whose parents did not participate in the program. "A change in the home environment which supports student achievement," explains Krasnow, "occurs as parents become more familiar with program expectations and the importance of their role as supportive parents."

the next lowest, and what he calls "authoritative" parents (strong but open to discussion and negotiation) are associated with the highest grades.

He concludes that parenting style is a more powerful predictor of student achievement than parent education, ethnicity, or family structure. He has not yet, however, presented data showing that low-income students from "authoritative" homes do as well in school as middle-class students.

Thomas E. Hart (1988) gives an example of how these parenting styles might differ in response to children's grades. The authoritarians would likely punish their children for bad grades; for good grades, they would tell them to do better. Permissive parents seem indifferent to grades, don't stress working hard, have no rules about TV, and usually aren't involved in education. Authoritative parents, however, would respond to good grades with praise, to bad grades with restrictions or offers of help and encouragement.

Authoritative parents tell kids to look at both sides of an issue and admit that children sometimes know more. All family members participate in decisions.

Dornbusch says that children of authoritative parents are more socially responsible, more independent, and exhibit more developed social and cognitive skills (cited in Olson 1990).

In a study of ten poor African-American families, Clark (1983) also found that parenting styles were a key to achievement and that the authoritative style (or what Clark terms "sponsored independence") is associated with students who do well in school regardless of social and economic backgrounds.

"His study strongly suggests that a family's overall cultural style—not the more commonly used variables of marital status, educational level, income, or social class—determines whether or not children are prepared to perform well in school," says Anne Henderson (1988).

The question arises, Can parenting styles be taught or influenced through parenting education, which is a component of many parent involvement programs? If so, some at-risk families may already have authoritative styles of parenting that are a good foundation to build on.

Family Involvement Programs Can Help

Programs for involving at-risk families can help enrich what parents already do "naturally" in the home to socialize their children and help prepare them for school, says Ascher. "One might say," she concludes, that the aim of educators is "to increase school effectiveness by improving the assistance they receive from parents at home."

Ziegler says that an important message of research is that school personnel *can* intervene positively to teach at-risk parents to be more effective. Families are *not* unalterable, she stresses:

> Research indicates that the attitudes of parents who have felt unimportant and powerless and the academic outcomes for their children who are performing poorly in school can be changed, by parent involvement which is well-planned and lasting.

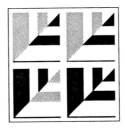

Chapter 10

PREPARATION: GETTING CHILDREN READY FOR SCHOOL

The fact that many children arrive at school apparently more difficult to teach has made it natural for educators to want to improve the preparation of students for school," says Ascher (1987).

Some children entering first grade from low socioeconomic homes come from impoverished backgrounds and lack the necessary motor, cognitive, and social/emotional developmental experiences that help ensure success in school.

Because of their own limited schooling, poor parents may not be able to provide the learning experiences that foster successful entry into school. Says Kurtz (1988):

> Parents of children in poverty have a low literacy rate, rely on electronic media rather than printed media, and find it difficult to afford educational materials, toys, and books. Thus poor children frequently enter school without readiness skills, often with physical and mental handicaps, and are at risk for school adjustment problems. Some kids reach kindergarten, for instance, without having been read to or even talked to and can interact with other children only by hitting them.

Children from Other Cultures Are Often Unprepared

Preparing children for the American public school system has been difficult for many at-risk families, but particularly so for those from other cultures. Why is this so? For one thing, parents who want their children to succeed in American schools must do certain things in the preschool years to produce in their children the skills that kindergartners are expected to have mastered.

Yet many other cultures may not stress these practices. "Although they teach their children essential social skills such as cooperation," say Nicolau and Ramos (1990),

> most low-income Hispanic parents are unaware of specific practices—such as talking and reading to children and encouraging their curiosity—that lay the academic skills foundation. These practices begin at home, and must be carried out by a child's first and most important teachers—the parents.

Low-income Hispanic parents may not realize the value of out-of-school educational activities, such as trips to parks, zoos, museums, and libraries that may provide a base for understanding the larger world and may reinforce what children learn in class.

While most Hispanic parents understand that children should do their homework, few are aware, say Nicolau and Ramos, that school-age children should spend up to twenty hours a week engaged in constructive learning activities outside the classroom, such as reading for fun, writing, pursuing hobbies, watching educational television, talking with adults about the day's events, spending leisure time with the family and going on family outings, and participating in sports.

However, Nicolau and Ramos are optimistic:

Knowing how to help your child succeed in the U.S. school system is an acquired skill and can be learned. Many low-income Hispanic parents— like other poor parents—are unaware of the crucial role they can play in supporting their children's sense of accomplishment and self-esteem.

Schools Uninformed about Other Cultures

Many teachers are uninformed about other cultures. They have values and expectations that stem from their own backgrounds and from teaching middle-class children. Frequently teachers don't know where to begin with a child who has been socialized differently from middle-class children.

Comments from two teachers of Hispanic children illustrate areas of misunderstanding: "Where have they been all their lives? The children don't know anything. They come into kindergarten without knowing colors or numbers. They can't hold a pencil." And: "The children are unresponsive. They won't look adults in the eye, and they refuse to participate in class unless directly called upon" (Nicolau and Ramos).

Hispanic parents comment in turn: "The teachers are professional people. They know what is best for my child." Or: "I teach my children to behave like the teacher says and not be asking questions or talking too much. She says my child is too quiet. I don't understand. My child is good" (Nicolau and Ramos).

TWO SUCCESSFUL HISPANIC PROJECTS

TEXAS. One project in Texas schools (pre-K and kindergarten) ran an Intensive Training Institute for Hispanic families. Although most families had expressed a willingness to assist their children and prepare them for school, most did not feel capable (45 percent of the parents did not have a high school diploma).

The project's goal was to train the parents to meet the educational and emotional needs of their children and to become involved in their children's education year-round.

To do this, they held an informal week-long Intensive Training Institute for interested parents. At the institute, Hispanic parents received information about child growth and development, motivation and self-esteem, and the process and techniques of language development. Parents also learned about the school system.

The institute was followed by monthly workshops on what children are expected to learn in kindergarten. The program was so successful that the mothers requested another training session for fathers and other relatives. By the end of the project period, fifty-three parents were actively participating in school activities.

BOSTON. A Boston K-1 school created Classroom-Based Activity Centers for Parents where parents were allowed to sit in on their children's classes once a week. This gave them a firsthand understanding of their children's day and helped them become familiar with the curriculum and their children's interactions. Parents were then able to reinforce at home what the children were learning in school. Parents took pride in watching their children, and the children liked having their mothers at school.

Source: Adapted from Nicolau and Ramos (1990)

THE LAFAYETTE PARISH EARLY CHILDHOOD PROJECT

By the end of the first project year, the creators of the Lafayette Parish Early Childhood Project hoped that 80 percent of the parents of preschool children would report specific knowledge of how children learn and understand the types of experience that foster physical growth, social/emotional growth, and academic readiness. The project was successful in meeting these goals.

It's interesting to note that the project was designed specifically for those children not accepted by Head Start, who thus had greatest need for this kind of program. The children participating were described as "high risk," and the population was heavily weighted in terms of African-American males.

Project personnel say there is always a tremendous gap between what is acceptable at home and the demands of the classroom. Given the socioeconomic background of these children, project teachers were not surprised that at the end of the academic year 39 percent of the thirty-one children in the project still demonstrated behaviors that their teachers felt would interfere with learning in kindergarten. Alexander and Lovelace conclude that support services should be provided for preschool children and their teachers to help the children acquire social skills appropriate for the classroom.

Parents appeared to be well informed at the end of the project about how much their children had learned. Specific accomplishments parents noticed in their children included:

1. Learning to get along with other children.

2. Learning to express themselves orally.

3. Recognizing letters of the alphabet, colors, and shapes.

4. Learning to write their names.

5. Improved ability to count and recognize numbers.

6. Improved listening skills.

7. Improved social skills (including better manners). Every parent surveyed felt this preschool experience would definitely help his or her child do better in kindergarten next year.

One parent explained that the teacher helped her to know what kind of behavior is appropriate for children at different ages, and each parent expressed satisfaction with his or her child's increased social awareness and ability to get along with family members and peers. In terms of readiness, all parents interviewed felt they had acquired valuable skills and information to help their children.

Several comments from parents in the project show how much these kinds of programs are needed:

• "It may seem like common sense things but little kids don't know them and they won't learn them unless we talk to them and teach them. I thought kids learned these things by themselves, but they don't."

• "They showed us how to do things and I'll do it with my baby because they showed us how."

• "It helped me to be a better parent—like teaching them and learning to do things with them—things I never realized."

Source: Adapted from Shirley Alexander and Terry Lovelace (1988)

Differences Stem from Countries of Origin

While most Hispanic parents want their children to succeed in school, they are simply behaving in a manner consistent with the way they were expected to in the countries in which they or their parents were born.

As it's been said, the U.S. school system assumes that parents will take some responsibility for their children's success in school by preparing them for school—teaching basic skills and later reinforcing what goes on in the classroom. Many white middle-class parents do this.

But in the countries of origin of most low-income Hispanic and migrant parents, the roles of parents and school are sharply divided: "Parents have a serious duty to instill respect and proper behavior in their children. *That is a parent's job.* It is the school's job to instill knowledge. *Teaching is not the parents' business*" (Nicolau and Ramos). Thus the majority of low-income Hispanic parents simply "hand over" their children—neat and respectful—to be educated.

As an example of cultural differences, consider that for Hispanics "respectful" often means not looking adults in the eye, not speaking to adults unless spoken to, and not asking questions. Casual conversations between parents and children are not the norm in most poor Hispanic homes.

Most Hispanic children are deeply loved, claim Nicolau and Ramos,

> but the parents' deep sense of responsibility to instill proper behavior and respect, and to protect the children from a world they themselves do not fully understand, frequently hinders their ability and willingness to build on their traditional parenting practices to include the skills that prepare children for success in the U.S. system.

Language Delay

Language delay is one of the most serious obstacles that many low-income Hispanic children (and other at-risk children) must overcome when they enter school. The typical Hispanic child is the good, obedient child. Yet conditioning them to be quiet among adults also conditions them to be nonverbal.

Different cultural norms, combined with the fact that these parents often do not read to their children, contribute to children from other cultures having underdeveloped language skills. "This is a challenge for any child," state Nicolau and Ramos, "but those who simultaneously must learn a new language *and* catch up on language development in general are truly disadvantaged at the starting line."

Parenting Behaviors Can Change

But there is hope. Projects that the Hispanic Development Policy Project funded (see Nicolau and Ramos) revealed that parent behavior and parenting styles *are* subject to change.

The partnerships created an awareness among the involved parents that they must play a greater part in their children's education. The projects familiarized parents with the skills that children require to be successful in school and showed them how they could promote acquisition of those skills.

Schools, in turn, learned to communicate cross-culturally and to build on the many strengths that Hispanic parents already have.

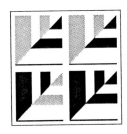

Chapter 11

HOME LEARNING:
THE WAVE OF THE FUTURE

*H*ome learning has become very popular recently. Once considered the most difficult kind of family involvement, this is becoming the most relevant type of involvement for families, schools, and student learning.

Reasons for Popularity of Home Learning

As Ascher (1987) says, "When parents' time is limited, becoming involved in home-learning is one of the most efficient uses of their time." But there are other valid reasons to pursue home learning, too.

For one thing, parent surveys indicate that this is a high priority for them (Krasnow 1990). Also, direct involvement in school activities isn't feasible for all working parents, single parents, or parents who have had negative experiences with schools.

Indeed, there are interesting differences between single parents and two-parent families. Joyce Epstein (Council of Chief State School Officers

1989) found that single parents spend more time helping their children in the home, whereas two-parent families spend more time helping teachers at school. Home learning activities seem to be a particularly good tool for single parents.

Research also shows positive effects of home learning: "Children given this support by families will excel far beyond their classmates who do not get this type of support," states the Council of Chief State School Officers (CCSSO). In addition, Janet Chrispeels (1991) reports that parent involvement projects using a traditional school-based format have been shown to have less impact on student achievement than programs that train parents to work with their children at home.

Home learning can be very cost effective compared to other programs. Ziegler (1987) gives the example of a simple series of specific, practical activities for home learning that was developed jointly by parents and teachers of grade 1 children who had less than average measured ability. The activities successfully built in family interaction and increased children's achievement without duplicating school activities. The cost of this program was $4.83 per student per year. In contrast, the cost for special instruction would have been $563 per student per year.

Reinforcement for the Work of the School

Dorothy Rich, founder and president of the Home and School Institute, has been working with home materials for the past twenty-five years. She says that parent involvement should no longer be defined as involvement only in the school setting, which usually takes the form of attending meetings and spending time at school. Not very many parents, especially employed mothers, can participate in this way anymore. But we need not despair. What we need to care about is involving families in children's education well beyond the school setting (Rich 1987).

Rich adds that children learn before school hours, after school, and on weekends and vacations. Yet there are still parents and teachers who are not yet aware of what can be done to help children at home. She stresses that parents need to learn how important they are and what they can do to help and that teachers need to be familiar with the research about families as educators.

Rich advocates learning activities at home (see sidebar next page) that reinforce and support but don't duplicate the work of the school. Her position, she says, is to mobilize the strengths that exist in every family into effective educational action, including at-risk families who simply need help to make the most of the time and resources they have (Rich 1986).

Teacher Attitudes

"To involve parents more often and more productively," argues Joyce Epstein,

> requires changing the major location of parent involvement from the school to the home, changing the emphasis from general policies to specific skills, and changing the major target from the general population of students or school staff to the individual child at home. (Quoted in Jennings, August 1, 1990)

However, says Chrispeels, most schools still want parents to come to them rather than going to the parents. Most of the efforts, she adds, have been directed at "fixing" parents rather than at changing school structures and practices.

A 1982 study of home/school relations showed that elementary teachers do not favor parent involvement in teaching at home (Newman 1989). However, those teachers in the study who did encourage home activity were able to work successfully with all socioeconomic levels. Teacher leadership, not the educational background or marital status of the parents, was the key to success.

Home learning activities can be extensions of what the child is learning in the classroom by helping the child develop specific skills in various subjects. Often these home learning activities are conducted in consultation with the classroom teacher. Or home learning activities can deal with basic attitudes and motivation.

The literature is full of techniques and tools for involving parents in developing both general and specific skills that are immediately applicable to the classroom. However, teachers may need training to know how to work with parents in using these materials.

Epstein is one of several experts nationwide who have developed models to help parents help their children at home with school-related skills. She also trains teachers to use these activities. Her program, Teachers Involve Parents in Schoolwork (TIPS), offers training for teachers to involve elementary and middle-school parents in their children's homework assignments. TIPS targets mathematics and science instruction at the elementary level and social studies instruction in middle school. The goal is to help teachers guide parents through structured homework assignments that must be completed by parent and child together.

Parent Competence

What about at-risk families? Can home learning really work with them?

DOROTHY RICH: HOME LEARNING PIONEER

Dorothy Rich, founder of the Home and School Institute, Inc., has been pressing for increased parent involvement at home for more than two decades.

What are Home and School Institute learning materials? They are like recipes, says Rich (1986), designed to teach reading, writing, and math in creative ways: "They do what the finest schools cannot do. They put the parent and child together for a few minutes each day to learn from one another and to talk together."

Six thousand families used these materials in 1985, and more schools and programs are being added each year. Responses, Rich says, have been remarkably similar, even though the materials have been used in disparate communities. In one survey, 99 percent of the parents said that the activities helped them spend enjoyable time with their children and 98 percent said they felt their children learned something useful doing them (Rich 1986).

Rich has created the MegaSkills Education Center, which offers parent training workshops across the country. The center draws on ideas from her book *MegaSkills: How Families Can Help Children Succeed in School and Beyond* (1988).

These "megaskills," as Rich calls them, include confidence, perseverance, teamwork, responsibility, and problem solving. The program teaches parents to provide their children with the motivation, basic skills, and attitudes to succeed in school. Students whose parents have participated in the program have shown improvement in reading, reasoning, and visual-aural skills, according to Rich (Jennings, August 1, 1990).

"Our programs, especially the MegaSkills workshops, reach out and make a big difference with at-risk youth," says Rich (personal correspondence, May 27, 1990). Here are some comments about how at-risk parents or families have been affected by MegaSkills programs:

- In Tampa, Florida, migrant families were targeted for program services by the American Red Cross. At the year's end, parents said, "This is the most wonderful thing we have ever seen!"

- From Petersburg, West Virginia: "The interaction between the parents was very open, honest, and unaffected—from the superintendent of the schools to the parents who didn't finish high school."

- From a single parent in Denver: "Not only has the program given me ideas on how to help my children, but it has also told me that I was already doing a lot right. The program gave me confidence."

- From the director of a Chapter 1 program in Bennetsville, North Carolina: "As I greeted parents at the sign-in desk I realized two of them could not read or write. I grouped them with parents they knew and everyone was comfortable and at ease."

- From a director of the programs for single parents and Chapter 1 groups: "Parents tell me they need the sessions; they seem so appreciative....The program helps get them thinking about what actually makes a person confident, motivated, and responsible." (Rich, "What People Are Saying about the New Partnerships/MegaSkills Curriculum")

Rich has worked with parents from all kinds of backgrounds, including bilingual parents, parents of severely handicapped children, divorced parents, and parents in Chapter 1 programs. "Across the states," she says,

> we have successfully reached thousands of what have been called "hard to reach" families. These families, who may not go to meetings in schools because they are employed or otherwise school-avoidant, given encouragement and ideas on how to get involved directly with their child at home, prove to be dedicated and remarkably able home-style teachers for their children (Rich 1986).

The Importance of Literacy

However, the CCSSO has something slightly different to say about certain at-risk families and home learning:

> Despite organized efforts on the part of school staff, family involvement in learning activities is often circumscribed by the level of literacy in the home. If the level of literacy is low, families are unlikely to motivate their children to place high priority on reading and other literacy skills, and they will not be able to assist their children with the most basic tasks.

What's the answer then? "Improving the home learning environment through family education," the CCSSO goes on to say, "is one way to enhance family esteem as well as child achievement. Family literacy programs...are designed to break the intergenerational cycle of illiteracy by simultaneously addressing the basic skills deficits of both parent and child."

Reginald Clark (1983) describes how home curriculum "stimulates and reinforces children's literacy skills development by increasing their access to experiences that encourage them to utilize school-related texts, words, ideas, and strategies." Besides home study programs, other examples of "home curriculum" are leisure reading, enrichment programs, hobbies requiring special knowledge, and games.

Research shows, Clark says, that students must have active lifestyles and practice literacy skills beyond the school day in order to become firm and automatic with their literacy. Classroom instruction by itself is not enough to produce this "automaticity that leads to above average performance of high achievers and effective learners."

Clark supports this claim by contrasting the number of hours that successful students spend in desirable literacy experiences with the number of hours spent by nonsuccessful students. He also lists a number of parent-child interactions that enhance children's literacy skills. His work encourages schools to develop home learning models and work with families to implement an informal curriculum of the home that reinforces the literacy skills necessary for school achievement.

Ziegler (1987) says that considerable research supports the effectiveness of parent involvement at home. She describes home reading programs (see sidebar next page), in which parents and children read together on a regular basis with teacher support.

Disagreeing with those who say that parental literacy is a prerequisite for home learning, she states that "such programs are shown to be effective with parents of varied language backgrounds and with no or low as well as higher literacy skills." However, she adds that recent research suggests that such programs may be of limited effectiveness if they don't include active and recurring communication between home and school.

Activities for Parents with Low Literacy

Epstein (cited in Ziegler 1987) has other suggestions for parents with low or no literacy, such as watching a specific television program and discussing it afterwards or asking teachers to give an assignment where the children have to ask their parents questions. In addition, she suggests games and group activities related to the children's schoolwork and also certain techniques for using learning materials that can be explained to parents.

For example, in a California elementary school, where about half of the students are Hispanic, many parents questioned their ability to help students in academic matters (many of them had little or no formal education). Thus a variety of workshops are planned to train parents to use and develop instructional materials for school and home use. The first workshops were attended by fifty-two parents (only half that number was ex-

SAMPLE HOME READING PROGRAMS

Suzanne Ziegler (1987) notes that while there is evidence that high levels of home involvement have high payoff, it is also true that programs requiring little special training can be effective. Here are examples she cites:

1. Project STEP (Systematic Training for Effective Parenting) included parents representing all socioeconomic levels from four elementary schools. Parents signed a contract agreeing to meet with their child twice a week to discuss accomplishments, thoughts, and ideas, and to spend time each week with their child on a reading-related activity. Children in the STEP program gained twelve months in reading compared to the control group, where the average gain was one month.

2. A similar project was conducted in two schools whose students were described as "culturally deprived." Parents were asked to read to their children daily, to listen to their children read, and to provide a quiet time for reading and study. Over five months their overall gain was 5.4 months in reading compared to the 2.7 months in the comparison school.

3. In two innercity Toronto schools, parents of problem readers agreed to listen to their child read for twenty minutes every school night over a six-month period. Improvement was noted for all children whose parents remained committed during the period.

4. In a project in London, children in two different schools read to their parents on a regular basis. Their reading progress was compared to those students who were given extra reading help in small groups by an experienced teacher who worked four half-days in the school. Both groups were compared with a control group.

   All the groups were in multiethnic areas, and many of the parents did not read English or use it at home. However, it was found to be both feasible and practical to involve nearly all the parents in such a program. Almost without exception, it was also found that parents welcomed the project.

Researchers reported that parent involvement had a pronounced effect on the students' success in school. Children who read to their parents made significantly greater progress in reading than those who didn't engage in this type of literacy sharing.

Most interesting of all, the small group instruction with the reading specialist did not produce improvements comparable to those obtained from collaboration with parents. In addition, involvement between parents and the schools was effective for children at all levels of performance. Teachers also reported that the children showed an increased interest in school learning and were better behaved.

5. Borrow-a-Book and Read-and-Share are Toronto programs modeled after the London-based program mentioned above. They usually begin by asking parents to spend ten minutes a night reading to their child or listening to him or her read. Suggestions are made about how to be positive and encouraging. Parents who don't read English are reassured about the value and validity of the process, no matter what language is used.

6. "Paired Reading" has been very popular in England. Children choose books to read with their parents; parents provide support and corrective feedback. Parents and children can be trained in one group meeting. Then they contract to do Paired Reading for a certain period of time.

   Studies show that children involved in Paired Reading generally make three times the normal progress in reading comprehension. Socioeconomic status, according to Ziegler, has not been found to correlate with the success of the projects. Even in disadvantaged areas, she states that parent involvement has been sustained over long periods.

   However, Paired Reading, because of the corrective feedback given by the parent, isn't workable for parents whose own literacy is extremely limited. For these parents, other kinds of programs or parent education may be required.

pected) and the other one was equally successful (Nicolau and Ramos 1990).

Other Examples of Home Learning

At Project Ahead in Los Angeles, family educators go into disadvantaged homes and recruit parents to participate in their kids' home learning. The family educators establish rapport with the parents, assess the family circumstances and lifestyle, then develop a written plan of action for the family. This plan is discussed with the parents and modified if necessary. The family educators also obtain "partnership agreements" from the parents, visit with the child's teacher to discuss how the family is supporting the teacher's objectives, and conduct bimonthly visits to the home to carry out the activities listed in their plan of action (CCSSO).

The Schools Reaching Out (SRO) program in Boston and New York decided to focus on developing materials for parents to use at home with their children. These materials are brief, easy-to-do activities that enhance reading and math development. Teachers and project personnel work together to develop their own parent materials that will coincide with instructional goals. Home visitors, who are parents of children at the schools, are hired to meet with the parents at home, discuss school and family issues, and provide the at-home materials (Krasnow).

Some programs are sending teachers directly into students' homes to work with the families on home learning. Project Care in El Paso, Texas, for instance, provides substitutes for teachers who would like to visit parents at home during the school day. Gloria Barragan, project director, says teachers have been impressed by how eager even the most hard-to-reach parents were to work with their children, once they were shown how they could provide educational activities at home (Jennings, August 1, 1990).

Future of Home Learning with At-Risk Families

As Epstein says, home learning is the type of involvement most parents want more help with.

We've learned that we can greatly increase this type of involvement when teachers design homework to include parents on purpose.... Some homework once a week in some subjects or twice a week in other subjects should be designed to require students to talk with someone at home about an interesting, important, exciting part of schoolwork. (Interviewed by Brandt 1989)

Home learning is definitely an area that has great potential for at-risk families.

HIGH SCHOOL HOME LEARNING

There are very few examples of home learning or parent-as-tutor programs at the high school level. Ziegler (1987), however, cites a program aimed at involving parents of grade 11 students in their children's writing assignments. This program took place at an urban school where 90 percent of the students are nonwhite.

The teacher developed a set of worksheets for students on elements of style, developing paragraphs, and other elements of composition. Worksheets were also developed for parents, advising them both on how to help with writing in general (discussing ideas, encouraging dictionary use, and proofreading) and with specific assignments.

After fifteen weeks, students in the experimental group improved significantly more than the control group. "This improvement," says Ziegler, "was considerably larger for the students with lower achievement records, suggesting that high school students most at-risk for poor performance may stand to benefit very significantly from planned parental involvement in their work." The experiment also indicates the willingness of parents to involve themselves with their teenagers' education.

Chapter 12

DECISION-MAKING AND ADVOCACY: THE IMPORTANCE OF EMPOWERMENT

*E*mpowerment is an important factor to consider when designing programs to involve at-risk families. Low-income and minority parents often feel a sense of exclusion, low self-esteem, and hopelessness—attitudes that they pass on to their children.

One of the best ways to increase empowerment is to provide opportunities for parent participation in school decision-making. This participation builds the skills that lead to both individual and collective empowerment (Davies 1989).

It's easy to see how empowerment helps at-risk families who have often felt powerless. If they can feel some measure of control in their children's schooling and in the home environment, it will have a ripple effect, extending outward from themselves, to their children, and to their neighborhood and community.

For example, when parents get involved with their children's education, they often gain a greater sense of adequacy and self-worth. These positive feelings can sometimes motivate them to resume their own education. This, in turn, emphasizes the importance of education to their children. Parent involvement in education also can lead to community involvement, which can further raise parents' feelings of competence and motivate them to participate in the political process.

Is there evidence that parent involvement in school governance and decision-making has a significant effect on children's achievement? Michael Fullan (1982) says that "there is little evidence to suggest that other, non-instructional forms of parent involvement directly affect student learning in school." But Fullan asks whether this might be due to poorly implemented councils; if they worked as they should, would there then be a positive impact?

Several school programs have sought to give poor and minority parents, who have been disenfranchised by the educational system, a greater role in school decision-making.

Head Start

Head Start was the first large-scale, organized attempt to involve parents in the education of their children. The program is often cited by experts as one of the finest examples of early childhood care and education. But it would not be as successful without the parental component.

Along with other programs during the "War on Poverty," Head Start was initiated as a response to the influx of African-Americans and Hispanics into urban areas. The idea, according to Slaughter and Kuehne (1987-88), was to push children beyond the limitations of their families so that they would become more "middle-class." Early Head Start programs, say Slaughter and Kuehne, stressed parent involvement and participation in order to radically improve the child's home environment.

Eventually, for many low-income parents, Head Start became the basis for grassroots training in political participation and decision-making, something that in itself was very important to these parents and central to the success of the children. Ultimately, Head Start empowered the parents, which, in turn, positively affected their children.

In the beginning, the program encompassed the social and political empowerment of parents and parent education. Over time, the latter focus has prevailed. Several experts would argue, however, that empowerment is equally important for parents helping their at-risk children.

"Parents are eager to learn how to help their children and improve their parenting skills if their self-esteem and cultural heritage are respected, and if they are permitted to make decisions for the program," says Avern Moore, executive director of the Institute of Community Services, a Head Start grant recipient in Holly Springs, Mississippi (Cohen 1990).

The Early Childhood and Family Education Program

A good example of the ripple effect of empowerment is the Early Childhood and Family Education Program (ECFEP), established in an economically depressed neighborhood in Albuquerque, New Mexico, through a process termed "respectful intervention" (Council of Chief State School Officers 1989). The staff looked for strengths in the community and wanted to learn from participating families how best to structure a program that would reflect the community's needs.

Although residents of the community were aware of their problems, they seldom realized their strengths. As Maria Chavez, project director, says, parents "do not know they are the experts on their needs and those of their families and children. Nor are they aware of the importance of their role as their children's prime educators, and of their unique ability to perform this crucial responsibility" (CCSSO).

By allowing parents to participate in the decision-making process and also to serve as teachers in the preschools, ECFEP soon found that parents were designing curriculum and setting policies as well. And they were realizing their ability to accomplish these tasks.

Parents enrolled in the program also began to see new opportunities for themselves in other areas. For instance, many returned to school to obtain GED certificates or specialized job training, or they enrolled in the local university. Program parents also initiated community action by petitioning for better school transportation, effective police patrols, and better cleanup services.

Other Programs

Family Matters at Cornell University stresses empowerment as one of the keys to overcoming social class and cultural barriers to parent involvement in the schools. Empowerment has been defined as a process through which people become more able to influence those individuals and organizations that affect their lives; it also helps in removing obstacles that get in the way of achieving equal status in our society (Davies 1988).

Davies' Schools Reaching Out program aims at increasing family empowerment through a home-based support program (involving home visits), support-network development, and use of community resources. One of the reasons empowerment is needed, says Davies, is that Americans need to rebuild a sense of competence and confidence in dealing with institutions in the face of increasing powerlessness and manipulation caused by our postindustrial society (Hamilton-Lee 1988).

Henry Levin's Accelerated Schools model sets specific achievement goals for all children to meet by the end of their elementary years. In addition, the program stresses changes in school management. Parents play central resource roles in Levin's schools and collaborate with teachers in making important school decisions.

"Unless we can create schools in which...there are decisions that parents can make that have meaning for their children," says Levin, "parental involvement must necessarily be limited" (Jennings, August 1, 1990). Jennings adds that involving parents in decision-making at the Accelerated Schools has often proven problematic because of the turf conflicts between educators and parents.

The School Development Program

James Comer, a Yale University psychiatrist, and his colleagues in several states have been working to reform schools that serve poor and minority children. Comer believes that parents must play a major role in all aspects of school life, particularly school governance and management. He contends that involving parents directly in school operations can lessen parents' distrust of educators. He also stresses the importance of fostering a democratic setting, where teachers, families, and specialists work together to promote the social and emotional as well as the academic growth of children.

History of the SDP Schools

Begun over fifteen years ago to combat school failure and severe disciplinary problems, the School Development Project (SDP) provides insights into how we might approach reform for at-risk children. Rather than define reform in terms of teacher credentials, didactic instruction, and curriculum, the two project schools in New Haven decided to focus on developing supportive bonds that empower children, parents, and the school (Jones 1989).

It had become obvious that the differences between home and school environments were affecting the psychosocial differences of at-risk children, which in turn shaped their behavior and academic achievement. Thus to bridge the gap in a way that respected the diversity of cultures, languages, and learning styles, parents in the program became involved as classroom assistants and volunteers. They were also encouraged to participate as members of a school governance committee—"a collaboration that energized the entire school" (Jones).

This process didn't happen overnight. It took time to build trust. The program began in a "no-fault" atmosphere, in which all concerned agreed that no single group was at fault and that no single initiative by itself would make a difference.

The outcome? The academic performance in the schools exceeds the national average, and truancy and delinquency problems declined drastically (Jones).

In fact, in 1969, the schools' first year, the two SDP schools in New Haven ranked thirty-second and thirty-third in the city academically, and attendance was among the lowest in New Haven. By 1986 the original project school, with no change in its socioeconomic makeup, tied for third in achievement out of twenty-six elementary schools, and its students ranked a year above grade level. This school has ranked among the top five schools in attendance in the last seven years, and there have been no serious behavior problems in the school for well over a decade (Ziegler).

The model is now being used in all low-income elementary schools in New Haven and has been replicated in over 100 schools throughout the country.

"An essential characteristic of the model is to move the school from a bureaucratic model of management," says Comer (1987-88), "to a system of democratic participation in which parents play a key role. The purpose of this team is to establish a representative body within each school to address the governance and management issues of the school."

A Three-Level Approach

The schools are based on a three-level approach that gradually moves parents from social events to volunteering and, finally, into policy making.

Level I: Broad-Based Participation. This level is designed to include most parents. Activities are culturally compatible with the community, such as gospel music nights, children's pageants, and potluck suppers.

Level II: Parent Participation in Day-to-Day School Affairs. At this level, parents become more active in the ongoing life of the classroom and school. A range of parent education activities is offered. The key component is the parent stipend program: about fifteen parents are employed as classroom assistants, tutors, and clerical and cafeteria aides. Parents are paid a minimum wage for fifteen hours a week. In addition, parents function as unpaid volunteers for an average of five hours per parent per month (Comer).

SDP schools claim that the importance of level II is often overlooked:

> We believe that the basic climate and tone of interaction of a school are greatly influenced by the presence or absence of parents within the school building on a regular and observable basis. Besides being visible to the children, it reduces barriers between staff and parents, both in the eyes of adults and students. Although this level of involvement will probably include only 10 to 20 percent of the parent population, its impact is considerable. (Hamilton-Lee)

Because of its importance, SDP schools don't leave this type of involvement to chance or self-selection. If they find only a handful of parents are volunteering, a recruitment program is conducted. If parents seem reluctant to volunteer because they feel inadequate or inexperienced, then informal training workshops are provided to discuss the skills needed and to reassure parents that professional training isn't usually necessary for most school assistance tasks. In many instances the principal or a teacher must offer personal encouragement to overcome a parent's shyness or anger, or the disbelief that their presence is actually welcome in school.

To accomplish both levels II and III, the school's teachers and administrators must have a genuine desire to include parents. Thus staff development workshops are often necessary.

Level III: Parents in School Governance. This level is the most sophisticated and innovative concept of the SDP schools. The Governance and Management Team is composed of twelve to fifteen individuals and is representative of all adults involved in the school, including three or four parents selected by the parents' organization. The group meets on a weekly basis to review and coordinate all aspects of the school, both academic and social (Comer).

Parent-staff collaboration is stressed and therefore parents tend to participate in the school's regular governing body rather than in a separate parent advisory group. Training in participatory skills is provided on an issue-by-issue basis and touches upon such topics as techniques of letter writing, telephoning, and mobilizing the larger parent-staff community.

Like level II, level III has both real and symbolic value for improving home-school partnerships. For one thing, parents are seen as equal partners with teachers and administrators. Also, by sharing in the "ownership" of the school, parents have more of a vested interest in the outcomes of all students and are thus more willing to invest increased time and energy in maintaining trust and collaboration. Symbolically, parents, students, and staff recognize that all are working together for common goals: there's a new climate of shared responsibility and power at SDP schools, according to Hamilton-Lee.

The Effects of SDP Schools

Research on SDP schools indicates that the overall model has produced significant improvement in both social and academic areas among student populations (Hamilton-Lee). An evaluation of the program conducted in schools in low socioeconomic areas showed significant improvement in attendance and achievement in classroom reading grades (Comer). However, "the most pronounced student improvements have occurred in those schools in which the parents' program is an active and integral part" (Hamilton-Lee).

The results indicate that the SDP program has a positive effect on school climate as well. Research has shown that, for African-American children in particular, school climate plays an important role in adjustment to school and ability to perform well. Thus the SDP schools, with their strong emphasis on changing attitudes, values, and ways of interacting among adults and children, have sought to create a climate that is sensitive to the needs of African-American children (Comer).

EXAMPLES OF DECISION-MAKING AND GOVERNANCE

1. **FLORIDA.** Thirty-three schools in Dade County volunteered to participate in a school-based management/shared decision-making model. Each school makes its own decisions, involving both students and parents. The long-term goal of this experience is to improve student achievement and educational administration. The participants have redesigned almost every aspect of their schools, from textbook selection to instructional goals, from restructuring the school day to creating smaller classes. Parents and other community representatives participate as advisors and partners (Jones 1989).

2. **NEW YORK/NEW JERSEY.** Parent participation on parent/teacher councils at P.S. 91 and P.S. 146 in New York helped bridge the gap between the schools and the communities they served and made the schools more responsive to parents' concerns. At Franklin School in Newark, New Jersey, parents, teachers, and business leaders led a school cleanup and antivandalism campaign. At Ward School, parents successfully collaborated against a school closing (Lawrence C. Stedman 1987).

3. **CALIFORNIA.** Hispanic parents at a California school were trained in the support services needed at school and were helped to become members of the school's decision-making bodies. The project significantly increased the number of parents on school committees, such as the PTA and school site council.

One parent became vice president of the executive board of the PTA and four parents became members of the school site council. This was one of the few Hispanic Development Policy Projects that worked directly to involve parents in the school decision-making process. However, this project director felt that it was very important for parents to be involved in every aspect of their children's schools and in the decisions that affected at-risk families (Nicolau and Ramos 1990).

4. **ILLINOIS.** The Illinois State Board of Education has long supported family involvement in programs serving at-risk populations. Parent involvement is particularly important in areas of program planning and service eligibility. The Chicago reform legislation has gone a step further, mandating local school councils to be predominantly made up of parent and community members. The school councils will transfer power from Chicago's Board of Education to the neighborhoods. That is, the councils have the power to hire or fire the principal, develop a school improvement plan, and decide how discretionary funds will be spent (Council of Chief State School Officers 1989).

How Shared Decision-Making Can Work

"The New Haven experience suggests," Ziegler concludes, "that a parental role in school governance may be related to very significant achievement gains, when that role is made truly integral to a school's central policy-making, and when a school has a very defined and significant decision-making focus and structure."

Davies agrees. No school's outreach strategy will be complete, he says, until educators and parents learn how shared decision-making can help them "put it all together." But he echoes Ziegler when he states that most past efforts toward school decision-making have been a disappointment and will continue to be so "until collaborative approaches to governance—like other forms of outreach—are integrated into an overall school restructuring effort that encompasses all aspects of school life" (Davies 1991).

When parents assume new roles in the schools, they may require training to make the most of their efforts. Epstein says that few parents participate in leadership roles and that those who do rarely communicate with the other parents they represent to solicit their ideas and to report committee or group plans and actions. "Schools need to consider new forms of recruitment and training of parent leaders," she says (interviewed by Brandt 1989).

PART 3
SUPPORT

Preview of Chapters in
Part 3: Support

Chapter 13. Families Need Support

Most families whose children are at risk lack the knowledge, skills, and resources to become involved or stay involved in their children's education. Family support programs promote child development by enhancing parents' child-rearing skills and providing other support from the community. This chapter examines parent education and parent centers (a space set aside in each school that parents can call their own), presenting the rationale, procedures, and examples of each. Although the initiative to develop family support programs must come from the schools, the funding and delivery of family support services require coordination between schools and community social service agencies.

Chapter 14. Teachers Need Support

To positively influence the social and academic development of children, teachers, too, need support. This chapter addresses the need for teacher preservice and inservice training to include information about family structures and processes, parental roles in education, and effective work with parents. Some school districts are hiring parent involvement coordinators to assist staff. Support for parent involvement and teacher training must also come from the school board, superintendent, and principals.

Chapter 13

FAMILIES NEED SUPPORT

*F*amilies with special needs require help to achieve overall health and well-being. Family support programs characteristically promote child development by enhancing childrearing and by drawing upon community resources.

The programs usually provide information and guidance, help with securing services, joint problem-solving, emotional and social support, and one or more concrete services (such as job training, early childhood development, respite care, transportation, health or developmental screening, employment referral, and adult education). Family support programs emphasize prevention and often incorporate paraprofessionals, volunteers, and information networks (Council of Chief State School Officers 1989).

Family support programs, according to the CCSSO, are based on the following assumptions:

1. All families need help at some point and can benefit from support.

2. A child's development is dependent on the strength of the parent/child relationship and on the stability of the relationships among adults responsible for caring for the child.

3. Most parents want to, and are capable of, helping their children grow into healthy adults.

4. Parents are likely to become better parents if they feel competent in other important areas of their life.

5. Families are influenced by societal and cultural values and pressures in their communities.

If they are to become involved in their children's education and schooling, many at-risk families must receive family support. Without support, many of these families simply lack the knowledge, skills, and resources to either become involved or stay involved in the education of their children.

Parent Education

Parent education is a large and increasingly popular component of family support. There has never been a time when childrearing has been more difficult or complex, according to Sally Provence at the Yale University Child Study Center (Cohen, May 9, 1990).

The Need for Parent Education

Less support from extended family members and greater demands from the workplace have isolated families and put them under increasing stress. Some working mothers and single parents have limited time and energy. And many parents are simply uninformed about techniques to stimulate learning but have nowhere to turn to talk about their fears and concerns related to child development and parenting. Thus, many projects that blend professional guidance with informal exchanges among parents are attempting to simulate the kind of advice and help that was traditionally available from the extended family.

Educators are also beginning to recognize parent education programs as one strategy to curb the school failure rate among children at risk from poverty, language and cultural barriers, and family breakups. Studies show that parents' attitudes about learning can have an enduring influence on their children's education, and this finding has bolstered the parent education movement.

In an effort to break the cycle of failure, particularly among vulnerable groups, many of the programs are being designed with specific populations in mind. Parenting education, for example, is an integral part of many efforts to aid pregnant teenagers and teen parents. And, it is often used to improve the confidence, skills, and employability of disadvantaged parents enrolled in vocational education, adult literacy, and welfare programs (Cohen, May 9, 1990).

The Link with Schools

Experts estimate that thousands of parenting programs are operating today. Interest in linking such programs with schools has dramatically increased in the last few years.

Cohen notes that the Harvard Family Research Project identified more than 200 local school-based programs. Missouri and Minnesota are in the lead in launching comprehensive, statewide programs funded and administered through public schools. But smaller-scale efforts modeled after Missouri's Parents as Teachers program have been started in twenty-eight states.

An underlying premise is that these programs will build stronger bonds between schools and parents. Thomas Keating, superintendent of the Kirkwood, Missouri, schools, told Cohen that the program "establishes in the minds of parents their importance in educational decisions and gives them an incentive to cooperate and offer schools ideas." Parenting programs also force schools to recognize that parents who have been involved on a partnership basis with their children's education for several years need to be taken seriously.

What Successful Programs Do

Successful programs show parents how to integrate learning activities into the day's routine and how to prepare the home environment so that it encourages development and learning. Many stress that the type of relationship parents develop with their infants can affect their child's ability to learn later on. These programs stress the importance of holding, talking, stroking, and responding to babies. A key goal is to show parents how they can pose questions, share books and play things, and use daily life experiences to teach their child.

Most programs also teach stages of child development so that parents will know what is realistic to expect of their children at various ages. Others specifically help parents to know how to aid their children with schoolwork.

One of the basic assumptions of the programs is that all parents want to be good parents. In an interview with Cohen, Aurelia Zoretich, coordinator of a parenting program in Canton, Ohio, says, "Those who fail to foster learning—or even resort to abusive behavior—may be lacking self-esteem, unable to communicate effectively, or simply unfamiliar with normal developmental patterns."

Focus on Parents

Parenting programs for at-risk parents must not only be focused on children's development but on the parents' development as well, says Cohen. Support for parents can be provided through education, training, counseling, and employment programs. "The evidence is really clear," adds Zoretich, "that parenting education alone does not provide the changes in behavior that are necessary, particularly in communities where there are other stresses. Information on the child is not enough to motivate changes in childrearing patterns."

"The more things you attack in one program, the better your success rate is going to be," says Janet Blumenthal, director of a followup study on the federal Parent Child Development Centers. "To the extent that these programs don't do just parent education, but really help parents get some training or better job situations, it might help change the whole family's living circumstances....Then you're really going to see some substantial changes for kids" (Cohen).

How Effective Are Parent Education Programs?

Epstein says that research documenting the effectiveness of these programs is inconclusive, that there are few hard data on the impact of these programs on parent behavior and even less on children's outcomes (Cohen).

However, one of the best arguments for parent education may be studies showing that the initial gains in early education programs are less likely to be sustained without parent involvement. To have long-term effectiveness, parent education programs should include some kind of classroom component and regular home contact.

Cohen emphasizes, though, that there is a danger that parent education programs can be oversold and that they are not a substitute for other programs or an inexpensive way to provide preschool education.

Alison Clarke-Stewart, a developmental psychologist, contends that the effectiveness of parent training varies widely among parents. For example, data indicating that some of the gains exhibited at age three by children enrolled in Parent Child Development Centers had eroded ten to sixteen years later left researchers with the awareness that "we simply were not able to inoculate them against the rest of life," said Clarke-Stewart.

However, Chicago's Beethoven Project has noted the dangers in setting unrealistic timetables for success in communities of severe distress. "At some point," Blumenthal notes, "we have to grapple with the fact that a child's experience has to be a good experience every year." Parenting programs, she adds, "present the hope of kids arriving at school where they need to be. I don't think we can ask for anything more" (Cohen).

Parent Education versus Parent Involvement

Epstein argues, though, that many people don't understand the difference between parent education and parent involvement. Parent education advocates are pushing for people to see these programs not just as add-ons but as an integral part of the larger educational system (Cohen).

However, Cohen notes that Epstein worries that many parenting programs focus on the "dynamics of family life" without exploring how it relates to schooling. It's the rare program, she says, that tries to be cumulative, to help parents be responsive to their children through all the grades and to help them grow with their children. To have an impact beyond the preschool years, she adds, parenting programs "would have to make stronger connections with schooling and with the child as a student. That's the kind of continuing education parents want and need and often do not have access to."

Support for Parent Education Programs

Cohen provides examples of evidence in support of such programs. In a 1989 second-phase followup to Missouri's Parents as Teachers program, children from the program were doing better in school than those who hadn't participated. Teachers also reported that significantly more program parents sought parent-teacher conferences and took part in school activities.

Additionally, parents who participated in Kentucky's PACE (Parent and Child Education) program showed increased literacy rates and improved educational expectations for their children.

And a 1983 longitudinal study of the Parent-Child Education Program, which began in Canton, Ohio, in 1974, showed that children scored above city and national averages on standardized tests from kindergarten through tenth grade. And 84 percent of the parents reported their own communication skills and discipline methods had improved (Cohen).

Some of the arguments for more family-oriented approaches are less related to data than to values. People are realizing that the

---

EXAMPLES OF PARENT EDUCATION PROGRAMS

1. At the David Ellis School in Boston, one of the Schools Reaching Out projects, workshops and classes for parents bring them into the school building.

2. Seven school districts in Mississippi, under the auspices of the Quality Education Program, have developed monthly seminars for parents on topics of the parent's own choice. The seminars are held evenings and weekends to accommodate working parents' schedules and cover subjects such as parenting skills, drug and alcohol abuse, and basic school procedures.

   Schools need to empower parents, says Ivy B. Lovelady, program coordinator, "to teach them how to discipline their children, or to turn off the TV to help them study" (Jennings, August 1, 1990).

3. Kentucky's PACE (Parent and Child Education) program is being piloted in twelve districts in response to the unusually high number of adults who don't complete high school. Its aim is to break the intergenerational cycle of undereducation by uniting children and parents in a positive education experience: both are taught simultaneously in a public school setting. PACE has served 700 parents and children at a cost of approximately $800 each and uses teachers and teaching assistants from the school system. Six states are now replicating the program (Council of Chief State School Officers 1989).

4. Other programs also focus on teaching parents and children together. For instance, the Family Math Program, which is used in schools nationwide, teaches problem-solving skills based on the use of "hands-on" materials.

5. In San Diego, community agencies have joined with the schools in an effort to educate parents. San Diego's Parent Institute has operated six-week courses for parents in about twenty-five schools over the past two years. The courses are developed by parents and taught at the schools by local college professors (Jennings).

6. In Indianapolis, the school district is collaborating with fifteen local businesses to provide parent education seminars at worksites during parents' lunch hours.

7. The United Federation of Teachers and two other New York City unions have announced an agreement to provide parent seminars in several languages at workplaces throughout the city.

8. The Parent-Child Education Program in Canton, Ohio, has been praised for its comprehensive approach, creative use of resources, and grassroots appeal. While the centers are located in areas that draw large numbers of low-income families and children at risk of learning problems, the program is open to all families and is free.

   Family life classes combine play and language development and learning activities for children with guidance on child development, communication skills, nutrition, consumer education, and health and safety issues. Parents also receive information on childbirth and prenatal care and learn to help children who are coping with separation, divorce, illness, and death. Evening seminars are held on such topics as family law, communication skills, sex education, and divorce.

   The program runs year-round and offers a dual parent-child curriculum on a fifteen-week cycle. Starting with one center serving seventy families, it has now expanded to four sites serving nearly 1,000 parents and children (Cohen, May 9, 1990).

family is critical in human development and that we need to strengthen and reinforce the role that families play in children's lives.

David L. Williams of the Southwest Educational Development Laboratory warns that schools should not intrude on the right and ability of parents to rear their children. But he argues that "without training on how to support their children's learning, parents will never become the resources that schools so desperately need (Jennings).

Parent Centers

The Institute for Responsive Education (IRE) in Boston suggests that if schools really want to make parents feel welcome, they should set up a room or place in the school that parents can call their own.

Vivian Johnson, IRE's project coordinator, estimates that about 30 percent of the parents use the parent center in the David Ellis School in Boston. Before the project started at the school, there was a sign on the outside of the school saying, "Parents: Wait outside for your children." "The fact that this center exists really sends a message to parents," says Johnson (Jennings).

Reasons for Parent Centers

An increasing number of communities and schools are creating parent centers in schools or at other locations in low-income neighborhoods for a variety of purposes. Besides letting parents know they are welcome in the school and giving them a sense of ownership, parent centers can also:

- Allow informal person-to-person contact between parents and teachers.

- Give parents written material and information on how to help their children in school.

- Serve as places for parents to practice new skills.

- Give parents the opportunity to meet other parents.

- Provide a pooling of resources between schools and communities to help families.

- Offer parent education workshops and other seminars on child development or topics of interest to parents.

- Act as an information clearinghouse for materials that parents can pick up or check out; even computers are borrowed by parents at some parent centers.

9. While the idea is catching on nationwide, Missouri is the only state that requires each of its school districts to offer a parent education program. Parents as Teachers, launched in 1981, is based on the premise that parents are best suited to be their children's primary teachers, but recognizes that parents sometimes need help.

The program makes a special effort to reach disadvantaged families but is designed to serve all parents. That way there is no stigma attached to participating in the program. Parent participation is voluntary.

Districts are expected to offer (1) information and guidance for expectant parents; (2) parent education services, including four home visits and four group meetings over an eight-month period for families with children from birth to age three; and (3) annual screening for children from ages one to four to monitor language and motor development, hearing, vision, health, and physical development.

The chief goal of parent educators in the program is to coach parents on how children are developing and specific ways they can encourage their child. Language development is emphasized, and parent educators serve as role models. Instead of focusing on weaknesses, the program helps parents build on family strengths.

According to the national center, twenty-eight states have started seventy-five smaller-scale programs based on Missouri's program (Cohen).

- Offer adult education or literacy courses for at-risk parents, such as GED or ESL classes.

- Serve as a referral center for other social services in the community.

- Act as a liaison between parents and teachers.

Part of the Schools Reaching Out (SRO) program at the David Ellis school, the parent center transformed the culture of the school. The tone and content of school conversations about parents and communities change when parents are physically present in the building, says Davies (1991). It is difficult for school employees to say "The parents just don't care" when caring parents are a visible presence in the schools.

Examples in England

In Liverpool, one of the locations where Davies conducted research for his SRO project, a Parent Support Program is operating in about seventeen nursery, primary, and junior high schools. The centers operate in surplus classrooms and each center has two staff members—a Teacher Keyworker (a regular teacher who thus has credibility with teachers) and an Outreach Worker (who is from the community and has credibility with parents).

The centers, in operation since 1979, have broad purposes:

> The aims include trying to break the cycle of deprivation through parent support and education, raising the level of academic achievement, responding to the educational needs of the community, raising the parents' level of expectation and aspiration for their children, and encouraging parent-school interaction. (Davies 1988)

These centers offer a wide range of activities:

1. Opportunities for parents to drop in for informal visits with other parents and staff

2. Mother-toddler sessions to help mothers increase understanding of child development

3. Home visits to help family stress and problems

4. Community newsletters and social events

5. Help with preparing and using home teaching materials

CHILD CARE

Child care is a significant issue for schools. "If there are not enough school-age child-care programs in place," says Donna Euben, program director of the Child Care Action Campaign, "families are not going to be able to deal with all of their stress" (Cohen, August 1, 1990).

The number of schools offering child care is increasing. Why do schools care what children do when the school day is over? "Because they know the children will bring it back to school with them the next day," says Kristen Amundson (1988). Even a majority of low-income parents said they would pay for educational afterschool programs.

Latchkey Services for Children, Inc. in Florida sponsors before- and after-school day care programs in schools in Pinellas and Pasco Counties. The programs are housed in cafeterias and other shared school space, and the amount parents pay is based on family income. Although the programs enroll 2,000 children, there is still a waiting list (Amundson).

Minnesota's Early Childhood Family Education program provides child care funds for adolescent parents who are in high school or who wish to return to school. They are eligible for child care funding on a sliding scale basis.

This funding is handled through county social service agencies. Child care can be provided by the school or by other providers (Council of Chief State School Officers 1989).

In recent years employers have taken more steps to upgrade the supply and quality of child care in their communities. In the past year AT&T, IBM, and U.S. West have each committed several million dollars toward child care and other parenting programs (Cohen, August 1, 1990).

EXAMPLES OF COLLABORATIVE SUPPORT

Examples of collaborative support programs for at-risk families include:

1. Minnesota's Early Childhood Family Education program (ECFE) has made efforts to provide specific services for at-risk families in urban districts with large budgets and high concentrations of special populations. Linkages with community resources include cooperation in sharing facilities, equipment, and staff; outreach for recruitment and referral purposes; and collaboration in which ECFE resources contributed to a jointly funded activity (CCSSO 1989).

2. The Citizen Education Center and the Washington State Migrant Council have launched a family literacy program for Mexican migrant farm workers in the Yakima valley. The program includes instruction in English as a Second Language, early childhood education, and a parent education component that helps parents understand the school and the need to reinforce learning in the home (CCSSO).

3. The Washington Department of Social and Health Services and the Olympia School District have collaborated on a demonstration project for high-risk children and their families. The purpose of the project is to promote early intervention in families whose children are at high risk of school failure. Family support services are mobilized through development of a school-based Family Help Center, early detection and referral services, and case management for children and their families (CCSSO).

4. New York's Community School Program at fourteen sites statewide provides human and educational services to hard-to-reach or special populations. School facilities are made available on an extended school day and year basis. Instructional services include tutoring, mentoring, and enrichment activities. Support services include day care and social and health services. Each school has a management team composed of school administrators, teachers, parents, community service providers, and other professionals involved in serving students (CCSSO).

5. Edward Zigler's school-based child care model provides onsite child care for three- and four-year-olds and early morning and after school care for six- to twelve-year-olds. The model has already been replicated in two Missouri school districts. Funding comes from the Missouri Department of Education and three local community organizations (Jones 1989).

6. In McAllen, Texas, Superintendent Pablo Perez has encouraged the formation of school/community partnerships as a way to expand the base of support for parent involvement. Today each school has at least one community partner that provides resources (donations, volunteers, in-kind services) to support school programs and children's learning. Not long ago two bond issues for new schools passed easily, and passage was attributed in part to greater community awareness of school needs (D'Angelo and Adler 1991).

6. A wide range of formal and informal courses and workshops (Davies 1988)

Suzanne Ziegler (1987) reports that many primary schools in England have seen an increase in parent involvement by converting a spare classroom into a parents' room. She cites one innercity school, also in Liverpool, where many parents are undereducated and unemployed, that has turned a parents' room into a parent center.

The center houses a successful parent volunteer program and well-attended adult education classes in English, computer studies, and parenting education (including helping children learn to read). Involvement remains high, and children's reading scores have improved. Teachers, Ziegler adds, have come to value parental help in the classroom, and parents have come to appreciate teachers' skills.

The David Ellis School

Davies (1991) found that several ideas that worked in the demonstration elementary schools in his SRO project can be adapted to almost any school without waiting for the central office to invest heavily in parent involvement. One of these ideas is the parent center.

The David Ellis School, one of the demonstration sites, is a good example of a successful, low-cost parent center. Two paid coordinators (both of them parents of children in the school) staff the center and serve to bridge the gap between families and the school. The center itself is a comfortable room with places for parents to sit and a play area for preschool children who accompany them. Parents drop in for coffee, a chat, and information.

The Ellis School provides good examples of the kinds of specific activities a parent center might be involved in. For instance, the Ellis parent center:

- Offered ESL and GED classes—both requested by parents and well-attended

- Organized grade-level breakfasts that brought together teachers, administrators, and families to talk informally in a nonthreatening atmosphere about curriculum and classroom concerns

- Sponsored breakfasts for fathers, designed to bring male family members into the school to discuss the contributions they can make to their children's education

- Served as a referral service for parents who need help in dealing with social service, housing, and health agencies

- Organized a clothing exchange and a small library of books and toys for children

- Offered various social events, such as a multicultural potluck

- Recruited parent volunteers requested by the teachers

- Provided a telephone for parents who do not have phones at home and for teachers to call their students' families (Davies 1991 and Jennings, August 1, 1990)

TWO CHAPTER 1 PARENT CENTERS

1. BUFFALO, NEW YORK. Buffalo's Chapter 1 Parent Resource Center is located in a convenient downtown area. Although not located in a school, the center has the support of the local schools, and the assistant superintendent frequently participates in center activities.

Parents are invited to drop in to review resource materials or to take part in workshops. One of the ongoing activities is Reading with the Stars, a program in which local celebrities read stories to children while parents meet separately with staff members to discuss effective strategies for reading to and with their children. Then each parent selects a book to give to his or her child as a gift.

The center also has a computer lending program that trains parents in computer use as a prelude to borrowing a computer to use at home for up to eight weeks. Parents learn how to select and use software to meet individual student needs. Adult education programs are also conducted in the computer lab.

2. NATCHEZ/ADAM, MISSISSIPPI. This parent center serves two primary, two elementary, one middle, and two nonpublic schools. The center's goal is to make education a part of parents' lives and to help parents work more effectively with their children.

Parents receive forms from their children's teachers that outline the skills their children need to practice. Parents then bring these forms to the center and are trained in the use of instructional materials to help their children. Once the initial materials have been used, parents can return and check out other materials on their own.

Source: Adapted from D'Angelo and Adler (1991)

THE IMPORTANCE OF ADULT EDUCATION

Adult education for at-risk parents is particularly important, because studies have shown a relationship between the academic attainment of the mother and the school progress of the children (although Ziegler [1987] has found that this relationship holds only when parental involvement actually occurs).

Researcher Andrew Sum was able to use family data to predict test scores based on parental education. When other variables were constant, he found an "extra grade of attainment for the mother was associated with an extra half-grade equivalent of achievement for her children" (Reeves 1988).

"Because of this intergenerational effect of the parents' education on the child's," Sum says, "it is unlikely that we will be able to make a major difference for the child unless we place equal priority on education and academic remediation for the parent" (Berlin and Sum 1988).

Some schools are trying to facilitate this either by having regular "drop in" days at school or by introducing or supporting adult education classes.

Parents reported feeling more positive about the school and being involved in their children's education as a result of the parent center (Davies 1991).

Other Ideas for Parent Centers

Parent centers, it should be added, do not have to be located in schools. Sometimes schools or parent involvement personnel find it more convenient or less threatening to locate centers in downtown areas or neighborhood settings.

Parent centers might also consider offering flexible hours, thus allowing parents to participate at their own convenience; providing help for parents in negotiating the school system; and acting as

a catalyst for developing adult education programs offered onsite to parents.

For instance, parent centers could be the central location for parent education and/or adult education. Centers can be bilingual, recognize the cultural backgrounds of parents, and provide child care, car fare, and refreshments.

Michelle Sarkees (1989) adds that parent centers might also offer pamphlets, books, and other literature on recent legislation, effective parenting techniques, drug and alcohol abuse, and community resources—in other words, act as an information clearinghouse as well as a community resource center where parents can seek counseling and other assistance.

Requirements for a Workable Parent Center

Based on the experience of SRO at the Ellis School, Davies (1991) lists the following basic requirements for establishing a parent center in your school:

1. *A physical space.* At Ellis, the center was located in a small classroom.

2. *Adult-sized tables and chairs.* Ellis also had a comfortable sofa that someone had donated.

3. *A paid staff of parents.* At Ellis there were two part-time coordinators; at least one of t h e m was present just before school started until the building closed at 4 p.m. Project funds paid for their salaries, but Chapter 1 funds or other state and federal funds can also be used for parent workers.

4. *A telephone.* Davies considers a phone a low-cost but crucial piece of equipment to encourage school/family/community connections.

5. *A coffee pot, hot plate, and occasional snacks.* It's generally agreed that food aids conversation, sharing, and conviviality.

Parent Support Groups

Parent support groups are another approach that can be helpful for at-risk families. They can focus on dropout prevention, dealing with a disabled child, or the like. In rural areas, parents can often be more effective than professionals in working with at-risk parents or families.

In a study of two innercity junior high schools, parents felt keenly the need for more information about their children's progress and a better grasp of their schoolwork, and wanted parent support groups for assistance, reports Oliver Moles (1990).

Parent groups can also organize an information and referral service for parents who need afterschool care for the children; they can operate a telephone service to reach parents who might need rides; or they might help immigrant families adjust to the community and school.

The Need for Collaboration

Family support services can't be provided solely by the schools themselves, especially for at-risk families. Although the responsibility of schools to provide social services to families has expanded, in most cases funding for such services has not. Teachers and staff are already overburdened. Also, at-risk families often have multiple needs that require access to more than one community agency and involve a coordinated approach. Thus pooling resources and coordinating services makes sense.

Some analysts suggest that home-school collaboration may no longer be adequate, that wider collaborative arrangements are necessary. But whichever institutions join in the endeavor, parents must play an active role in the partnership.

The New York State Department of Education (1988) suggests that accountability for the conditions that put children at risk educationally must be shared among schools, families, and the community.

For example, consider the burden of teachers at Miami Beach Senior High School. The school and its teachers must acculturate a student body of 2,100 students representing sixty-seven nationalities. Principal Daniel Tosado says there is no other institution to help poor immigrant families. But John McCormick (1990) asks if that isn't missing the larger point:

> If South Florida mobilized church groups, nationality associations or elderly volunteers to help families with language training and social service referrals, couldn't Tosado's staff devote more

SCHEDULING

To effectively reach low-income parents, scheduling of activities must be carefully considered. As Kristen Amundson (1988) says, "Parent involvement activities must be scheduled for the convenience of parents, not the schools."

In 1987 a Metropolitan Life survey found significant discrepancies between when parents preferred to meet with teachers and when teachers preferred to meet with parents. Only a small percentage of teachers (9 percent) preferred to meet with parents in the evenings. But one-third of the parents favored evening meetings (Harris 1987).

Working parents frequently prefer evening meetings, though it should be kept in mind that some single parents prefer to spend evenings with their children and will pass up school events to do so. The Metropolitan survey noted that unless this mismatch in schedules can be overcome, "there remains a need for working parents to occasionally take time off from work, or else forego direct contact with teachers" (Amundson).

Creative solutions are needed, such as collaborating with businesses to convince them to provide parents with time off for parent-teacher conferences or other school meetings, offering home visits for those unable to come to the school, and scheduling events where both children and single parents can participate in a joint activity.

time to the class work students will need if they're to achieve their dreams of a better life?

Collaboration may not be easy. Warren Chapman (1991) states that to date there have been few connections between schools, families, and other community groups. "The development of these links," he says, "will take a great deal of effort, because both the schools and the social service agencies are accustomed to operating autonomously."

Still, there is no other way to meet the varied needs of at-risk children and families. Recent statements from the Council of Great City Schools, the Council of Chief State School Officers, and the Education Commission of the States have called the coordination of children's services, especially in urban areas, a top national priority. These groups are encouraging schools to forge more effective alliances with social service agencies, community-based organizations, and businesses.

As Davies (1989) sums up, "The schools can't solve these problems alone; neither can low-income families. Schools and families both need each other and they need other community resources and support."

The School as a Starting Point

In spite of the need for wider community support, schools may be the place that at-risk parents start. Siobhan Nicolau and Carmen Lydia Ramos (1990), in their report on Hispanic parents, point out:

> The school that is serving large numbers of at-risk families has to function in place of the parents while it goes about the task of seeing to it that the troubled families get the help they require to stabilize their lives and home environments. This has not traditionally been the schools' role....But school may well be the only connection an alienated and isolated Hispanic family has with any source of help. The schools may have to fill the outreach referral role by default, and the government and private sectors may have to give them the resources to do so.

A major study by the Institute for Educational Leadership concurs: "While schools do not have the resources to meet all the needs of 'at-risk' students, schools can provide referrals to a variety of community agencies that serve 'at-risk' students" (Amundson 1988).

"The time is ripe for reform in how our school systems interact with families and other agencies," says the CCSSO. "To be successful, policies and programs cannot concentrate solely on the child but must simultaneously address the needs of two generations—the parent and the child—for they are interdependent."

The CCSSO report proposes that state education agencies require all schools to develop family support initiatives and emphasizes that state edu-

cation agencies must become the "prime movers in connecting schools with health and social services" to meet a variety of family needs.

"A key to this idea," says Gordon Ambach, executive director of the CCSSO, "is for schools to become genuine community centers, offering services on site, or nearby, to make sure all needs are met" (Jennings, February 14, 1990).

The report also recommends that:

1. Schools collaborate with local governments, agencies, community and social organizations, and businesses

2. Community involvement in schools be increased through greater recruitment of volunteers, the extended use of school facilities, and the provision of social, economic, and recreational services

3. Resources be made available for hiring school-family liaisons, establishing state and local family centers, and providing the services of such professionals as psychologists and social workers in schools

Ziegler (1987) says that widespread support among parents, teachers, businesses, and other segments of the community is an element found in a number of successful parent involvement programs. "The utilization of a wide variety of resources among business people, parents, social agencies and other community sources," she concludes, "seems to have contributed to the development of a positive climate by expanding the number of individuals and organizations that become stakeholders in the program."

Chapter 14

TEACHERS NEED SUPPORT

*W*ithout a school's active assistance, efforts by parents to help children succeed depend heavily on the parents' social class or previous education. Nevertheless, research suggests that this can be changed by good teaching practices and teacher training programs.

"There is growing evidence that the involvement and caring of even one adult in the life of an at-risk child can prevent lifelong disadvantage," says Judith E. Jones (1989). Teachers alone, of course, can't be expected to change what has been called a child's "master setting" (Krasnow 1990). Still, they have enormous influence on the social and academic development of children, often greater than teachers realize.

Joyce Epstein's studies and emerging theory stress the key role of classroom teachers in school-home interaction. She has also recognized how important it is to give teachers specific, practical help in learning to draw parents into the learning process.

Dorothy Rich (1987) has concluded that the new role for teachers today is to coordinate what is learned inside the classroom with what is learned elsewhere. This means teachers must work not only with children but with adults, too. However, most teachers are not taught how to work with adults.

Teachers, like families, have both strengths and problems. Teachers need support, too. "Like many of us caught up in our daily routines," says Jones, "teachers have little access to new knowledge and new approaches.... Teachers need support in an ever-changing and complex environment, and if our children are to succeed, our teachers must succeed."

Teacher Training

Information about family structures, family processes, parental roles in education, and working effectively with parents is not part of most preservice and inservice teacher training programs. Only 1 percent of teachers surveyed by Epstein had completed a course in parent involvement (Krasnow). Oliver C. Moles (1990) also reports that few teachers receive training in parent involvement during their college preparation. Only

4 percent of teacher training institutions in the Southwest, he adds, offer a course on parent-teacher relations.

Preservice Education

Data collected in a five-year study showed that although parent involvement was strongly supported by teachers and principals, school personnel needed additional training. Very little has been written about effective ways to train teachers to involve parents in the education process (Chavkin and Williams 1988).

Chavkin and Williams suggest three essential components for an ideal teacher training program:

- An understanding of the framework of a teacher

- An understanding of the effective models of parent involvement

- Knowledge of the research on parent involvement and the development of a framework for using it in teaching

Experts agree that new modes of teacher education are necessary. In a study of educators and parents in six states, it was found that both groups supported mandating parent involvement training for teachers during their undergraduate education (Slaughter and Kuehne 1987-88). The Council of Chief State School Officers (CCSSO) (1989) also recommends that family involvement information be a mandatory part of teacher training coursework, not an optional interest area.

Washington has a requirement that competence in parent involvement be one of the "generic standards" for state certification of teachers and administrators. "Were this activity to be undertaken in many states," says Epstein (1991), "more courses would be instituted at colleges and universities to work more productively with parents as partners."

Educators need to be trained in interviewing skills and in parent development. Teachers also need instruction in communication techniques and effective group or team management.

The University of Houston-Clear Lake in Texas has developed a parent education model for preservice teacher training. Students have the opportunity in this program to learn about potential barriers to parent involvement and also gain practice in minimizing those barriers. Eight out of every ten program participants reported a positive attitude change toward ethnic and racial minority parents after participation (Texas Education Agency 1989).

Inservice Training

Many teachers of at-risk students may need help initiating home-school programs. First, they are seldom trained to undertake such a task. Second, many have little understanding of the characteristics, needs, and strengths of at-risk children's families.

"Teachers are increasingly expected to develop skills for working with families and leadership in working with advisory groups in addition to their traditional role," the CCSSO points out. However, teachers have received little direction and training for this new role. Not only is there a lack of inservice training, but few materials on working with at-risk parents (let alone parents in general) are readily available to teachers.

"Parents are usually portrayed in mainly negative terms, as problems, not partners," Krasnow (1990) says. Thoughtful inservice programs, she suggests, similar to the Home School Communication model offered by Cornell's Family Matters Project, provide an opportunity for parents and teachers to work together and develop an understanding of each other's role.

For inservice training, the CCSSO recommends that schools help teachers discover how working with families has the potential to improve their work, develop better relationships with parents, and improve community support for schools. They suggest that training should first address teachers' attitudes toward and motivation for working with at-risk families. Then teachers can move on to knowledge and research, and finally to actually developing the necessary skills to work with various families. This sequence implies a series of workshops rather than one-shot sessions.

Specific topics that state-of-the-art inservice training for classroom teachers might offer include:

1. Ways of providing information and advice to parents in writing, by telephone, in home visits, in parent/teacher conferences, and workshops

2. Methods of helping parents encourage their children's progress in each school goal and subject

3. Ways parents can help children make successful transitions across school levels

4. Techniques for helping families prepare their children for taking tests (Solomon 1991)

Changing Behavior and Attitudes

Oralie McAfee places teacher training within the overall field of adult education.

Adults who deal easily with difficult and abstract ideas in their own field may need to start at a very basic level to learn something new, especially which can be threatening to the routines through which they currently work. The more unpredictable and ambiguous the setting in which to try out new skills, the more difficult is the transition to a new skill. (McAfee 1987)

Teachers in innercity settings, with limited training in parent involvement, who see themselves as quite different from the parents of the children they teach, may not face an easy transition to new behaviors.

An action research project for staff training in Portugal had as one of its aims changing teacher attitudes toward working-class families. Interestingly, the project used a combination of observation, studies, and reflection to help teachers understand and modify their own behavior with children and families.

In the first two years, teachers were brought out of the school into the community to study, observe, and better understand the culture of working-class children. For instance, some teachers discovered the rich and varied language used by children on the street and in play areas.

Action research techniques were also used to help teachers see the sometimes subtle factors that operate in the classroom to prevent the success of poor and working-class children (Davies 1988).

The Schools Reaching Out (SRO) project provides funds for teacher training and staff development activities—including trips to other schools, workshops, courses, a library of materials, and opportunities to visit other programs—to help teachers develop skills, attitudes, materials, "and most importantly, new mind-sets about shared responsibility for teaching and learning (Krasnow).

Sometimes creative ways can be found to relieve teachers' doubts or reservations about working with parents. For example, Pacific Oaks College in California is working with the Pasadena Unified School District to enhance teachers' roles in state-subsidized prekindergarten programs for language minority children.

Explains Jones (1989):

The college is helping teachers address the issue of language development among poor Hispanic children, some of whom are newly arrived immigrants while others are from undocumented families. Since the district has few dollars for inservice training and staff development activities, the college is providing resource consultants to work right in the classroom to help teachers solve problems directly.

Unfortunately, Jones adds, there are few examples of creative approaches to teacher training.

Commitment

Suzanne Ziegler (1987) says that appropriate staff training and orientation in such areas as human relations and cross-cultural training, conferencing techniques, and career counseling appear to have a significant impact on family involvement with schools. This has been especially true, she adds, in areas where there are large numbers of low-income and minority families. "Appropriate training," she concludes, "can make a difference to teachers' readiness to involve parents and to the level of communication skill they bring to the telephone call, conference, or classroom visit."

While communication and related skill training is useful, gaining commitment is the essential key for teachers. The ability of motivated teachers to successfully involve a wide cross-section of parents is attributable to the skills that are associated with good teachers—for example, caring, relating, individualizing, personalizing, selecting appropriate activities, reinforcing, teaching, explaining, reteaching, and evaluating.

"For the majority of teachers," Rhoda Becher says,

it is a lack of awareness, priorities, and attention that hinders the development of successful involvement programs. Once teachers develop commitment to parent involvement, they can begin to more systematically use the skills they already possess in achieving optimum and successful involvement. (Cited in Ziegler)

Parent Coordinators and Teacher Specialists

Coordinators for parent involvement are often a necessity.

"We've learned," states Epstein,

that the strongest programs are usually developed in schools where there's a part-time coordinator to work with teachers and develop materials. The position of coordinator or lead teacher for school and family connections is just as necessary as a guidance counselor, an assistant principal, a school psychologist, or a social worker. (Interviewed by Brandt 1989)

Parent coordinators can guide staff, provide inservice training, offer services to parents, and perform other tasks that promote partnerships.

Schools Reaching Out (SRO) emphasizes the key role of the classroom teacher in developing school-family relations. In each SRO school there is a *key teacher* who has been freed from teaching for two years and is paid by the district to be a specialist in school-family relations. The key teacher works full-time making connections with families and community agencies.

In SRO, the key teachers play a central role in forming new partnerships with parents and the community. Key teachers also serve as coaches and troubleshooters for other teachers and foster use of community resources.

In McAllen, Texas, Chapter 1 funds are used to hire parent liaisons. While district staff members and teachers make some home visits, parent liaisons visit families new to the district as well as those who have not come to school or have not

---

SAN DIEGO DISTRICT STAFF SUPPORT AND DEVELOPMENT

District policy in San Diego recognizes that building the capacities of teachers, administrators, and other staff members to work effectively with families is a prerequisite for family-school partnerships. To accomplish this goal, the district established a department to oversee policy implementation and to assist schools. Some of the department's actions include:

1. *Staff Newsletter.* A quarterly staff newsletter contains articles on parent involvement research, suggestions for school-based activities, and information on upcoming workshops.

2. *Parent Involvement Handbook.* The department compiled its own parent involvement handbook for principals. The manual discusses the district's parent involvement policy and describes steps for schools to take in developing family outreach programs. It also emphasizes that staff members' attitudes and behaviors toward parents are keys to the level of parent involvement the school will be able to achieve.

3. *Workshops.* Workshops are an essential component of staff development. Those for principals introduce them to the handbook and other district resource materials. Other workshops focus on the areas of parent-teacher conferences, family-friendly homework and study skills, and developing parent involvement plans.

Source: Adapted from Janet H. Chrispeels (1991)

---

responded to attempts to contact them. The parent liaisons take information directly to these parents and introduce them to the local parent center and the variety of other services and activities available to them.

School Environment and Organization

The SRO project recognizes that the environment of some schools inhibits both learning and teaching. "The ecology of the school has a profound effect on the sense of control, empowerment, and motivation of teachers," says Krasnow. "Creating schools that are positive learning environments for children may have to start with the creation of positive work environments for teachers."

Several studies have examined the effects of the school's organizational climate on teachers. One of the most striking findings is the sense of isolation teachers feel—they do their work alone, interact with students but not peers, and yet they are all part of a common mission (Krasnow).

Thus SRO schools include teachers in planning and decision-making. Faculty collaborate in setting meeting agendas. Problem-solving teams study problems and issue reports on the faculty's perspective. Ziegler claims that the organizational climate is greatly enhanced when teachers are included in the planning and decision-making aspects of the program.

Modifying school structure for genuine participation and staff empowerment is seen as critical at SRO schools and linked to the success of their parent involvement programs. "Isolation contributes to resistance to change," says Krasnow. "Apprehension is reasonable when a teacher faces the prospect of implementing changes alone."

Therefore, SRO schools strive to develop a nonthreatening, collegial environment where examination, reflection, and change can take place so that work with at-risk families can proceed productively.

Commitment from the Top

It goes without saying that for home-school relations to really make a difference, principals, other administrators, and school boards must believe in the power of parent involvement. Williams and Chavkin recommend including principals and other administrators in staff training since they often set the rules and policies in schools.

Solomon suggests that states might offer inservice training to district and school administrators and policy leaders to enable them to guide teachers in parent involvement. The training she

suggests for administrators includes topics such as:

- Why parent involvement is worth it
- How to integrate effective homework procedures into the instructional program
- How to encourage, support, and reward teachers for partnership activities
- Basic strategies for mobilizing "out of school" opportunities for learning
- Facts about families' diversities and strengths that affect student achievement
- Ways to help parents support, learn, and motivate one another (Solomon 1991)

Board and Administrators Must Demonstrate Support

The school board's commitment to the implementation of parent involvement programs has been identified as crucial by a recent review of parent partnership programs. Ziegler says that board policies significantly influence parent communication and involvement practices and that board-level influence can be achieved through recruitment practices, inservice training, or clearly expressed directives and expectations.

A junior high school principal in McAllen, Texas, illustrates the concept of commitment from the top. This principal, who believes that the best strategy involves face-to-face meetings with parents, gives teachers two planning periods a day during which they may confer with parents or set up appointments for meetings at other times. In other schools in the district, administrators teach classes while teachers conduct home visits; the principal of one school conducts the home visits himself (D'Angelo and Adler 1991).

The Importance of Formal Policy

Davies notes that authoritative policies are needed whenever a proposed change represents a significant departure from existing norms or whenever the new activity requires individual or organizational risks. The wording of the policy, he adds, is crucial since the minimum requirements

ACTION RESEARCH TEAMS

One of the innovations in the Schools Reaching Out project (SRO) was the establishment of action research teams to involve teachers directly in home-school-community relations and in devising actions to improve their own practices. "School/family/community partnerships will amount to little more than empty rhetoric," says Davies (1991), "unless teachers help design the partnerships, are devoted to making them work, and eventually find themselves benefiting from them."

What are action research teams? In both of the SRO demonstration schools, a researcher/facilitator organized a group of four teachers who met at least monthly. After background reading in parent involvement and training, the action research team in each school interviewed the rest of the faculty to determine how teachers felt about parents and parent involvement, what past activities had been successful, and what concerns teachers had about parent involvement.

The teams used the results of the interviews to design several projects aimed at increasing collaboration between the school and its families. They also came up with the idea of awarding a series of minigrants (each totaling $150 to $200) to teachers who were not on the team to encourage them to reach out to families to encourage children's learning. This strategy, says Davies, produced a number of imaginative activities at little cost.

Each teacher on the team received a stipend of between $400 and $600—modest, but an acknowledgment of professional effort.

To incorporate a school-based action research team, Davies suggests that only a few changes are needed:

1. At least a small number of teachers must be willing to participate in the process of improving parent involvement.

2. Funds for small grants or stipends are necessary. These may be available from a local community source.

3. A researcher/facilitator who is sensitive to teacher concerns can help teachers write proposals, design interviews, analyze results, and lead discussions that encourage reflection. A facilitator might be found already on the school staff, at a local university, or on the school district's central office staff. Volunteers might also come from a local corporation, a community organization, or a senior citizen center.

"The action research teams of teachers," concludes Davies, "operate on the assumption that change and improvement in schools are most likely to occur when there are opportunities for teachers to collaborate with time for reflection and with support for trying new strategies."

---

tend to become the maximum performance (Davies 1987).

This means that if a local school board decides it wants to increase a particular type of parent involvement, such as with at-risk families, it should translate this decision into a set of clearly written policies that can then be adopted through the usual legislative or collective bargaining channels.

Merely expressing support for at-risk parent involvement, says Ziegler, or adopting a policy of good intentions is not enough to produce change.

Successful district initiatives also recognize that teachers must learn from the families of their students. Says Chrispeels:

The most important role for families from ethnically and racially diverse backgrounds may be to help teachers understand the educational experiences, customs, and values of parents as well as their expectations for their children. Opportunities for teachers to visit the homes of their students and learn directly from parents about their children may not only be the best training for teachers and parents but also may be a way to craft meaningful partnerships.

PART 4
SPECIAL AGES

PREVIEW OF CHAPTERS IN
PART 4: SPECIAL AGES

Chapter 15. Preschool Years: Early Intervention

Because the process that contributes to school success begins at birth, proponents of family involvement urge schools to reach parents early. This chapter looks closely at four preschool programs: The Perry Preschool Program, the Lafayette Early Childhood Project, Project HOPE (Home-Oriented Preschool Education), and Home Instruction Program for Preschool Youngsters (HIPPY). Because it was described in chapter 12, the Head Start program will not be mentioned in this chapter.

Chapter 16. High School: Dropout Prevention

At the secondary school level, involvement of parents can be helpful in keeping students in school. First, the chapter acknowledges the difficulty of involving parents of disadvantaged high school students. But the critical impact a student's home environment has on his or her decision to drop out is reason enough for schools to take the initiative. A sidebar presents five examples of parent involvement programs in high schools, and the final section offers several suggestions for involving at-risk families.

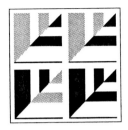

Chapter 15

PRESCHOOL YEARS:
EARLY INTERVENTION

*7*t used to be that infancy to kindergarten were considered empty years. It was a period when parents took care of things. Not so today. Now these years are recognized as the most formative ones.

Edward Zigler, professor of psychiatry at Yale University, notes, "There is an absolute growing recognition that if we want to optimize the development of children, we have to get in there even before they are born with prenatal care—and then do everything we can to see that the environment of the child is optimal for the period from 0 to 5" (Cohen, May 9, 1990)

Preschool programs for at-risk kids have shown us the importance of early intervention and its long-lasting effects and the importance of parent involvement. In fact, the latter can make all the difference in the world.

Head Start was really the first program to involve parents in the education of their children. Parent experience with the program is detailed in chapter 12.

Although Carol Ascher (1987) mentions that the effects of parent involvement in public school years are open to interpretation, she states that preschool studies that include extensive parent involvement show notable and apparently long-term effects in students.

Preschool programs for at-risk children are especially important because of their early intervention into these families' lives. The process that ultimately leads to students' dropping out of school, says Judith E. Jones (1989), begins before students even enter school: "Reaching parents early is the key, because the process that contributes to school success begins at birth. Many children drop out before they drop in. The seeds of failure are sown early, and early intervention is critical."

Preschool Programs and Parent Education

An increasing percentage of impoverished families are headed by young couples or young single mothers. In part, this is due to rising teen pregnancy rates. Poverty and teen parenthood can work against a child-centered approach that includes parent involvement, which is why parent education and support is so important for these families.

Many school districts, Erica Gordon Sorohan (1988) notes, are turning to preschool programs to address the needs of at-risk students and the national shortage of day care facilities. Preschool programs offer practical advantages: established physical and administrative structure, continuity and stability for children, and convenience for parents.

An integral part of many public preschool programs, Sorohan reports, is parent education. Classes focus on topics such as discipline, time management, helping with homework, basic skills, and interpreting test results.

For example, a cooperative preschool involves parents during the day as classroom aides and then asks them to return to school at night for training sessions. The program, says Kristen Amundson (1988), is "living proof of the inaccuracy of the popularly held notion that low-income parents will not turn out for school programs."

EARLY CHILDHOOD FAMILY EDUCATION

ECFE, funded by the Minnesota Department of Education, is a center-based program designed for children from birth to kindergarten that operates in more than 300 school districts in Minnesota. The program is available to all families, with the goal of serving hard-to-reach families in proportion to their representation in the community.

On average, parents and their children spend two hours a week at centers located in housing projects, low-income apartments, store fronts, and former elementary schools. Classes include parent-child activities supervised by early childhood educators, parent-to-parent discussions facilitated by a parent educator, and children's activities to promote cognitive and motor development.

Source: Goodson and others (1991)

The implication for school board members is that "preschool education may become a cost-effective way to reach 'at-risk' children. By investing in preschool programs, school districts may save thousands of dollars per student per year in reduced special education costs" (Amundson).

Benefits of Parent Involvement

The benefits of parent involvement can be seen in evaluations of preschool programs such as Head Start, where the program variable that contributed most was parent involvement (Krasnow 1990). Urie Bronfenbrenner's (1972) review of early intervention programs also found that the most successful programs—those in which the gains in ability persisted long after the children left the program—built in the involvement of the mother. "Such effective programs are family-centered rather than child-centered," says Ziegler.

Another reviewer also concludes that parent involvement is the key to long-lasting effects from preschool programs. "Evidently a change occurs in the home environment which supports and maintains school achievement" (Sattes 1985).

A closer look at four preschool programs shows how this happens.

The Perry Preschool Program

The Perry Preschool Program is often cited for its longitudinal studies, which have been very positive. The studies followed 128 children for more than a decade after they left the program. These children came from a crowded slum area in a city in Michigan, an area with consistently high school failure rates and crime rates.

Children in the program attended preschool five half-days a week for one academic year. Perhaps most importantly, weekly home visits encouraged parents to structure household activities that included their children.

"The Perry Preschool Program," says Krasnow,

> demonstrated better grades, fewer failures, fewer absences, and fewer special education placements during public school years for those children

HOME INSTRUCTION PROGRAM FOR PRESCHOOL YOUNGSTERS (HIPPY)

Home Instruction Program for Preschool Youngsters (HIPPY) is an Israeli-designed program for disadvantaged children that has been slowly making headway here in the U.S. since it was introduced in 1984.

Begun in Israel to help children of poor immigrants from Africa and Asia, it is based on research funded by the U.S.-based National Council of Jewish Women (NCJW). In the beginning the NCJW was divided over whether supplementary education should take place at home with the mother or in class with a teacher. Studies showed that the kids who worked with their mothers did better. Avima Lombard, who devised HIPPY, also witnessed positive changes in the mothers studied. Many went back to school.

Impressed with the results, the NCJW brought the program to Oklahoma in 1984, then to Miami in 1985. Since then the program has spread to thirty-three sites in thirteen states.

By sending tutors into homes to show parents how to teach their children, HIPPY tries to give poor children the developmental stimulation a middle-class home would provide. But it goes beyond parent education. HIPPY also tries to teach, through a step-by-step approach, how to stimulate minds and make it possible for children to succeed in school.

A typical HIPPY program hires mothers from the community, trains them, and sends them into their neighbors' homes every other week for thirty weeks. Tutors show the parents—often mothers in single-parent households—how to work with their preschool children. First they role play, working through prepared lessons and storybooks. Then the mothers work directly with their children and their progress is charted during home visits. On alternate weeks, the mothers meet as a group with the tutor.

The program is offered for two years, starting with four-year-olds in preschool and continuing through kindergarten. This program is only offered to children who are already in school (whether preschool or kindergarten). That's because it was found that the program works best when the efforts of mothers can be directly reinforced by the teachers.

The program's goal is to help both generations. Mothers can gain as much as their children do. One mother, for instance, who was unemployed and poorly educated, went to vocational school after her eldest child completed the HIPPY program. "It just made me feel so good about things," she says.

"This program puts the parents back in the driver's seat," says Michael Honore, a coordinator of early childhood programs for the New Orleans Public Schools. "It's a common perception that project moms are negligent. They're not. They just need a vehicle to help them help their kids. Once they have that, it makes them feel good and it helps them, too."

Source: Adapted from Nina Darnton (1990)

whose parents had been involved in a weekly home visitor program, in addition to the preschool program, than for those children not involved.

In fact, Ziegler says the positive effects have been shown to persist throughout children's entire school careers. During secondary schooling these students showed a greater commitment to schooling. At age fifteen they were more willing to talk to their parents about school, spent more time on homework, and had a higher self-rating of school ability.

In addition, fifteen years after preschool, at age nineteen, program students were far less likely than their peers to have dropped out of school, been arrested, or become involved in the court system. Far more of them graduated and were employed and self-supporting. Thirty-eight percent were attending college, and 48 percent were employed at a time of high unemployment, especially for African-American adolescents (Ziegler).

Ziegler admits that it is impossible to know to what extent the involvement of parents of Perry students, independent of the children's school-based program, made a difference. Parent involvement, either at home or school, has been built in to many of the most successful preschool programs. She adds:

> Long-term follow-up of several models of preschool programs, all of which included parent involvement, are consistent in finding effects that include fewer instances of grade repetition and of placement in special education (both of which are also important indicators of cost-effectiveness).

The Lafayette Early Childhood Project

Although small, the Lafayette Early Childhood Project, mentioned in chapter 10, was another very successful preschool program designed to meet the needs of at-risk children who had not been accepted into Head Start.

The Louisiana project involved two certified teachers and one teacher assistant who provided individualized instruction for thirty-one preschool students in two schools. Parent involvement, a strong component, was evaluated as part of the report on the project (Alexander and Lovelace 1988). If parents learned how to assist their children in learning, the project leaders hoped, parents would also be equipped to help other children in the family, thus benefiting siblings, too.

The program continued for nine months. Classes met seven hours every day, five days a week. The whole project and inservice staff training were based on preschool education principles.

The parent involvement program included four components:

1. An initial interview, designed to determine the degree of commitment, and culminating in the signing of a contract acknowledging the parents' responsibilities

2. Workshops for parents, including dissemination of calendars with daily activities reinforc-

ing classroom activities and learning packets containing books, toys, and instructional games

3. Home visits that allowed the staff to gather information on student needs and to make provisions for necessary support services

4. Followup assistance to parents with siblings (Alexander and Lovelace)

Inservice programs stressed the importance of coordinating services as well as providing regular written and oral reports to parents.

At the time of the evaluation, students previously enrolled in the project had completed second grade, first grade, or kindergarten. Evaluation of the parent involvement component was conducted through structured telephone interviews and selected indepth interviews. Every parent or guardian interviewed responded positively to the questions asked. Thirty of the thirty-one parents had visited the classroom at least once in addition to attending regularly scheduled parent meetings in the evenings (one parent said she visited her child's class every day!). Parents were impressed by the teachers and their willingness to have them observe classroom activities.

Many parents reported daily conversations with teachers about their children's progress. "Every day when I would pick him up, the teacher would talk to me about how he did that day," one parent said. Several parents commented on the communication between home and school. One parent, when asked how she found out how her child was doing in class, replied,

> The teacher sent work home every day and also my child talked all the time about what they were doing at school. I attended three night meetings. I visited the school on several occasions, and I had two conferences with his teacher. (Alexander and Lovelace)

Home visits were also favorably referred to:

• "If we didn't understand the home study program, they explained to us what we needed to do to help our children."

• "She gave us great ideas of things to do at home. It made us closer as parent and child."

• "It was helpful and it was nice to meet the other parents." (Alexander and Lovelace)

For comments about what the children and their parents learned, see chapter 10.

This was a well-received program. All the parents surveyed felt their children would do better in kindergarten. Two mothers even said their kids could probably do first-grade work. Other comments were as follows:

- "A lot of kids, you throw them up in school at six years of age without this program—they won't make it."
- "It will give him a 'way-boom' start."
- "I could never pay for the kind of education my child got." (Alexander and Lovelace)

In summary, all parents surveyed acknowledged the favorable impact of their newly acquired skills on both the children enrolled in the project and on other siblings in the family.

Project HOPE

Project HOPE (Home-Oriented Preschool Education) is another preschool project that has something to teach us.

Begun in 1968 in rural Appalachia for disadvantaged children, Project HOPE consisted of three groups of participants: one group of children was exposed to daily TV lessons, another had TV lessons plus home visits and were given printed materials related to the TV lessons, and the third group had, in addition to TV lessons and home visits, a group experience with young children once a week in a mobile classroom van. In addition, a control group had none of these experiences, although they were from similar backgrounds and attended the same schools as the children in the project.

The home visits appeared crucial to the program in the followups conducted in 1975 and between 1985 and 1988 (project children were followed from preschool through high school graduation). By 1975, the results from the TV-only kids had "washed out," as has been found in other preschool programs that are oriented to the child only. But in the groups that received home visits, the children surpassed local norms (Gotts 1989).

EXAMPLES OF FAMILY-CENTERED PRESCHOOL PROGRAMS

Early childhood development programs are now beginning to reach out to families as well as to children. Besides fostering children's development, the new "family-centered" programs are striving to be a place where the whole family can be involved. Two such programs are in California and New Jersey:

1. CALIFORNIA. Besides serving disadvantaged preschoolers, the Parent-Child Development Centers in Oakland, California, offer parents support groups, cultural programs, parenting classes, respite care for ill children, and the chance for a recreational "night out."

   The parent involvement program of the centers—known as the Parent Services Project—is funded by a private foundation and was designed by mental health professionals. Its aim is "to raise parents' sense of importance and diminish their isolation," says Barbara Shaw, executive director of the Parent-Child Development Centers.

2. NEW JERSEY. The Rand School in Montclair, New Jersey, is described as a "family magnet" school for four- to eight-year-olds. The principal and a social worker interview each family before children enroll to establish initial contact and invite communication. Teachers periodically contact parents simply to have a positive conversation about their children, and some send children home with written "logs" that allow parents and teachers to exchange comments. The school also offers parent workshops and family activities on weekends and encourages families to volunteer in school projects. A central goal is to "support the growth not only of the child but of the family," says Sandra Yark, school principal.

   Source: Adapted from Cohen (November 28, 1990)

It could be inferred, then, says Gotts,

that the superiority of the home-visited families' children did not result from the original treatment; instead, the families had become more effective as mediators of their children's school experience. It was, therefore, the behavior of parents in the home-visited groups that constituted an ongoing treatment during the years following the program. The parents had been treated, now they "treated."

In the final followup stage (1985-88), HOPE parents maintained a stronger academic orientation—the most powerful single variable for predicting school effects in their children. This orientation consistently exceeded the effects of socioeconomic status. Both boys and girls expressed more positive self-concepts when their parents had a higher academic orientation. Home environment improved, but for boys only. In general, participation in HOPE led to more favorable outcomes in parenting, school-family relations, school performance, and children's adjustment (Gotts).

HOPE's home visitation program empowered and trained parents in essential skill areas. However, the parents didn't become different in a fundamental sense. Families were not asked, for example, to espouse some new philosophy or to consciously commit themselves to a lifetime of changed behavior. Nor were their parenting practices treated as inferior or lacking in cultural value.

In fact, all the valued parent practices were found in the control group as well. Moreover, these parenting variables were generally associated with the same desirable child outcomes in the control group as were demonstrated in the experimental group. "What changed," says Gotts, "was only the frequency and consistency in which the HOPE parents engaged in these practices...HOPE promoted parent actualization more than it did parent change."

Gotts says it's a mistake to focus on the actual content of the program. Rather, attention should center on involving parents as mediators in their children's education. Yet, to the extent that schools emphasize preschool education as a solution, Gotts stresses, "the risk increases that they will fail to ask to whom these experiences should be directed."

Gotts answers that *both* parents and children, but especially parents, must be assisted. In conclusion, he says, "Ask not how parents can help the school, but how schools can help the parents."

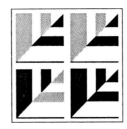

Chapter 16

HIGH SCHOOL:
DROPOUT PREVENTION

*D*ropout prevention is one of the most important issues in education. Dropouts include large numbers of minorities, those who are limited English-speaking, and low-income children. For instance, in New York City, which enrolls more than 77 percent of the state's African-American and Hispanic students, as many as three out of four African-Americans and four out of five Hispanics fail to complete high school within the traditional four-year period (New York State Department of Education 1988).

Involving parents can be an effective step toward keeping students in school. A recurring theme with dropouts surveyed in Atlanta, Georgia, was "the feeling that their parents were not concerned/involved with their education" (Jonas 1987).

Difficulty of Involving Parents of High School Students

"Bringing parents of disadvantaged students into a meaningful relationship with the school," says Larry F. Guthrie and others (1989) "is one of the most difficult practices to implement successfully, especially at the secondary level." These parents are reluctant to become involved for reasons mentioned in chapter 6, including negative educational experiences in school and limited English proficiency.

In general, it is harder to involve parents at the secondary level than it is at the elementary level. High schools are usually larger than elementary schools. Also teenagers are experiencing newly developed autonomy and independence that discourages some parents from participating in school activities if schools themselves do not encourage it (Bauch 1987).

Because of subject specialization, it's also harder for parents to know their children's teachers and to feel competent to help older children with homework.

"The literature on parent involvement in their children's secondary education," says Suzanne Ziegler (1987), "suggests that parent involvement at that level is potentially as effective as at the elementary level, although it is much rarer to expect parents of secondary students to become involved as home tutors."

Nonetheless, she says, "when secondary school parental involvement is successfully sought, it proves to be effective in increasing students' achievement and in preventing dropping-out."

Importance of Parent Involvement

Home environment is just as important in high school years as it is earlier on. Commenting on a recent study based on comprehensive information on dropouts from American high schools, Ziegler concludes that students' home environment has a critical impact on the decision to leave school. She suggests that policies be developed to help parents increase their interest in and monitoring of their teenagers' school progress.

Izona Warner, director of the Parents in Touch program in Indianapolis, says that she would like to see a stronger emphasis on keeping parents involved in their children's education. Currently, she says, their involvement tends to drop off dramatically between elementary and middle school (Jennings, August 1, 1990).

S. M. Dornbusch and P. L. Ritter (1988) studied the link between parents and academic achievement at the high school level. Parental attendance at school events was consistently associated with higher student grades.

However, says the Texas Education Agency (1989), some high school personnel may not be ready to encourage a high level of parent involvement. "The students who suffer most when this lack of involvement occurs at the secondary level include average-ability students, ethnic or racial minority students, and students from single-family or step-family homes."

Parent Empowerment and Dropouts

An interesting issue is that of the link between parent empowerment and high school dropouts. Deborah Meier, principal of Central Park East Secondary School in East Harlem, cites two elements that are critical for helping "disaffected" youth reconnect to schools and their families:

(1) breaking up huge schools into smaller units, and (2) changing the power relationship between parents and their children (Council of Chief State School Officers [CCSSO] 1989).

"This means empowering parents in their children's eyes," says the CCSSO, "such that parents can better realize their role as protectors, 'bread winners,' counselors and the like. Once empowered, parents are better positioned to direct their own lives and those of their children."

Studies Encourage Schools To Take Initiative

Actually, few studies have been conducted on parent involvement at the high school level. But what little research has taken place suggests ways to begin at-risk parent involvement.

F. Montalvo (1984) reports on the notion of transforming ineffective schools into effective schools in his study of parent involvement and high school education for ethnic and racial minority youth. Montalvo believes that it is up to local schools to build a bridge between home/community and school. He also notes that many parents need help in supporting education for their children. Of the ten sites he visited, the schools that were most successful in educating at-risk children made extensive efforts to involve parents in the school and to provide training for parent involvement. Educators in this project also attempted to bridge any cultural differences between home and school.

Following up on a finding that at-risk students felt their parents weren't concerned with their education, Jonas found that parents could lessen students' feelings of separation from the educational setting by engaging in activities designed to show their support for education. Further, he found that parents can assist in reducing the feelings of alienation that preceded dropout behavior.

Capistrano Unified School District in California, which embarked on a long-range plan "to shatter the myth that you can't achieve parent involvement at the high school level," believes that schools must reach out to parents (Hester

EXAMPLES OF HIGH SCHOOL PARENT INVOLVEMENT

1. TUCSON. An example of parents working to help other parents is employed by the Tucson Dropout Prevention Collaborative in Tucson, Arizona. This is a target program for at-risk elementary and secondary students in forty-two schools. A special feature of this collaborative is an innovative parent leadership program called the Commadre Network.

   Developed with a Ford Foundation grant, this program involves a group of approximately fifty parents who work to convince other parents of the importance of education. They make presentations to other parents, work to re-enroll students who have dropped out (in 1987, 250 students were retrieved), and act as mediators between students with problems and their families. Each parent leader receives a stipend of $100 (Guthrie and others 1989).

2. NEW YORK CITY. The Parent Support Group is run by Middle College High School, a New York City alternative school known for its innovative approaches to dropout prevention. Each month two counselors meet with parents who are experiencing difficulties. The parents define specific areas of need, then counselors arrange for speakers on topics such as effective communication, teenage lifestyles, letting go, college preparation, and financial aid. Various exercises help parents see how their responses affect their children's behavior and how they can make adaptations.

   The group has filled a vacuum for parents who might be reluctant to seek therapy but who feel comfortable coming to the school group. The group also deals with personal adult concerns, such as alcohol, drugs, illness, sexuality and sex roles, managing finances, ambitions, and fears.

   Teenagers have encouraged their parents to come to this group. The children of group members show a pattern of improvement in behavior, attendance, and grades (Berman and others 1987).

3. ONTARIO. A secondary school in rural Ontario held a coffee and doughnuts get-together. The idea might work with other at-risk families if the get-together is scheduled at parents' convenience. The intent is not for parents to discuss their children's progress or for staff to make school-related announcements, but simply to allow parents and staff to visit with each other, exchange impressions of the school and its program, and develop mutual respect (Ziegler 1987).

4. SAN DIEGO. Lincoln Prep High School demonstrated effective ways to link high schools with the broader community. The school helped students and their families find community resources through a school-sponsored telephone referral system. They also invited parents to a series of parenting workshops, not only to improve parenting skills, but to let parents know that to be most effective, their involvement needs to be sustained throughout their children's school years (Chrispeels 1991).

5. CALIFORNIA. Partners for Success is a project in Gilroy, California, that addresses the problems of at-risk high school students with limited English proficiency. The project director and resource teacher recruit students and parents through personal contact, promotion of the program at school and in community media, and use of students to refer other students. A commons room at the school is used by parents and students for informal conversations and organized events. Besides tutoring, classes, a work-study arrangement, and other events for the students, family meetings are also arranged (Cross and others 1991).

1989). Parents want more responsible roles, says Hester, but no one recipe or blueprint works for every school.

Good home-school communication, says Hester, relies on direct, personal contact between educators and parents. However, in comparing elementary and secondary levels, he says it is unrealistic to expect the same degree of participation at the secondary level that you would expect at the elementary level. Instead, he recommends increasing the parent-student involvement at home as a priority goal.

Avenues for Parent Involvement in High Schools

The following are suggestions based mainly on the programs cited by Hester and Jonas, modified to apply to at-risk families.

Parent-Teacher Contracts: Parents enter into contracts that state they will: (1) help their children do school work at home, (2) attend PTA meetings (this may not work with at-risk families), (3) maintain regular communication with the school, and (4) provide assistance when requested by the teacher. Contracts with at-risk families set forth specific parental activities to support instructional approaches (Jonas).

Parents as Supporters of Activities: "It may not be realistic to expect parents of secondary school students to be as involved in school activities as elementary students," says Hester. "However, getting more parents involved is a powerful component of a comprehensive high school parent involvement plan."

Ideas you might try:

1. Sponsor parent-student socials, where cost is not a factor in participating, and where awards are given for teamwork, attendance, and school spirit.

2. Conduct new student orientation activities that are scheduled over a period of four to eight months to welcome new parents and children. Focus on grade 9 for high school. Activities could include reviewing school rules and curriculum, for example.

CAREER INFORMATION

One of the most important roles of parent education programs for at-risk populations, says Michelle D. Sarkees (1989), is to provide information concerning career and occupational development for their children.

According to Sarkees, research shows that parents contribute directly to the aspirations of their sons and daughters and, in many cases, are the principal influence on their children's occupations. Other researchers also claim that career aspirations, along with maturity and expectations, are heavily influenced by family structure and parental association with children.

Sarkees states that a student's success in choosing a career can be greatly enhanced by parents who are "able to encourage role modeling and career exploration, provide career-related materials, and build a healthy self-esteem."

She emphasizes that it is important to include parents of at-risk youth as an integral part of the planning team, instead of leaving testing, evaluation, and placement to the school. If parents are to be prepared to provide career guidance, they must also be provided with specific information. Career-related knowledge, she adds, will greatly affect parents' attitudes and the amount of time and energy they will expend exploring career options with their children.

Sarkees suggests that schools provide the following activities to assist parents in exploring career opportunities with their children:

1. Informal meetings to discuss vocational programs offered in the schools

2. Joint meetings of parents with school personnel and employers to discuss employability, entry-level, and job-seeking skills

3. Opportunities for parents to visit business and industrial settings

4. Materials with suggestions for activities to do at home that will reinforce career development experiences at school

3. Enlist parent-teacher mentors for groups of students, to assist with transitional problems.

Parents as Educators: "A parent involvement approach can teach parents to be better educators and to utilize family resources to reinforce dropout prevention efforts at home," say Nancy Peck and Raymond Eberhard (1988).

Parent training might include the following activities:

1. *Workshops* that bring parents, teachers, and administrators together (try topics such as homework, vocational education programs, drug abuse, teenage suicide, college admission, dropout prevention, and parenting skills).

2. *Parent education activities* that address helping students master basic skills, preparing for parent-teacher conferences, and learning tips for helping students with homework. Provide individualized instruction if parents can't attend group meetings.

3. *School tours* held after school for those who work to help familiarize parents with the school environment.

4. *Demonstration classes* conducted for parents to help them better understand how school classes operate.

5. *Field trips and joint classes* for parents and students; consider offering classes in the evenings so working parents can participate.

6. *Community resource information* for parents; it's advisable to have someone at the school who can make referrals.

7. *Home visits* with parents of truant students ("The parents might be more willing to work with the school if they feel the principal and teachers are genuinely concerned about the student," says Peck); also, try employing parents to visit other parents.

Home visits might be a good time to introduce packets of simple homework activities keyed to instructional objectives. Other ideas include offering suggestions on creating a good study environment at home and discussing homework, providing parents with complete information on their children's progress, and developing a test that parents can administer to

---

A GAME FOR DROPOUT PREVENTION

The Junior Achievement of Lane County, Oregon, has developed a game called *The Game of Success* that is designed to reduce dropout rates by teaching at-risk students the personal and economic costs of dropping out of school.

Students play the game in the first of a four-session class called "The Economics of Staying in School."

"The kids tend to think it's not that difficult out there, really," says Marnie Chambers, Junior Achievement vice-chair of community involvement. But after playing *The Game of Success,* she says they change their minds.

The game uses charts and graphs to explain the rewards of education and also involves looking at classified ads for jobs that don't require a high school diploma. By the fourth session, students acting as "peer counselors" are full of advice for the "dropouts." "The kids just take over at that point," says Chambers.

The one-hour sessions are currently incorporated into the social studies programs at four middle schools in Lane County.

Source: Adapted from Laura Price (1991)

---

their students at home to check their progress in meeting skills required for high school graduation.

Parents as Advocates: At-risk parents probably will feel most comfortable with this role only after they have first gotten involved at home, then perhaps as supporters of activities at school.

It is important for school personnel to (1) encourage parents to develop policies on school problems, such as drug abuse and smoking on campus; and (2) offer training for parents who are willing to serve in leadership roles or who are interested in exploring the possibility.

HELPING WITH HOME-WORK

Here are suggestions on how parents can support their children's education at home:

1. Create a routine and establish a regular study time; set aside a place that is quiet and away from the distractions of phone, radio, and TV.

2. Assume that your child has homework. Review material he or she learned that day.

3. Know homework guidelines for each class and what your child is expected to accomplish.

4. Help to manage the workload by dividing the tasks into manageable doses.

5. Set an example. Use the homework time as your time to read, pay bills, or write letters.

6. Participate in homework assignments. Review work. See if it's complete. Ask questions about it.

7. Use lots of praise and reward progress. Avoid using homework as a punishment.

8. Encourage study groups. Children can learn a lot from each other through group study. Organize a group at your church, in community centers, or at home.

9. Reinforce formal learning with informal learning activities, such as visits to museums, theatres, parks.

10. Monitor grades and keep abreast of text and quiz scores. Look for patterns that suggest additional work is needed.

11. Reinforce individual strengths by talking about them and finding ways to use them in everyday life.

Source: Adapted from the National Urban League (1989) and Ron Brandt (1989)

The Capistrano school district cautions that it may take time to develop a comprehensive parent involvement plan. But Hester advises, "If there are things that can be done immediately, do them. Almost anything and everything you can do to improve parent involvement yields immediate returns." Just keep in mind, however, that Hester is speaking of high school parents in general, not of at-risk parents specifically.

Efforts to reach kids must be ongoing. Epstein (1991) reiterates that programs must continue throughout childhood and adolescence. "Educators and policy makers, who may once have thought that family involvement was an issue only in the early years of schooling, now recognize the importance of school/family connections through the high school grades," she says.

Yes, the first five years of life are extremely important. But in some ways an overemphasis on this "magic period" can be counterproductive, says psychiatrist Edward Zigler. It can promote the attitude that "if we just do everything we can during the preschool years, then everything is going to be wonderful in school. That's just not true" (quoted in Olson 1990).

Instead, he says that changing the trajectory of a child really calls for consistent, ongoing effort. "That is why the family is so important," Zigler emphasizes, "because the family is there year after year after year" (Olson).

PART 5
SPECIAL GROUPS

PREVIEW OF CHAPTERS IN
PART 5: SPECIAL GROUPS

Chapter 17. Rural Families

A close look at the nation's rural areas turns up a surprising number of at-risk youth. This chapter surveys some of the aspects of rural life that either contribute to the problem or make it more difficult for at-risk students to obtain help. Then it recommends some ways to reach at-risk rural youth.

Chapter 18. Divorced and Separated Parents, Single Parents

In a recent survey, teachers said that 41 percent of their students had parents who were separated or divorced. The school work of approximately half of these students was adversely affected, the teachers reported. Schools can play a significant role in the family adjustment process.

One out of every four children—for African-American children, it's one out of two—live with a single parent. Studies show that single parents want more contact and consultation with teachers, but teachers tend to mistakenly believe that these parents won't help their children. Schools can take several steps to help.

Chapter 19. Teenage Parents

Teenage mothers tend not to finish high school, live on welfare, and aren't ready, in many cases, to assume responsibility for a child. Unable to reach teen mothers, a Hispanic project turned to the extended family. Programs dealing with life skills and focusing on jobs and training were useful in reaching teen fathers.

Chapter 20. Fathers

As a general rule, fathers are less involved in school matters than mothers. Coordinators of the Hispanic project learned what works and what doesn't work in reaching at-risk fathers.

Chapter 21. Children with Disabilities

Involving families is especially important if schools are to help children with special needs, because it is the family that knows the particular strengths, needs, and problems of their children.

Chapter 22. Immigrants

Many immigrants, driven to improve their status through hard work, fare better in the U.S. school systems than do native-born minorities. But many immigrant parents face obstacles that may thwart the good intentions they have for their children's success in school. For schools, therefore, effective communication with immigrant families is a must.

Chapter 23. Asian-Americans

Since the fall of Saigon in April 1975, over 800,000 Southeast Asian refugees have settled in this country. Today they number over a million. This chapter reviews several demographic and social factors that influence the level of Southeast Asian parent involvement. Then it recommends steps schools can take.

Chapter 24. African-Americans

The history of racism in this country has left African-American families with a deep sense of alienation from most institutions, including schools. This chapter suggests that the most effective way to reach out to African-American families as partners with the schools is to bolster their sense of control. A major element in James Comer's solution to involvement with African-American families is *empowerment*.

Chapter 25. Hispanics

Forty percent of Hispanics drop out of school—half of these before they reach ninth grade. No matter what causes Hispanics to fare so poorly in school, the bottom line is that Hispanic families need support. Guidelines for planning programs to involve Hispanic parents are provided, and recommendations for reaching out to Hispanic families are offered.

Chapter 17

RURAL FAMILIES

$\mathcal{R}$ ural families tend to get overlooked in the research on at-risk youth; by far, the majority of that research has been done in innercity areas. Also, because media coverage emanates from cities, rural areas often receive inadequate attention.

A closer look at the nation's rural areas turns up a surprising number of at-risk youth. In fact, a recent study by the National Rural Development Institute found that rural children were significantly more likely to be described as "at risk" than their counterparts in cities and suburbs (Helge 1990). Rural children came out worse on thirty-four of thirty-nine statistical comparisons within various risk categories.

Responses indicated that rural children were far more prone to be living in poverty during elementary and middle school years and to be involved with substance abuse in elementary school than were urban children. It seems that rural children may be more vulnerable to social and economic problems than their urban counterparts.

One of the difficulties in comparing this study with research on innercity students is that the term *at-risk* is defined slightly differently by Helge. Her "at-risk" categories include, for instance, low self-esteem, suicide attempt, depression, disability, child abuse, and child of an alcoholic parent—far broader categories, and yet also more specific, than those used by studies that simply concentrate on low-income and/or minority students.

One-third of the nation's students live in rural areas, and two-thirds of U.S. school districts are rural. While Helge says it's true that some rural communities are thriving, many are experiencing economic and social difficulties that are contributing to the development of at-risk children.

Obstacles Confronting At-Risk Rural Youth

The irony for rural kids is that some of the positive characteristics of rural communities can actually contribute to problems and lack of help for rural students. For example, pride and fierce individualism ("taking care of their own") can work against families' acceptance of counseling services. Also, the intimacy of rural settings can make it difficult to maintain confidentiality when reporting child abuse or seeking help for alcoholism.

Rural residents may be less willing to report child abuse because they have known the parents for years and may see them frequently at community functions or even be employed by them. In addition, in many rural communities a stigma is still attached to counseling. If counseling is sought, often it has to be done secretly so that neighbors won't find out.

Another obstacle to receiving counseling and other social, psychological, recreational, and medical services is that many of these services are nonexistent or inadequate in remote or impoverished rural areas. Many rural communities, says Helge, have inadequate medical and prenatal care, special education, foster care, sex and drug education, and career training and vocational education.

Some rural areas are also receiving an influx of refugees but lack bilingual staff and programs. Finally, many rural communities have comparatively few recreational opportunities, so teenagers may turn to drugs or sexual activity, claims Helge.

In communities with long-standing social, educational and economic problems, some develop low aspirations regarding education, graduation and employment. Education may not be highly valued. Sexual activity, teenage parenting, drug and alcohol use, delinquency, and dropping out of school becomes commonplace in such communities. Low self-esteem is accepted and becomes pervasive. Students have wider ranges of "deviancy" before their behavior attracts the attention of the school or community.

Suggestions for Reaching At-Risk Rural Youth

Recommendations include the involvement of parents, as well as social agencies, businesses, and civic and volunteer organizations. Resources are too scarce to deal with the problems in isolation. The entire community, Helge maintains, must play a part, including police, churches, the justice system, and civic groups.

TWO EXAMPLES OF RURAL FAMILY PROGRAMS

1. VIRGINIA. Family/School Partners in Education: A Model for Rural Schools is a program in Emporia, Virginia, that trains parents as tutors. The business community will also be actively involved, providing "work-release time" for parent training. A mobile resource center will travel to the different districts, serving as a training site.

2. TENNESSEE. The Washington County Learning Is for Everyone (LIFE) program promotes family involvement in rural areas to increase student achievement. Parents are encouraged to establish high educational expectations for their children and to pass these along through home learning activities and research-based techniques in parenting and behavior management.

Source: Adapted from Christopher Cross and others (1991)

Helge also suggests that parent groups are an essential resource in program planning and implementation, and she further advises the use of parents to approach other parents, community groups, and school employees. It is especially critical to involve the parents of students in dysfunctional family situations, if at all possible.

Helge focuses a great deal of attention on self-esteem, not only of children but of all family members. "The most basic ingredient to changing the serious problems of at-risk students, their families, and communities can be best affected by consistently enhancing self-esteem," she says.

Rural community members, who tend to value helping one another, can be key players in rural outreach efforts. "Frequently, rural family members will listen to their peers (e.g., neighbors, cooperative extension workers, or extended family members)," she says, "more easily than they will to school personnel. Thus all natural outreach agencies or unique rural resources should be involved in reaching at-risk families in those areas."

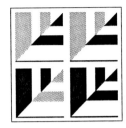

Chapter 18

DIVORCED AND SEPARATED PARENTS, SINGLE PARENTS

*B*oth children in families going through divorce or separation and those in families headed by a single parent are more likely to be at risk than their peers in stable families with both parents present.

Children of Divorce

Can parental divorce or separation really affect children's academic performance? Yes, says a recent teacher survey in which an average of 41 percent of the respondents' students had parents who were separated or divorced. The schoolwork of approximately half of these students was adversely affected. In addition, many of these students displayed school behavior problems, such as aggression, moodiness, daydreaming, withdrawal, and nervousness (Kurtz 1988).

This survey echoes other studies that have found children whose families have experienced marital disruption to be more at risk academically and psychosocially. Research demonstrates significant differences between students from disrupted families and students from intact families in their involvement in school problems such as tardiness, absenteeism, suspension, and dropping out, with those from intact families having fewer problems (Kurtz).

Services for Families in Transition

Schools can play a significant role in the family adjustment process. Kurtz suggests schools provide the following *direct* services:

1. Support groups for single parents to share and reduce loneliness and isolation

2. Parenting classes to help divorced, single parents understand the effects of divorce on children and how to manage those effects

3. Family transition groups for children who are adjusting to life in a divorced family

Indirect services might include:

1. Teacher inservice training to broaden teachers' sensitivity to family dynamics surrounding divorce and children's reactions to family breakups

2. Updated recordkeeping to ensure that school records reflect current family situations

3. Curriculum development to give children an opportunity to understand and discuss family transitions

4. Abolishing school policies that may be unfair to single parents (Schedule parent-teacher conferences after work, for example, and don't require parents to come to school to get children's makeup assignments when absent.)

5. Referral of families with chronic and severe problems to appropriate community agencies (Kurtz)

For instance, in regard to collaborating with other agencies, a social worker might be brought in to work with children and families. Robert Constable and Herbert Walberg (1988) mention Jimmy, a seven-year-old boy with learning disabilities whose parents were going through a divorce. The boy, who cried often and was very dependent on adults, was having trouble staying "on task" in school. The classroom teacher found him difficult and thought he was simply being uncooperative.

The social worker consulted with both his classroom teacher and resource room teacher and worked with them so that their expectations would be similar for him. Both teachers gained a better understanding of what Jimmy was going through and how the divorce was impairing his ability to concentrate. They agreed on a program of support.

The social worker also observed Jimmy and visited his parents. She helped the family see some of the effects of their conflict on him and referred them to a family service agency for indepth family counseling. The social worker developed a contract between the parents and teachers so that their efforts to work together and set common rules and expectations were supported. In addition, she worked with the parents' counselor.

"Jimmy was clearly triangulated into the marital issues," say Constable and Walberg. "Both parents were concerned about Jimmy's reactions to their problems but the school's work with Jimmy gave them enough space to get to other issues." This is a clear example of the benefits of parents and teachers working together to solve problems.

Some schools have taken steps to support children of divorce or remarriage. Many teachers have learned to work with children who are from different kinds of families. Textbooks have been adapted to be more sensitive to the needs of these children. Yet at the same time, says Jane C. Lindle (1990), the needs of the parents themselves often go unaddressed.

School administrators may be aware of the custody issues in divorces, and teachers are sometimes aware of where and with whom a child lives. But often school personnel stumble accidently upon difficult family situations. "Rarely do teachers and administrators actively seek to identify the students' family structure and then address the educational needs of both the child and the parent," says Lindle.

Involving Stepparents and Noncustodial Parents

Two such needs often occur with stepparents and noncustodial parents. In many cases, stepparents struggle with their role in the family. Generally, they are less involved in parent-school activities. Noncustodial parents also wrestle with their ongoing involvement with their children. Dorothy Rich (1985) encourages schools to reach out to noncustodial parents. "Almost always the more parents that are involved with the child, the better. Rather than discouraging this interest of noncustodial divorced parents, schools will want to encourage it."

Other experts agree. Know the custody situation in each family. Home life is so tied to school performance, says John McCormick (1990), that he claims 70 percent of elementary principals now keep formal records of each child's family structure. This practice is advisable for all children, at all ages.

Consider sending duplicate notes and report cards to noncustodial parents and scheduling separate parent-teacher conferences with them. Many researchers think this is definitely worth the extra postage and time it may require to ensure that all noncustodial parents who want these materials—and who want to be involved—receive them.

Rich suggests that allocating school funds for these extra mailings may be one of the least expensive but most effective ways of building parent involvement with at-risk families.

Single Parents

One-parent families now account for 22.3 percent of all families in the nation with children under eighteen, nearly double the rate in 1970. In 1990, 53 percent of African-American families with children were headed by a single parent, compared with 17 percent of white families and 26 percent of Hispanic families. By far, the majority of these single-parent families were headed by women: 82 percent of white families, 91 percent of African-American families, and 84 percent of Hispanic families (U.S. Bureau of the Census 1991).

The percentage of children under age eighteen who live with only one parent continues to increase, especially for African-Americans. In 1980, 44 percent of African-American children lived with their mother only; by 1990, the proportion had increased to 51 percent. For whites, the corresponding numbers were 14 percent and 16 percent (Bradley 1991).

Fully 97 percent of the members of the National Association of Elementary School Principals think children from single-parent homes pay a price academically, says McCormick.

A review of studies for the National Institute of Education shows that children from one-parent homes tend to receive lower grades, display more disruptive behavior in school, and have poorer attendance. Girls seem to adjust better than boys, and children who are very young fare better psychologically when their parents divorce than do their older brothers and sisters (Rich 1985).

The biggest factor that puts single parents at risk is poverty. Families headed by a woman with no husband present represented 53 percent of poor families in 1990; for poor African-American families, the figure was 75 percent (U.S. Bureau of the Census 1991). In fact, the Census Bureau reported that the growing numbers of families headed by females with no spouse present accounted for 84

FEMALE SINGLE-PARENT FAMILIES, RACE, AND POVERTY

Single-Parent Families Headed by Females with Children under Eighteen Years in 1990

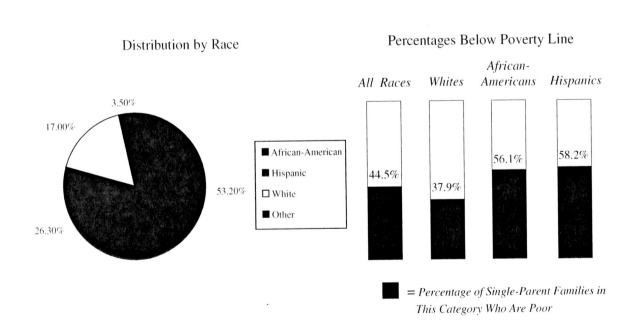

Source: Calculated from U.S. Bureau of the Census data (1991)

percent of the net increase in poor families between 1989 and 1990. Poverty, as has been pointed out, is one of the primary factors that place families at risk.

Schools Discriminate Against Single Parents

According to a study by Joyce Epstein (1984), single and working parents can and do spend as much time helping their children as parents who have more leisure time. It is often teachers who mistakenly believe that single parents won't help. But Epstein found that when teachers reached out to these parents, the parents were generally more willing to help. And when teachers assisted parents in helping their children, single parents were just as effective as parents with more education and leisure time.

"Whatever their potential for being involved," says Ascher, "research indicates that single and working parents may be discriminated against by school personnel, who tend to decide in advance that these parents cannot be approached or relied on."

The Metropolitan Life Survey (1987) showed that single working parents, as well as dual working parent families, are especially likely to want more contact and consultation with teachers. Although teachers see these parents as hard to reach, the parents themselves are often equally dissatisfied about lack of contact.

In fact, another survey noted that 71 percent of single parents who work full-time *had* taken time off to visit school, compared to 73 percent in two-parent families where both partners work full-time (Amundson 1988).

"There is evidence," says James B. Stedman (1987), "that single-parents find it difficult to participate in their children's education to the full extent they want because schools have not been sensitive to their time and resource complaints."

Among the complaints from single parents are that schools schedule events as though each family had two parents, only one of whom works, and that school staff may have negative expectations of single parents and their children.

What Can Schools Do?

Stedman's recommendations to schools include the following:

1. Be more flexible in arranging parent conferences; schedule them at times to accommodate working parents.

2. Provide staff with inservice training on ways of responding to single parents and their children, and deal with negative expectations staff may have about these families.

3. Consider child care both before and after school; provide child care facilities at the school during parent meetings and events.

4. Arrange transportation so that single-parent families can participate in all school activities; don't assume that parents have their own transportation.

5. Work with single parents in dealing with in-school behavior problems.

6. Develop a list of suggestions that single parents can use at home.

Chapter 19

TEENAGE PARENTS

*E*ach year more than one million teenagers in the United States become pregnant and more than half of them give birth (Nicolau and Ramos 1990). The physical and emotional changes that come with adolescence, plus increased freedom and peer pressure to become sexually active, can create problems, especially for female adolescents. That pressure, coupled with a lack of information about birth control or a willingness to use it, has led to high adolescent pregnancy rates.

Teenage mothers are definitely an at-risk group. They tend not to finish high school, live on welfare, and aren't ready, in many cases, to take on the care of a child, so many still being children themselves. As Nicolau and Ramos explain, "Being a mother is a big responsibility. Surviving the teenage years can be a real challenge. When you put them together, being a teenager and a mother at the same time can be an overwhelming task."

Many adolescent females are unhappy at home, do poorly in school, or believe that their parents don't understand them—and think becoming pregnant will solve their problems. They see having a baby as a way out, a way to become adults. Ironically, these young mothers often end up being bound to the home, living on welfare, and almost always mired in poverty.

Among Hispanic teen mothers, very few complete high school. If they marry, the marriage often ends in divorce or separation. More children are usually born. By her midtwenties, a woman who has had her first child in her teens may have several more, few marketable skills, and little chance of escaping poverty. Even though they may have planned otherwise, most Hispanic teenage mothers live with their own mothers, or, if they marry, with their mothers-in-law (Nicolau and Ramos).

The Difficulty of Reaching Teen Mothers

Project coordinators for Hispanic parent involvement projects found teen mothers very unresponsive. Many would make a commitment to attend activities and then fail to show up, even when they had proposed the activities during home visits.

A special initiative focusing on teen mothers shed some light on what was happening. Most of

EXAMPLES OF SPECIAL PROGRAMS FOR TEEN PARENTS

1. **ILLINOIS.** The Teenage Single Parent Initiative is a collaborative project among the Illinois State Board of Education and three organizations already active in working with teenage parents (Parents Too Soon, Ounce of Prevention Fund, and The Illinois Caucus on Teenage Pregnancy). Nine pilot sites have been funded to address the education and employment of teenage single parents, and parenting education is an important component of the program.

2. **CONNECTICUT AND PENNSYLVANIA.** Connecticut's Young Parent Program provides opportunities to acquire information on child development, parenting, and day care. Pennsylvania provides parent effectiveness training for teen parents.

3. **MINNESOTA.** Minnesota's Early Childhood Family Education (ECFE) program has a comprehensive plan that includes:

   • *Education for Pregnant Minors and Minor Parents.* School districts must make available an educational program to help pregnant teens and minor parents complete high school; the program must use appropriate community resources, a good example of collaborative action.

   • *Mandatory School Attendance for AFDC Young Parents.* All custodial parents through age nineteen who don't have a high school diploma must attend an educational program; school districts are required to report attendance to county social services.

   • *Adolescent Parent Planning.* Minor parents are required to plan for themselves and their children (including consideration of education, parenting skills, health care, living arrange-

ments, self-sufficiency, and personal problems); the county social service agency is required to assist in developing this plan.

   • *Transportation Aid for Adolescent Parents.* School districts are legally permitted to provide transportation for custodial parents and their children between home and day care facilities and school, according to criteria established by the local school board.

   • *Child Care Funds.* Adolescent parents who are in high school or who wish to return to school may be eligible for child care funding on a sliding scale basis.

   • *Other Services.* All children and parents are eligible for weekly classes. Children's classes are held simultaneously with parents' classes; in addition, home visits and access to toys, books, and special events may be provided.

The Minnesota statute requires substantive parental involvement, and parents comprise the majority of members of required local advisory councils. However, whether teen parents in Minnesota get involved with their children's education in any way is not reported; whether they actually attend the parent class is not mentioned. Still, providing support services and focusing attention on keeping adolescent parents in school is a start—both for teen parents and their children.

Source: Adapted from Council of Chief State School Officers (1989)

the thirty-two teen mothers who were interviewed were clearly dependent on their mothers, most of whom had been teen mothers themselves. "The girls were not only locked in a cycle of welfare dependency," say Nicolau and Ramos, "they were trapped in a cycle of emotional dependency as well.... Their misguided attempts to achieve adulthood through motherhood had produced the opposite result. It had prolonged the child/parent relationship with their mothers."

Thus the project coordinators decided these teen parents could best be reached by programs that targeted the extended family, rather than focusing on teen mothers alone. For instance, programs with incentives—like having a raffle or drawing—seemed to appeal to the practical sense of the grandmother. If more family members were needed to increase their chances of winning, the grandmothers seemed to see to it that their teen daughters showed up (Nicolau and Ramos).

Teen Fathers

Teen fathers are even harder to reach. However, Nicolau and Ramos cite a number of programs sponsored by Banks Street College that seem to indicate that programs dealing with life skills and focusing on jobs and training, as well as on children, attract young men. It is noteworthy that these programs also placed emphasis on including the parents of the teen fathers. But not all Banks Street models were school-based. Nicolau and Ramos contend that many teen parents may have to be reached in nonschool settings.

For example, AVANCE, a neighborhood-based San Antonio project, "has been enormously successful in turning around the lives of young mothers and fathers" (Nicolau and Ramos). The project started by offering free neighborhood babysitting. Mothers and grandmothers who used it paid for it by attending parenting classes, which led to education and training opportunities for the mothers—and, later on, the fathers.

The problem of teen pregnancy isn't going to disappear, because the daughters of teen mothers tend to become adolescent mothers themselves, perpetuating the cycle. "Extraordinary measures may be called for," Nicolau and Ramos stress, "and schools may want to consider making radical departures from the way in which they historically have viewed their role vis a vis parents." If teen parents can only be reached outside the schools, then schools may want to establish partnerships with neighborhood centers and other community-based organizations as a way to convey information.

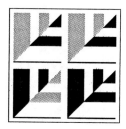

Chapter 20

FATHERS

$\mathcal{W}$hile American mothers spend less than half an hour per day directly interacting with their children, fathers spend only about fifteen minutes a day. So if it's difficult to involve mothers in their children's education—especially at-risk mothers—it's even harder to reach at-risk fathers.

With the changing roles of mothers and fathers in our society, policymakers need to find a way to involve fathers in the education of their children. With an increasing number of mothers working outside the home, it seems only equitable that fathers should be expected to assume greater responsibility for their children's schooling. But that's only theory, of course.

Dorothy Rich (1985) proposes media campaigns showing fathers working with their children; Kristen Amundson (1988) suggests that fathers be encouraged to serve on parent organization boards, visit classrooms, and become "room parents."

However, none of the proposals mentioned above would likely be effective with at-risk fathers. But what would? Unfortunately, in my research for this book, I found only one project

that tried to involve teen fathers. The program was designed specifically for Hispanic fathers, but since many of the characteristics of Hispanic fathers apply to other fathers, too, this chapter focuses on Siobhan Nicolau and Carmen Lydia Ramos's work with at-risk fathers.

The Difficulty of Working with Fathers

Regardless of race, ethnicity, or socioeconomic status, most fathers are less involved in school matters than mothers. The Hispanic project directors described trying to work with Hispanic fathers as "next to impossible." "The vast majority of low-income Hispanic fathers perceive education and anything related to it—like child-rearing—as a woman's job," explain Nicolau and Ramos.

As in several other cultures, the Hispanic father is the head of the house and presents a serious, stern, macho image. Generally, he doesn't express affection openly and doesn't communicate with the children. Sometimes other members of the family are afraid of him. Project coordinators report that when they visited homes, the fathers usually were not seen. When fathers were present, they seldom participated in the conversations.

The coordinators report that Hispanic fathers avoid functions that are promoted as, or can be construed as, "learning" activities:

> It threatens their control, their dignity, and implies that the father needs counseling, or is not a good father, or has flaws and weaknesses. An uneducated Hispanic father, even more than a Hispanic mother, fears professionals. What if questions are asked that the father does not know how to answer? How will that reflect on him as head of the family? (Nicolau and Ramos)

Suggestions for Recruiting Fathers

Over time, project coordinators discovered the types of involvement that at-risk Hispanic fathers are most receptive to:

1. Hispanic fathers like down-to-earth projects where they can use their unique skills, such as building playground equipment, overseeing sports events or garage sales, painting a classroom or mural, or moving furniture into a parents' room.

2. Hispanic fathers want to do the above things with other men; they are not comfortable working with women.

3. Fathers will attend events that are celebrations—appreciation dinners, assemblies, open school nights, sporting events, and graduations.

4. Meetings are almost never attractive to Hispanic fathers, but when they did agree to attend, it was, in most cases, to hear a male speaker.

5. Fathers generally prefer activities held in the evenings or on weekends.

6. Hispanic fathers like activities that offer incentives. As an example, one project gave raffle tickets to each parent who attended its meetings. If both mother and father attended, it increased the family's chances of winning. This incentive raised attendance of fathers.

7. Fathers enjoy accompanying a son or daughter to a "High School Night," a program to assist in reviewing high school options.

8. Generally, Hispanic fathers are willing to participate in "action projects," but are not willing to attend meetings and conferences.

Even though the attitudes of low-income Hispanic fathers in this project were distressing to many teachers, by doing the kinds of activities listed above, fathers were nevertheless sending a message to their children that said, "School is important. That's why I'm willing to build playground equipment or plant trees for the school on my day off."

School personnel can probably think of additional ways to involve at-risk fathers. Some fathers may come to parent-teacher conferences if specifically invited to do so. Or you might want to consider setting up family conferences, as the Central Park East Schools of District 4 in New York City have done, as a way of encouraging teachers, parents, and children to work as allies in the learning process. Through the family conference approach, the teacher, parents, and child develop a cooperative plan for addressing problems or areas that need improvement (Council of Chief State School Officers 1989).

Also, keep in mind what was learned about teen fathers in chapter 19—that programs dealing with life skills and focusing on jobs and training tend to attract men and thus open the door for male involvement in their children's education.

Chapter 21

CHILDREN WITH DISABILITIES

*A*s with other special needs groups, in families where a child has a disability, effective communication between home and school is especially important.

Importance of Family Involvement

According to Madeleine Will, former assistant secretary for special education and rehabilitative services in the U. S. Department of Education, the assumption is often made that children with special needs are burdens and that therefore these families are dysfunctional or deficient in some way.

Not so, she says:

Many of these families achieve happiness and well-being. School and service professionals, however, must be flexible and willing to go the extra distance if families with special needs are to receive the information and services necessary to ensure the best quality of life for the family unit. (Council of Chief State School Officers 1989)

The involvement of these families in their children's education and service programs is especially important because it is the family that usually knows the particular strengths, needs, resources, and problems of their children. Thus parents can help ensure that services are appropriate and sensitive to their family's unique characteristics. Also, because children with special needs often require services from more than one source, parents are frequently the most knowledgeable and effective case managers.

Parent Involvement Is the Key in Colorado

In Loveland, Colorado, parents have helped children with learning disabilities succeed. The Thompson school district is a good example of a special education program with strong parent involvement. "We have tried a variety of different approaches," says Barbara Benjamin, special education coordinator. "Involving parents in the process is the approach that seems to work best" (Decker and Decker 1988).

The Parent Resource Program serves parents whose children have been identified as having a learning disability or handicap and is designed to involve them in the development of an individual educational plan for each child. "It's a scary time for parents when children are singled out in this way and we feel that by helping the parents we are helping the children," says Benjamin (Decker and Decker).

The program involves parents helping other parents in a supportive way. For example, certain experienced parents are selected by the district to go through a twelve-hour training session. During this time, the parents discuss their own concerns and how they coped with problems when their children were going through the diagnosis and planning process. Then these parents are trained in communication skills, familiarized with the school-based programs available, and taught exactly what is involved in developing an educational plan and individual goals for a learning-disabled child.

The chief purpose in starting this group was to give parents of children who were experiencing learning problems contact with other parents who had already been through the process. "Knowing what to expect and having sympathetic support reduces the inevitable stress on the parents, enabling them to be more supportive and helpful to their child," explain Decker and Decker. "Most important, parents are better prepared to assist in the planning and be active participants in the education of their children."

The program's staff has also developed a booklet that tells parents about the planning process and the different steps involved. Regular group meetings are held to explain policies and procedures to parents and to provide them with resources. Guest speakers have included a variety of experts from different sources.

The group also presented a workshop for parents, special educators, and even bus drivers who transport the children, to help them better understand the frustrations and joys of working with handicapped children. The workshop focused on what it felt like to be the parent of a handicapped child or common emotions experienced by those responsible for providing education or service to the child. Both the group and the workshop have been very successful.

"We believe that parents play an important role in their children's education," says Benjamin, "and at times the responsibility can be overwhelming for parents of disabled children. We have tried to develop a system of supporting the parents to help them share the responsibility" (Decker and Decker).

Chapter 22

IMMIGRANTS

*I*mmigrants in the U.S. often fare much better educationally than native-born minorities. That's because immigrants generally perceive their status as outsiders to be a temporary one that they can overcome through hard work.

In contrast, "blacks and other nonimmigrant minorities tend to see their life conditions as permanent and unchangeable," says anthropologist John Ogbu. This perception, he says, gives "rise to such counterproductive school attitudes as the recently explored phenomenon of labeling high academic achievement as 'acting white'" (Reeves 1988).

As these native-born students get older, they apparently become more aware of the reality that, as members of a subordinate minority group, they will encounter more difficulties obtaining good jobs, even when they have a good education.

Immigrants Face Obstacles

In spite of the good intentions immigrant parents have for their children's success in school, they face several obstacles that they may not be able to overcome by hard work alone. Immigrant parents frequently lack knowledge about U.S. customs and American school traditions, which results in their children being ill-prepared for school. In addition, their limited English proficiency puts them at a disadvantage in dealing with their children's education.

Parents from some cultures—Hispanic and Asian in particular—are reluctant to challenge a teacher's authority or openly air their concerns with the schools. Some even feel uncomfortable approaching a teacher or school administrator. Finally, immigrant parents may have different notions than schools on what makes a child a good student.

Schools Must Reach Out

Schools must make extra efforts to develop effective communication with immigrant families, keeping in mind that there are differences between and within cultures. Here are some basic steps schools can take:

FAMILY LITERACY PROGRAMS

Schools unknowingly have often created rifts between immigrant parents and their children by teaching the children English at school while their parents remain non-English speaking. Students sometimes become frustrated when they have to translate for their parents, who understand little about their children's new life. Parents often report feeling isolated from their children and disadvantaged by having to rely on them for information about school.

In an effort to bridge the gap between generations and help limited English proficiency (LEP) parents participate in their children's education, English literacy classes and family literacy programs have been springing up nationwide.

The following are examples of projects or programs that are working with LEP families to improve literacy skills:

PROJECT LEARNING ENGLISH THROUGH INTERGENERATIONAL FUNDING (LEIF). Gail Weinstein-Shr, a professor of education at Temple University who was working with Southeast Asian refugees in the Philadelphia area, established LEIF in 1985. Privately funded, LEIF pairs adult refugees with college students who teach them English so that they can then teach their children and grandchildren about their native land and customs. Today the program includes more than 200 volunteers at four locations in Philadelphia.

NORTHWEST EDUCATIONAL CO-OPERATIVE in Des Plaines, Illinois, is a nonprofit agency that operated a demonstration project from 1986 to 1989 that taught LEP parents basic survival skills and how to understand and interact with the American school system. More than 200 copies of their curriculum program, *Home English Literacy for Parents*, have been distributed since then.

FAMILY LEARNING CENTERS is a network that has been created by Service, Employment, and Redevelopment, a nonprofit, Dallas-based organization founded by Hispanic groups. The centers are designed to improve the education of Hispanic students and reduce Hispanic illiteracy rates. After being piloted at three sites in 1986, today there are thirty-seven sites funded with $6.5 million in federal grants and private donations.

PARENTS AS PARTNERS INTERGENERATIONAL LITERACY PROJECT. Funded by a federal Family/School Partnership grant, this project represents collaboration between the Chelsea Public Schools in Boston, Boston University, and several community organizations. Its objectives are to improve the literacy skills of adults and to diminish reading disability among children. University staff members work out of a community center and offer "story time" programs for children while their parents are taught specific strategies for improving their own literacy and ways to become involved in their children's education.

OFFICE OF BILINGUAL EDUCATION AND MINORITY LANGUAGES AFFAIRS (OBEMLA) FAMILY ENGLISH LITERACY PROGRAM, part of the U.S. Education Department, is conducting a two-year descriptive study of fifteen demonstration projects that it has funded. However, even without data to support the effectiveness of the Family English Literacy Program, OBEMLA has been expanding its commitment to the program since 1984. In 1985, it funded four three-year demonstration projects; by 1989, OBEMLA had funded thirty-five such projects with a total of $4.7 million in grants.

All the projects attempt to improve the academic performance of LEP children by teaching their parents to teach them, by maintaining the cohesiveness of language-minority families, and by getting these families more involved in their children's schools. The projects vary widely in curriculum and methods, however, since they must accommodate diverse adult populations.

The OBEMLA-funded Family English Literacy Programs are evenly divided between those that stress bilingual instruction and those that provide lessons in English.

Examples of four such diverse projects are:

- **Michigan.** A project begun by the Grand Rapids, Michigan, schools in 1988 requests that

(continued on next page)

(continued from previous page)

parents and teachers sign a contract to collaborate in the education of LEP preschoolers. Parents can take home books from a library to read to their children. Teachers assist the parents in understanding the vocabulary and concepts in the books.

• **California.** A program in the Baldwin Park Unified School District in California includes both ESL and bilingual education techniques. It provides certificates of completion to immigrant parents who can then use them to help meet the language training required for U.S. citizenship.

• **Colorado.** A program operated by the Bilinguals United for Educational Opportunity Center at the University of Colorado in Boulder attempts to reach Hispanic and Asian families in remote rural areas by collaborating with local social service agencies.

• **California.** The Family English Literacy Through Books and Beyond program in the Solana Beach, California, school district is modeled after a highly successful districtwide project. Participating families meet at an elementary school for two hours each week. Parents and children spend the first hour working together on an ESL lesson that teaches them how to adapt to American society. During the second hour, the children focus on literature, while the parents receive training in English and parenting skills.

Although little is known about the effectiveness of such programs, supporters report a growing level of enthusiasm and funding, spurred partly by interest in the broader area of family literacy, which Northwest Education Cooperative project coordinator Laura Bercovitz calls a "hot issue." In addition, according to Meta Potts, director of the National Center for Family Literacy, new family literacy programs are being established as a result of the Family Support Act of 1988, which requires provision of educational services for welfare recipients.

Source: Peter Schmidt (1990)

1. Provide translators for those parents who don't speak English.

2. Prepare all information and messages sent home in the parents' native languages.

3. Recruit volunteers to promote communication with parents who don't speak English.

4. Learn about cultural differences in attitudes, styles, and practices related to education and the school in order to avoid practices that alienate culturally different parents.

5. Offer ESL classes or family literacy programs.

6. Develop a plan to help families of bilingual/bicultural students understand the role they can play in the educational process—both at school and at home—and share information about issues of concern with them. (Council of Chief State School Officers 1989)

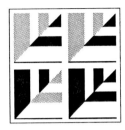

Chapter 23

ASIAN-AMERICANS

S ince the fall of Saigon in April 1975, over 800,000 Southeast Asian refugees (Vietnamese, Cambodians, Laotians, and Hmongs) have settled in this country. This high incidence of immigration, added to their above-average birthrate, has increased their number to over a million. California has nearly 40 percent of this population, with the rest centered mainly in the urban areas of Texas, Minnesota, Pennsylvania, and Illinois Morrow 1991).

Factors Affecting Involvement of Southeast Asian Parents

Several demographic and social factors influence the level and quality of Southeast Asian parent involvement. All the following factors, discussed by Morrow, should be considered if schools are to successfully involve these parents in their children's education.

Different Values and Behaviors

In contrast to Americans' emphasis on egocentric, independent behavior, Southeast Asian children are taught to think of family first and subjugate personal desires and concerns. Each child develops a sense of moral obligation and primary loyalty to the family, which includes unquestioning loyalty and obedience to parents and, by extension, to all authority figures, including principals, teachers, and other school personnel.

Like Hispanics, Southeast Asians tend to believe that professional educators have the expertise and right to make all the decisions and know what to do with their children, without parental assistance.

Literacy Level

In a 1985 study of 800 Southeast Asian refugees, Paul Strand found that the Vietnamese were far more literate in both their native language and English than Laotians, Cambodians, and Hmongs. There were also significantly higher levels of literacy among the early (1975-78) refugees than among those arriving later.

Prearrival Education

Twenty-six percent of the Vietnamese had no formal education, compared to 44 percent of the

Cambodians, 53 percent of the Laotians, and 81 percent of the Hmongs. Also, 46 percent of the Vietnamese attended or graduated from high school, compared to 53 percent of the Cambodians, 43 percent of the Laotians, and only 19 percent of the Hmongs (Strand 1985 and Tran 1982).

In addition, the Vietnamese had a decided advantage in higher education, with 28 percent having attended college or trade school, compared to 4 percent of Laotians, 1 percent of Cambodians, and none of the Hmongs (Morrow). These wide variations in both literacy and educational levels have obvious implications for schools in working with Southeast Asians.

Size of Their Native Community

One factor often overlooked, says Morrow, is the size of the refugee's native community. Most Southeast Asian refugees have settled in U.S. urban areas, and their ability to adjust can be dependent on their previous experience in such an environment. While the Vietnamese and Laotians are largely urbanites, most Cambodians and Hmongs are rural people. Among the most recent arrivals, however, all but the Cambodians tend to be from rural areas.

Perceptions of Parental Involvement

In the U.S., we expect that parents will be involved in school functions and work with their children. This idea of parents being involved in schools is completely counter to Southeast Asians' beliefs.

In their native countries, school administrators and teachers are expected to decide all matters, from curriculum to discipline, without regard to parent concerns or desires. The Vietnamese especially revere education and educators, and, like other Southeast Asians, hold teachers in high esteem, second only to parents. But little or no contact with the school is expected or practiced by most Southeast Asians in their native countries.

Consider also that these parents come from poor countries where educational resources are far inferior to those in American schools. Large classes (up to sixty students), lack of textbooks, didactic teaching methods, and harsh physical punishment are accepted as normal conditions in Southeast Asia. It is no wonder, then, as Ascher notes, that "few parents can see that the American schools are not equally equipped and staffed, and that children are not treated according to their cultural, linguistic, and socio-economic backgrounds."

The Pride and Shame Principle

American children are often referred to the principal's office when they show inappropriate or disruptive behavior. When a Southeast Asian child is sent to the office for this reason, the principal must be aware of the cultural "pride and shame" principle.

According to this principle, all individual behavior reflects either positively or negatively on the whole family. Thus while academic achievements are highly valued and promote family pride, negative behavior—disobedience, disrespect, shirking responsibilities—results in collective family shame and can trigger severe punishment by the parents on the child (Morrow).

Families Emphasize Success

Many Asian children do well in school. "The remarkable school success of recently arrived Asian immigrant children has prompted questions about what these children have that American youngsters don't," says Rich (1987).

What's their secret? Apparently it's not Asian parents' discussions with their children. Contrary to common perceptions, a 1988 poll found that Asian parents were less likely than parents from other ethnic groups to talk regularly with their children about school experiences (Rothman 1990).

Some experts have cited cohesive family structure as a reason for Asian children's success at school. But other cultural groups whose children do not do as well also have cohesive family structures.

However, in another sense, the family of Asian children may play a large part. The section on effort versus ability in chapter 9 perhaps explains why Asian children generally do well in school compared to other ethnic groups. Parent attitudes toward education may provide students with the motivation to succeed. If effort is the key to success in school, as a majority of Japanese and Chinese parents have said, then these parents expect more of their children and believe that they *can* succeed in school.

As Lester Thurow of MIT said recently, the big reason for Asian-American success in public schools is family: family means having a parent who tells you that education is important (Jones 1989).

Recommendations for Schools

If schools want to involve Southeast Asian parents in their schools, Morrow suggests that it's essential to do the following:

Offer inservice training for teachers, counselors, and support personnel to raise their awareness of cultural differences. For example, when working with Southeast Asian families, it is important to first determine whether the family is Vietnamese, Laotian, Cambodian, or Hmong. Also, remember that Southeast Asians vary considerably in education and literacy levels, urban orientation, and, to a lesser degree, in perceptions of the parental role in schools.

Provide resources for school personnel to help them understand cultural differences. Many excellent books, films, and other resources are available (see sidebar) from various agencies. Remember that many traits that Americans take for granted, such as openness, independence, and directness, are not equally valued by Southeast Asians.

Respect the "pride and shame" principle. When a Southeast Asian child is referred to an administrator, counselor, or psychologist for behavioral problems, keep in mind that the child's family suffers intense shame, guilt, and anxiety. "When working with parents in such cases," says Morrow, "school personnel should proceed cautiously and sympathetically in discussing the child's problems, since Southeast Asians typically 'talk around' any subject."

Develop and maintain a sense of trust. Because Southeast Asians rarely question educators' decisions, school personnel have tremendous power over both Southeast Asian children and parents. Therefore, ensure that your treatment of Southeast Asian children is both caring and professional.

Consider hiring native-speaking community and classroom aides, especially if you have a sizeable number of Southeast Asian students in your school. Carefully selected aides who have the respect of the Southeast Asian community can provide valuable assistance in increasing the level of parent involvement.

Find out how Southeast Asian parents feel about American schools. A 1980 survey by Rupp found that most were generally satisfied with their children's education, felt that teachers' ideas were more important than their own, but thought that schools should emphasize the basics and teach good morals and behavior.

However, many also felt that schools in their native countries were more difficult than American schools, that their children were not getting enough homework, that schools were "Americanizing" their children too quickly, that school discipline was too lax, and that students lacked respect for teachers.

Is it possible to effectively involve Southeast Asian parents in school activities and in their children's education? Morrow answers a qualified yes. "If principals, teachers, and other school personnel," he says, "make an effort to understand their different value systems, take time to look at each family as a unique entity, and work patiently and sensitively with each child and family, a higher degree of Southeast Asian parental involvement can indeed be achieved."

Chapter 24

AFRICAN-AMERICANS

*K*eep in mind that, when compared with other racial groups, African-American families in general have:

 • a higher incidence of female-headed households (and teen mothers)

 • an intergenerational history of employment in lower-skilled, lower-paying occupations

In comparison to other American families, African-American families have been more vulnerable to changes in the labor market in the past fifteen to twenty years because African-American adults do not have equal access to prosperous sectors of the job market. This new source of deeply entrenched poverty affects even the hardiest of African-American families.

Chronic poverty is one of the major elements that places African-American families at risk, which the above factors play a major role in maintaining. The majority of African-American families in the U.S. are middle- to low-income households. One out of five American children lives in poverty, but the rate is twice as high among African-Americans. In 1990, 45 percent of African-American children were poor, compared with 16 percent of white children and 38 percent of Hispanic children (U.S. Bureau of the Census 1991).

African-American Males

Has the African-American male become an "endangered species"? With the crisis in educational performance, economic productivity, and employability among African-American males, this question has spawned national debate.

African-American males have much higher poverty rates than whites. Among high school dropouts of all ages, African-American males are twice as likely as white males to be poor. Among high school graduates, the poverty rate for African-American males is two and one-half times higher than for white males (U.S. Bureau of the Census). African-American men earn only about three-fourths of what white men earn, regardless of education level attained. Median income for African-American men between the ages of thirty-five and forty-four in 1989 was $15,320, compared to $22,160 for white men (Bradley).

Among male African-Americans who were twenty-five to thirty-four years old in 1990, 16.6 percent* had dropped out of high school and had not reenrolled. In contrast, the dropout rate for the same age group of white males was 13.9 percent (U.S. Bureau of the Census). However, the African-American dropout rate has improved markedly since 1968, when it was 27 percent for both sexes.

As early as elementary school, African-American males begin to experience failure at rates much higher than their counterparts. "It is imperative," says the Orleans Parish School Board (1988), "that we act now to remedy the academic and behavioral problems of black male youth, with particular emphasis on raising their self-concepts and self-esteem so that they will succeed in school."

In the report *Toward a More Perfect Union*, economic analysis shows how inadequate basic academic skills are intertwined with problems of youth employment, dropping out of school, out-of-wedlock parenting, welfare dependency, and decline in work-force productivity (Orleans Parish School Board).

Thus we must do everything possible to ensure that African-American children—particularly African-American males—are prepared for living and working successfully in twenty-first century America. That means changes in the education of African-Americans, including an emphasis on parent involvement.

James Comer of the School Development Program (SDP), who has worked with African-American children for years, has said, "It has become increasingly evident that too few parents of black children are intimately involved in their children's educational experience and that ways must be found to involve them" (Comer and others 1987-88).

Barbara Richardson (1989) also speaks of the importance of involvement by African-American parents:

---

* This percentage was calculated from table 11 (p. 84) in the Bureau of the Census report *Poverty in the United States: 1990.* Another Bureau of the Census report, *Educational Attainment in the United States: March 1989 and 1988,* gives a figure of 19.1 percent. Although both reports were issued in August 1991, the *Poverty* report uses 1990 data, whereas the *Educational Attainment* report uses 1989 data.

It is critical that parents play a role in the education of their children. The school should have groups and activities specifically for parents, such as the PTA, parent-teacher nights, pot-luck suppers, and so on. Parents should be very involved in the education process and take responsibility for their children's educational environment and achievement. Ideally, parental influence should extend to what is taught in the classroom. African-American parents should ensure that books and other learning materials used in school include positive African-American representation.

African-American Parent Involvement: A History Lesson

To find a way to involve African-American families, we must start by examining the history of African-American education in the U.S., for it contains a key to reaching African-American parents in the public school system.

The history of American education has been different for African-Americans than for whites or middle-class groups. In nineteenth century rural America, teachers were often boarded with "kith and kin" to those they taught. However, such symbiotic relationships rarely characterized the connections of most African-American families (or other ethnic minorities) to schools (Olson 1990).

Racism Causes a Crisis of Confidence in Schools

A history of racism and discrimination through the years has left African-American families with a deep sense of mistrust and alienation regarding most institutions. As Comer explains, "Alienated, rejected and suppressed people everywhere develop passive-aggressive and anti-social relationships with those in power and control" (Hamilton-Lee 1988).

Most African-American parents have experienced continued crises regarding their children's education. Sara Lawrence Lightfoot (1987) points to a history in which the children of slaves were, both by national and local policy, to be kept undereducated and illiterate. Further, in northern states, where slavery was abolished prior to the Civil War, African-American children were generally forbidden to attend schools with white children, and public dollars were not allocated for African-American schools, without repeated pressure by African-American parents and communities for adherence to the "separate but equal" education of African-American children.

"Even today," Slaughter and Kuehne (1987-88) add,

> once allocated, the dollars are rarely allocated equitably. Desegregation efforts, initially pursued by black parents and communities to ensure that black children would have equal access to a high-quality education, have been systematically resisted and thwarted by white communities in all regions of the country.

In short, then, it's easy to see, as John Ogbu and others have suggested, that the African-American community's "crisis of confidence" in the benefits of public education for its children is justified. "There have been numerous efforts within the community for years that have attempted to maximize parent involvement and participation in schools," Slaughter and Kuehne assert. "Although the majority of black Americans still favor public education, they express continuing concern about the public schools' influence on their children's learning and development."

Schools' Lack of Respect for African-American Families

Today, especially in schools where white middle-class faculties teach low-income minority groups, an understanding of historical and psychological realities that have influenced minority groups is necessary to improve home-school relations and thus involve these parents in the schooling of their children.

"Even those schools that claim to have a positive attitude toward the families of minority students and offer outreach programs to involve parents," says Hamilton-Lee, often "operate on the rather naive assumption that the children's problems are the result of their parents' inadequacies."

> In far too many situations (though not all), schools serving minority students show little respect for their students' parents and make no effort to include them in school affairs—other than calling them in to deal with a discipline crisis involving their particular child. Communication is one-sided,

consisting mainly of rules or criticisms of the school to the parent. The not-so-subtle message often seems to be: "You parents are not doing a very good job at raising your children, as demonstrated by their behavior or academic problems at school."

With this kind of history, African-American parents may simply view school "as a necessary evil, mandated by law but clearly outside the family's control or best interest—just like all other social services" (Hamilton-Lee).

Empowerment of African-American Parents

Perhaps the most effective way to reach African-American families as partners with the schools is to restore the sense of control that has been taken away from them, and to ensure that schools *are* serving the best interests of their children.

A sense of greater control can be achieved through empowerment—discussed in chapter 12—and through African-American parents' involvement in decision-making, planning, and development of their children's education. This has been a major element in Comer's strategy for involving African-American families.

Self-Determination and Empowerment

Empowerment is a major issue for African-Americans. It's been mentioned earlier that the Head Start program gave African-American families their first real involvement with education. For many African-Americans, this opportunity served as a basis for grassroots training in political participation. However, over time, greater emphasis has been placed on parent education.

Still, as a program designed to reduce poverty, several researchers conclude that without a strong emphasis on empowerment, Head Start will be significantly compromised because of the parents' and community's need for control and self-determination (Slaughter and Kuehne).

"If the exercise with parent involvement in Head Start has taught us anything, it is that self-determination is not only an important component of quality education but the link between education and the material and social progress of the poor," say Slaughter and Kuehne. Evaluations of Head Start shouldn't focus simply on children's skill development and related parenting behaviors, but also on parents themselves and their self-perceptions.

Comer believes that preschool programs, while perhaps useful, have had debatable long-term effects with at-risk children, particularly those that have had limited parental involvement. "While such programs may have reduced parental alienation from their children's educational experience," he says, "they did not involve parents in school management and operations in a meaningful way" (Comer and others 1987-88).

For Comer and his colleagues, parent involvement is a key to increasing African-American children's success in school, since many African-American children perceive home and school as being less closely related than other students do.

However, school climate and parent involvement in school management and decision-making are the components of parent involvement programs that Comer considers essential, particularly for low-income and African-American families. Slaughter and Kuehne agree that we must not only look at the level of African-American parent involvement in the schools, but also at whether African-American families feel a sense of inclusion and belonging in the school community.

It has been reported that 90 percent of all children in America are educated in public schools. Yet among African-American children the figure is higher because few of them attend private schools. Those African-American children who are enrolled in private schools appear to do better academically than African-American children in public schools. Dropout rates among African-American children in private schools are also lower than rates among African-Americans in public schools (Comer and others).

Involvement in an African-American Catholic School

Many Catholic schools operate much like communities. However, in a study of five metropolitan Catholic high schools that serve low-income students, great variance in parent involvement was found (Bauch 1987).

Three predominantly African-American schools served a smaller proportion of low-income families than the other two schools (one being a white working-class school and the other primarily a low-income Hispanic girls' school).

A coed African-American school was the smallest school studied. Along with familiarity and ease of interaction, this school had a number of organizational advantages that contributed to a higher rate of parent involvement. First, the school had been established through the efforts of a group of concerned parents who were highly organized and active. These parents continued to participate in the school in a number of monitoring roles. Here is how observers described this school:

> Parents were found in the school nearly every day and felt welcomed. They communicated informally and easily with teachers and administrators. While the research team was in the school, a problem arose concerning students' coming late to class. The principal immediately implemented a solution suggested by one of the parents.

> Parents wanted the best for their child and did a great deal of monitoring of their child and of the school, and the school enjoyed the support and benefit of a motivated and involved group of parents to assist in reinforcing school policy and discipline. (Bauch)

Half of the parents were involved in decisions about home-school relations. Clearly it is a school that focuses on empowerment, where parents *started* the school (an important factor connected to control and self-determination), and where parents are not only welcomed but also actively involved in school decisions.

SDP Schools and African-Americans

The increase in student achievement and parent involvement documented in SDP schools is no accident. SDP schools build "human capital" through their emphasis on staff development training, which equips teachers and staff to deal with sociocultural issues. They also increase "social capital" through emphasis on school management, in which administrators, teachers, and parents work together to determine the climate, priorities, and objectives within the schools. (See chapter 12 for more information on SDP schools.)

Comer and his colleagues conclude that

the School Development Program, with its strong emphasis on changing attitudes, values, and ways of interacting among adults and children in schools, seeks to create a climate, an ethos if you will, that is sensitive, challenging, and conducive to high academic achievement among African-American children in public schools.

Further Evidence

In a study reported by Ziegler (1987), empowerment is again seen as a crucial issue for involvement of African-American families. In a large-scale study of elementary schools and school achievement in Michigan, she reports, parent involvement in the school was found to significantly correlate with school achievement. "The relationship was particularly strong in schools with a majority of Black students," she adds.

Other researchers, too, have found that, for African-American children, high levels of parent-teacher contact and parent and community involvement in school decision-making were associated with higher reading scores.

Lightfoot (1978) describes an African-American urban school in which teachers encouraged and welcomed parents:

From selling cakes, in the traditional volunteer role, mothers began to work in the library, finding readable books for children; in the lunch room, managing the traffic of hungry children; and in the halls, keeping track of wandering children or having private conversations with children who needed special attention. Finally, mothers began to work actively *within* classrooms and became actively involved in the schooling process.

Ziegler says it's important to recognize that the presence of parents in the school transforms the culture of the school—that with African-American mothers present, there's no way that the curriculum and environment could remain unchanged. With their mothers there, school felt more like home for African-American children.

African-American families, we must remember, are among the most vulnerable of all families today. It seems clear that, along with providing support and help with resources, increasing empowerment is also a key to increasing African-American parent involvement with the schools.

Recommendations for Schools

The recommendations of the Committee to Study the Status of Black Males in New Orleans Public Schools (Orleans Parish School Board 1988) include the following, along with ideas of my own. Schools can:

• Use teacher conferences, school forums, and home visits to communicate to African-American parents the importance of teaching their children the value of education.

• Give special assistance to teenage parents and those who haven't completed their education.

• Encourage parents to make sure their children are in school daily; this message can be communicated through home visits, special parent-teacher contracts, or social worker followups on absences.

• Invite parents to visit the school to monitor their children's academic progress; they should also be encouraged to monitor how their children spend their free time (perhaps limiting TV viewing).

• Sponsor parent-staff get-togethers; one principal of a 90 percent African-American school eats lunch with ten different parents each month. During these lunches, parents may ask questions and express concerns (Kneidek 1990).

• Find ways to increase the number of African-American parent volunteers in the classrooms or increase their presence in other parts of the school.

• Train African-American parents to become an active political group that can assist educators and be part of the planning and decision-making process; Parent Effectiveness Training has been suggested as a way to facilitate this process.

• Suggest that businesses provide rewards and incentives to employees' children who have above average grades and who have good attendance records.

• Provide parenting education and other events in the evening or at other times that are convenient for parents; these events should be scheduled at several school or neighborhood sites.

• Make child care and transportation available; offering homework assistance is a good idea, too.

Chapter 25

HISPANICS

*I*t's important to remember that, although they share a common language and heritage of Spanish colonization, Hispanics are not a homogeneous group.* They differ on such variables as race, age, socioeconomic status, geography, the nature of their arrival in the U.S. (immigration, migration, exile, or asylum), the length of their residence in the U.S., and their country of origin.

Mexicans, for instance, account for 63 percent of Hispanics in the U.S., Central and South Americans for 13 percent, Puerto Ricans for 12 percent, and Cubans for 5 percent (Nicolau and Ramos 1990). Differences among Hispanic subgroups—in poverty, education, family structure, and age distribution—often are greater than the overall differences between Hispanics and non-Hispanics (Haycock and Duany 1991).

Fastest Growing Ethnic Group

Nationally, the Hispanic population—now exceeding twenty-two million people, according to

early 1990 census figures—is growing faster than any other ethnic group. Since 1980, the Hispanic population has increased by 53 percent; if this growth continues at its present rate, Hispanics will outnumber African-Americans in the nation by the year 2080 (Western Interstate Commission for Higher Education and The College Board 1991).

Today about one in ten children enrolled in U.S. elementary schools is Hispanic (just fourteen years ago the ratio was one in sixteen); by 2030 Hispanic children will make up 20 percent of the school population (Haycock and Duany). WICHE and The College Board project that the number of Hispanics enrolled in elementary and secondary schools will increase 54 percent between 1985-86 and 1994-95, from 3.3 million to more than 5 million students.

The median age of Hispanics is lower than that of other Americans. Add their relatively high birth rates and continued immigration, and it's clear there is considerable momentum for future growth.

Eighty-nine percent of the Hispanic population is concentrated in the urban centers of nine states—Florida, New York, Illinois, Texas, Cali-

---

*For a discussion of our reasons for using the term *Hispanic* instead of *Latino*, see the "Introduction, page" 3.

fornia, Arizona, New Mexico, New Jersey, and Colorado. Mexican-Americans, who account for two-thirds of the Hispanic population and are the segment that is growing the most rapidly, are concentrated in the southwestern United States.

Poverty and Unemployment

Of course, not all Hispanics are poor. There is a growing Hispanic middle class. However, a sizeable portion of the Hispanic community has lower average incomes and higher rates of unemployment and poverty than does the general population.

The median U.S. income for Hispanics is $21,769, compared to a national median family income of $33,915 for whites (Statistical Abstracts of the U.S. 1990). In a population where one in three Hispanics is under fifteen (Haycock and Duany), the rate of poverty for Hispanic children (38 percent) is nearly twice as high as it is for American children in general (21 percent), according to the U.S. Bureau of the Census (1991) figures.

The National Council on Educational Statistics reports that 8.5 percent of sixteen- to twenty-four-year-old Hispanics were unemployed, compared to 5.8 percent of their white counterparts. The unemployment rate for Hispanic high school dropouts was 21.1 percent (Ochoa 1990).

Hispanics have the same problems with employment as African-Americans do: the well-paying, unskilled jobs that supported the first generation immigrants are rapidly disappearing, and today's entry-level jobs offer lower salaries and require higher skills. In other words, an individual entering the job market "must know more to earn less" (Nicolau and Ramos). Thus poverty is a real trap for the Hispanic working family and often locks them into welfare dependency.

Most of today's new jobs require workers who can read, write, and compute at high levels, as well as analyze and interpret data, draw conclusions, and make decisions. Unfortunately, most Hispanic students, along with their minority peers, do not excel in these areas.

High Dropout Rates and Low Academic Achievement

Like African-Americans, Hispanics have a high dropout rate. Four in ten Hispanics leave school without a high school diploma—and half of these dropouts leave school before completing ninth grade (Haycock and Duany). Of the 55 percent of Hispanic students who do graduate, only 10 percent have sufficient skills to pursue a college education (Ochoa).

Not only are Hispanic dropout rates among the highest, they do not show any of the recent improvement seen in other racial/ethnic groups. According to the September 1991 National Education Goals Panel report card, between 1975 and 1990, high completion rates for 19- and 20-year-olds improved 12 percentage points for African-Americans, 2 percentage points for Whites, and 2 percentage points overall. Completion rates for Hispanics remained consistently low.

As an example of low Hispanic academic achievement, data collected by the California State Department of Education showed that in 1984-85, 46.3 percent of California's Hispanic twelfth graders attended schools where the average reading scores ranked in the state's lowest twenty-fifth percentile (compared to 11.8 percent of Anglo students). Only 9 percent of Hispanic students attended schools with average reading scores in the top twenty-fifth percentile (compared to 34.1 percent of Anglo students). This contrast remains if we look at scores for third- or sixth-graders or math instead of reading (Ochoa).

Research indicates that a mother's level of educational attainment is a good predictor of her children's school success (although Ziegler [1987] contends that this is true only when the mother is actually involved with the schools). That being so, Hispanics are at a distinct disadvantage, because the Hispanic mothers most likely to have school-age children are over three times as likely to have dropped out of high school as are other American women in that age group (Nicolau and Ramos).

As Nicolau and Ramos say, "Low educational achievement has been—and continues to be—a major barrier to the advancement of Hispanics in the U.S. society."

Why Hispanics Fare So Poorly in School

For some time, it has been clear that Hispanics and African-Americans do less well in school than most other groups. Why is this so?

Many educators point their fingers at the children themselves and the families. According to Haycock and Duany, however, several other factors are at the root of the low academic achievement that is present among Hispanics and other minority students.

"Schools put less of everything into the education of Latino and other minority students," they say. "They get less in the way of experienced and well-trained teachers, rich and well-balanced curriculums, and adequately equipped libraries and laboratories. More importantly, they get less in the way of a belief that they can really learn."

A Segregated School System for Minorities

Despite what we might think, Haycock and Duany maintain that minority students in this country are still educated separately and that the

---

A PROGRAM FOR MIGRANT FAMILIES

Prestame una Comadre is Spanish for "loan me a godmother." This program in Springfield, Illinois, is an extension of Head Start parent involvement that targets migrant Head Start families identified as high risk and who have limited English proficiency. Begun in 1984, the program utilizes social workers or "family life trainers" who conduct home visits as often as three times per week to help parents increase self-reliance, learn about child development and educational opportunities in the home, and improve family functioning. Small group meetings are held weekly to discuss topics such as nutrition and family relationships.

Source: Goodson and others (1991)

---

problem has been getting worse for Hispanics. In 1986, more than 70 percent of Hispanic students, compared to 63 percent of African-Americans, were enrolled in schools with a minority enrollment of 50 percent or more. Worse yet, almost one-third of Hispanic students attended heavily segregated schools, where minority enrollment was 90 percent or higher.

Some minority-dominant schools do provide high quality education, say Haycock and Duany. But most, they claim, do not: "In general, segregated schools lack the resources to provide students with a competitive education. Their teachers are not as well educated as those in the suburbs, and they often use out-of-date curriculum materials. Virtually everything is watered down."

The Tracking System

For those Hispanic students who do attend schools with more resources, the problem is "tracking" (ability grouping), which Haycock and Duany contend has essentially the same effect as segregation. "In these schools," they say, "we tend to herd the poor and minority students into low-track classes with the worst teachers and the oldest books—and expect little or nothing from them."

For example, Hispanic eighth-graders are twice as likely as their white counterparts to take no English or science classes, and they are most likely to take remedial math. "We often force them to choose between learning to speak and read English," Haycock and Duany continue, "or trying to keep up with their classmates in math, science, or literature."

When we teach them less, say Haycock and Duany, it should hardly be surprising that these students do less well on academic achievement tests. And because schools and teachers often assume that Hispanic parents have little to offer the school or their children, "we isolate ourselves from the very community that we should be trying to involve and serve" (Haycock and Duany).

Hispanic Families Need Support

The other major reason Hispanics do less well in school has to do with the demographic statistics cited earlier: many Hispanic communities suffer from inadequate resources, financial and otherwise. Sheer survival is often very difficult.

"The fact that one-third of Latino kids have parents with less than nine years of schooling," say Haycock and Duany, "means that schools should provide additional support for families that have low literacy skills, fewer skills to help with homework, and negative views about their own school experience."

The effects of these characteristics, both in schools and communities, they point out, are devastating for many Hispanic children. Although they enter school only slightly behind other children, the gap grows as they progress through the grades. The average Hispanic student is about six months behind by the third grade, two years behind by the eighth grade, and more than three grade levels behind by the twelfth grade—if he makes it there at all (Haycock and Duany).

Guidelines for Working with Hispanic Families

When planning parent involvement programs for Hispanics, remember these points:

Hispanics have different cultural backgrounds: Because they are socialized differently and have different cultural backgrounds, as explained in chapter 10, many Hispanic children are unprepared for U.S. schools. As part of the National Educational Longitudinal Survey, a federally sponsored study of eighth-grade students, their parents, and teachers, 25,000 parents were polled in 1988. This poll found that Hispanic parents were less likely than their white or African-American peers to talk with their children about school, which may be due in part to the division their culture makes between school and home (Rothman 1990).

But it's not because they don't care about their children's education. "I want what is best in life for my children," says Maria Cano Gutierrez of Portland, Oregon. "Now that we're here in the United States, I want them to go to school and to get a good education" (Kneidek 1990).

Actually, Hispanic parents don't talk with their children about many subjects that parents in

---

HISPANIC RESOURCES

There are two organizations schools should know about if they have Hispanic populations:

Hispanic Policy Development Project
250 Park Avenue South, Suite 500A
New York, NY 10003
(212) 529-9323
Siobhan Nicolau, President

ASPIRA: Hispanic Community Mobilization for Dropout Prevention
ASPIRA Association, Inc.,
1112 16th Street NW
Washington, DC 20036
(202) 835-3600
Janie Petrovich, National Executive Director

For more information about these organizations, see the Appendix.

---

other cultures freely discuss with their kids, and the reason is that Hispanic children are socialized differently than other American children. Although Hispanic children are usually warmly loved, Hispanic culture does not promote casual conversations between parents and children in most poor Hispanic homes. Thus teachers may find it hard to understand or reach Hispanic children and may encounter delayed development and "different" behavior.

Hispanics have different attitudes toward schools: Hispanic parents have different attitudes toward the school system and its personnel than do most middle-class American families. Hispanics

BARRIERS/SOLUTIONS TO HISPANIC PARENT INVOLVEMENT

BARRIERS	POSSIBLE SOLUTIONS
	### Communication Problems
• Language differences. • Tradition/cultural differences.	• Conduct meetings, seminars, and workshops in Spanish. • Have bilingual aide available when Hispanic aparents visit the school. • Encourage parents to bring a bilingual relative or friend. • Sensitize school personnel to the Hispanic community, its culture, and its special needs. • Use cultural enrichment activities to bring school and families together.
	### Feelings of Inferiority
• Limited or no education.	• Involve parents in decision-making, planning, and implementation of activities. Let them know they are important partners. • Give parents opportunities to demonstrate and use their special skills and talents.
	### Feelings of Alienation
• Not welcome at school.	• Welcome parents by conveying a positive attitude when they visit the classrooms and at meetings and activities. • Let parents know you appreciate their presence and the time they are devoting to school.
	### Lack of Understanding of the Educational System
• Belief that school is an omnipotent force much wiser than parents.	• Hold workshops for Hispanic parents on the mechanics of the school system, and on school curriculum. Remove the mystery from "the sytem." • Have parents instruct other parents.
	### Lack of Time
• Fathers and mothers who work full time find attending daytime activities very difficult.	• Attempt to accommodate working parents and mothers of small children by holding activities and workshops in the evenings or on weekends. Hold some of the functions in their neighborhoods.
	### Problems Finding Child Care
• Affordable child care or baby sitting is difficult to find, especially for low income parents with more than one child.	• Provide child care for parents who want to attend meetings and workshops. • Plan activities in which parents and children don't have to be separated. • Utilize extended family members or teenage siblings to provide child care at meeting site.
	### Transportation Problems
• Many low-income families may not be able to afford transportation to and from activities.	• Provide transportation, if possible, to and from activities. • Set up carpools. • Get help from people and groups in the community. • Hold activities in the community.

Source: Nicolau and Ramos (1990)

are often in awe of the school and teachers and don't question educators' authority. Therefore, Hispanic parents may strike white middle-class teachers as being reserved, nonconfrontational, and uninterested.

"The hardest part of a parent program for Hispanic parents," one project director reported, "is to humanize teachers and to let parents know that teachers want to talk bilaterally if not bilingually about their students" (Nicolau and Ramos).

Most Hispanics have a background of poverty: Almost all poor Hispanic families are simply struggling to survive. Often the scenario goes like this: both parents work, sometimes at more than one job. Mothers may have a number of young children in their care. Or mothers may be single and on welfare. Their neighborhoods may be dangerous, and transportation and child care expensive or nonexistent. Some may desperately need help, but do not seek it because "we do not discuss family affairs with strangers" (Nicolau and Ramos).

Use personal contact: It's easiest to reach Hispanic parents through personal contact, as emphasized in chapter 8.

Focus on family strengths: Hispanic families have many strengths that schools can build on, such as the fact that they teach their children cooperation and respect.

To those who argue that many of the problems facing Hispanic children are typical of immigrants and will disappear with time, consider Haycock's and Duany's response: *"There is no time. We need these young people now."*

Recommendations for Schools

Schools must make special efforts to reach and involve Hispanic families. Consider the following suggestions:

• Institute home visits, at least in the beginning, with a bilingual staff or an interpreter.

• Communicate regularly with parents about their children's progress.

• Translate all notices sent home into Spanish. A humorous example of *not* doing this occurred in a Portland, Oregon, school when memos were sent

home with the children saying they needed to bring bathing suits to school to go swimming. However, the memos weren't translated; they were only in English. Many Hispanic parents were understandably confused when their children told them they needed swimming suits to go to school! Now the school translates all notices intended for parents (Kneidek 1990).

• Be aware that some Hispanic parents may not be able to read, even in their native language. Ways to reach this group include bilingual volunteers, bilingual parents (use Hispanic parents to reach other parents whenever possible), and paid aides or staff.

One school in California found a way to get limited-English parents more involved and to develop their children's reading skills at the same time. Parents in this school are encouraged to check out tapes where one side is in English, the other in Spanish, so that parents can share with their children (Levy 1989).

• Make inservice workshops for teachers a priority—not just on parent involvement techniques, but also on cultural differences. Teachers and staff, for instance, might explore their own attitudes toward minorities. Encourage awareness and acceptance of cultural differences in activity planning and scheduling.

• Offer parent education programs for Hispanic parents, particularly at the preschool level, in order to help them prepare their children for school.

• Provide transportation and child care; they are not frills. Meals, too, may be helpful.

• Educate Hispanic parents about the U.S. school system. This might be combined with family education and support programs. For instance, Gloria Rodriguez of the AVANCE Educational Programs for Parents and Children in San Antonio, Texas, has sought to fill what many feel is "an abyss between the Hispanic home and culture, and the public education system" (Council of Chief State School Officers 1989).

She does this through programs designed to help parents gain knowledge in child growth and development and child management skills, while also exposing them to community resources, strengthening their support network, and preparing them to become part of their children's educational experience.

• Try bilingual newsletters. The 1987 Metropolitan Life Survey found that Hispanic parents feel a need for increased home-school communication. For example, 80 percent of Hispanic parents believed a school newsletter would help "a lot" in improving education (Amundson 1988). Yet that's contrary to what Nicolau and Ramos (1990) discovered. They found that printed materials went unread by parents and that it was personal contact that counted, at least in the beginning. But each school has to find what works best for them—and *when*.

• The California school noted above publishes a bilingual newsletter called "Parent-Assisted Learning," and an elementary school in Portland, Oregon, with a population that is 25 percent Hispanic, is planning on publishing a school newsletter next year in both English and Spanish.

This latter school, Cornelius Elementary School, has been successful in their efforts with Hispanic parents, as Hispanic parents are now involved in the Parent Club, serve as translators at community meetings, and chaperone field trips (Kneidek).

• Be prepared to refer Hispanic parents to services in the community that they may need—and have someone at your school who is knowledgeable about community resources.

PART 6
THE PROCESS

PREVIEW OF CHAPTERS IN
PART 6: THE PROCESS

Chapter 26. Elements of Successful Programs

What characteristics set apart successful parent involvement programs from those that do not succeed? They include committed leadership, innovation and flexibility, personal outreach, positive communication, nonthreatening activities, active support by the principal and staff, attention to format and scheduling, meaningful activities, child care and other essentials, and high visibility.

Chapter 27. The Recruitment Process

Here are a number of suggestions of ways to get parents to that first event or meeting. The first step is to assign a recruiter. Then you can survey your community, arrange home visits, use parents to recruit other parents, choose a neutral site for your first meeting, and use the meeting to capture parents' attention and ease their nervousness.

Chapter 28. Keeping Parents Involved

Finally, this chapter tells how to maintain parents' attendance and hold their attention. Among the twenty ideas for keeping parents involved are the following: give parents a sense of ownership by consulting with them, establish a caring environment, organize special interest groups, be generous with recognition and awards, try new ideas and projects, and don't give up if the first response isn't overwhelmingly positive.

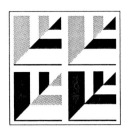

Chapter 26

ELEMENTS OF SUCCESSFUL PROGRAMS

*W*hat elements do successful parent involvement programs for at-risk families have in common? Nicolau and Ramos (1990) sum up features of various effective Hispanic projects. Many of these elements could be applied to programs aimed at other at-risk groups.

The following sections, compiled from Nicolau and Ramos and other sources, review essential elements for positive family involvement programs.

Committed, Dedicated Leadership

Overcoming the barriers to reaching at-risk parents doesn't require huge sums of money, but it does take energy, patience, and persistence. Halfhearted efforts don't accomplish much.

Nicolau and Ramos found that leadership was the single most important element in launching a successful program with Hispanic parents. Project leaders did not necessarily have to be Hispanic. In fact, two of the most innovative and successful partnerships were led by a Chinese principal in one case and an Anglo principal in the other (both, however, spoke Spanish).

One plucky Hispanic project coordinator, when talking about high-risk parents, said, "Be committed to give it all you have, both perspiration and inspiration. The parents are out there; we just have to make that first move, because they cannot" (Nicolau and Ramos).

An Innovative, Flexible Approach

The programs that failed in the Hispanic projects were those that had second thoughts about trying new techniques and went back to "the way we always have done it" (Nicolau and Ramos). Officials may have maintained the status quo, but they gained little or no increase in Hispanic parent involvement.

On the other hand, projects that built on activities that had *not* worked before—such as simply increasing the number of meetings per school year—were also likely to fail.

Strong, Personal Outreach

This element has been emphasized throughout, especially in chapter 8. In fact, some have

PARENT INVOLVEMENT AT AN INDIANAPOLIS SCHOOL

The Edgar Evans Elementary School in Indianapolis has attracted hundreds of parents through its effort to develop closer ties with neighborhood families. This school is a success story in a districtwide initiative, known as Parents in Touch, begun in 1979 to promote stronger school-home partnerships.

Seventy-eight percent of families in the Edgar Evans neighborhood have incomes below the poverty line; 75 percent of students walk to the school from nearby housing projects.

In 1988 when Mamie Thompson arrived as principal of the school, parent participation was minimal and barriers between staff and the community ran deep. After conducting a needs assessment, Thompson concluded that the school desperately needed to reach out to families. "We knew we couldn't do our job without them," she says. "But that meant we had to go out and get them."

Today the school has a parent center that includes resources for families on parenting skills and education. School textbooks are also available in the center to enable parents to follow their children's assignments.

The school also offers monthly workshops in the evenings and on weekends on such topics as Discipline with Love and Preparing Children for Tests.

Social events are designed to make parents feel more comfortable at the school. Signs welcoming parents line the hallways and there is a "parent involvement" bulletin board that lists the names and contributions of particularly active parents. Thompson says she will take over the classroom of any teacher who wants to meet with parents during the day.

Most teachers keep a chart in their classroom with gold stars to indicate how often individual parents have visited the school. Thompson sends a certificate of appreciation to frequent visitors to encourage them to return.

In addition, the school has hired a local parent as a community liaison to visit families at home and encourage them to become involved in their children's learning. The liaison also acts as a buffer to help dispel negative feelings between parents and teachers.

While Thompson says the school still has a long way to go to strengthen school-home ties, the efforts to date have demonstrated that low income parents want to be involved in their children's education. "If you ask them to come, they'll come," says Thompson.

Teachers, too, are learning what a contribution parents can make. "Before, a lot of teachers would say they wanted help from parents, but they would try to limit how much," says Sandra Anderson, a teacher at the school for seventeen years. "Now, teachers are really happy to have the parents around."

Although no formal evaluations have been conducted, Anderson says student achievement has improved since the program began. Two years ago, 66 percent of students were reading below grade level. In 1990 that figure dropped to 51 percent.

In addition, attendance rates topped 96 percent this year, up from 80 percent last year. "It's because parents know more what we expect," says Thompson.

Source: Adapted from Jennings (August 1, 1990)

questioned the term *parent involvement,* since it presumes that we want them—the parents—to be involved in our school, whereas instead we need to think of schools reaching out to parents and the community.

Warm, Nonjudgmental Communication

This aspect goes along with the above, but can't be overstressed. Obviously, personal outreach and adequate communication with parents cannot be handled by a single person in his or her spare time.

The Hispanic partnerships that succeeded all had project coordinators who were genuinely interested in working with the Hispanic community, sensitive to their needs, and determined to make the program work. It might also be pointed out that these coordinators had supervisors who gave them *time* to do their jobs. Besides creativity, perseverance was found to be crucial to a successful program.

Nonthreatening Activities

Most of the Hispanic project coordinators found that it was best to begin with a nonthreatening social activity. Examples of activities that might be too frightening or ambitious are inviting parents to attend a college commencement exercise or holding a social event at a university.

All the schools that expected poor Hispanic parents to begin their involvement by joining the existing parents' organization failed as well. "Low income parents are intimidated and made exceedingly uncomfortable when expected to cope with unfamiliar organizational structures and procedures," say Nicolau and Ramos. Moreover, these new parents weren't always welcomed by the existing parents' group, which sometimes perceived them as competing for control of the group. Particularly when the school population was predominantly Hispanic or nonwhite, these parents were seen as a threat.

Eventually, when at-risk parents have acquired the skills and confidence they feel they need to compete as equals, they can then join parent advisory committees or the like. Exceptions are schools set up from the outset to include parent governance, like the SDP schools or schools with predominantly African-American populations, where a different approach might be advised (see chapter 24 on African-Americans).

Active Support by Administrators and Staff

No matter how energetic a project coordinator might be, the Hispanic programs illustrated the fact that "the best efforts of a project coordinator will fail if he or she does not have the active support of the school principal and staff" (Nicolau and Ramos).

When everyone sincerely wants Hispanic parents to become involved and is willing to try new strategies and be flexible, parents sense this and respond. All the Hispanic programs that lacked the support of teachers and principals failed to increase Hispanic parent involvement.

Formal approval by the superintendent and the school board may give sufficient legitimacy and momentum to overcome initial resistance. A school district budget commitment, even if not a substantial dollar amount, gives further legitimacy and importance to the plan (Hester 1989).

The district can also build support for parent involvement by stressing that it is a districtwide goal and will be a criterion for staff evaluations.

Attention to Environment, Format, and Scheduling

Where, when, and how a meeting or event is held is extremely important. A nonjudgmental atmosphere is critical, along with selecting an appropriate topic for the first meeting or event.

Events may be more successful if held on neutral turf, such as neighborhood homes or community centers, rather than schools.

CHAPTER 1 FUNDS IN MCALLEN, TEXAS

For the past seven years the McAllen, Texas, schools have been combining Chapter 1 support with other support to build stronger school family connections in a comprehensive program. The task has not been easy, as the community is mainly Hispanic and many recent immigrants and migrant families have little or no proficiency in English.

However, under the leadership of Superintendent Pablo Perez, the staff has grown from one parent coordinator to five parent coordinators and several federally funded community aides. The position of facilitator was created at each building to help with instructional leadership and to free the principals to spend more time directly involved with parents and parent activities.

To broaden family involvement to include all parents—not just those targeted for Chapter 1 funds—required increasing the district's investment in school and family activities. The district budget has tripled and parent involvement is no longer supported solely by federal funds.

All parents of children in McAllen schools are eligible to become involved in five major types of activities: parent education programs, school/home and home/school communications, opportunities to volunteer for school projects, helping their children at home, and participation in the parent/teacher organization.

Most staff members involved with parent activities are bilingual. At each school the handbook is provided in English and Spanish versions. Families benefit from community aides, home visits, evening family study centers, computer-assisted language programs, and programs on parenting skills and other topics.

Each principal is responsible for the design and direction of a school's parent involvement program. For instance, at one school the parent teacher organization trains parents and other volunteers to run a self-esteem program for students in the school. This program was initiated and implemented by parents, though it is supported by the administration and teaching staff.

District staff now estimate that nearly 99 percent of parents have some productive contact with their children's schools. The staff are working to reach the other 1 percent and to continue to improve the level, extent, and quality of involvement for all families.

The McAllen approach can be adapted to local conditions in any district or school, although it will take time and commitment. Comprehensive programs to involve parents require long-term leadership and some additional resources, but McAllen's example shows that Chapter 1 and other categorical programs can be combined and coordinated with local initiatives to promote school-family partnerships.

Source: D'Angelo and Adler (1991)

Staff members, including receptionists and janitors, must commit themselves to making parents feel welcome. That's why inservice workshops should include everyone, so that a less-than-welcoming secretary won't spoil all the work you have done.

Also, *when you* hold an event is important. You may want to try different times, since no single time is likely to work for everyone. Here again, the key word is flexibility.

Meaningful Activities

Obviously, activities for parents should be relevant to their lives and concerns. Find out what parents are most interested in and design your programs accordingly.

The Chapter 1 programs discussed by D'Angelo and Adler (1991) are all variations on a basic recipe: combine the needs of a specific parent audience with creative ideas for generating activities, then blend in understanding of good communication. An awareness of the range of parent interests, ideas, needs, cultures, languages, and lifestyles must be present before programs are developed and activities designed," they advise.

The Essentials of Child Care, Transportation, and Meals

Providing childcare, transportation, and meals will make a big difference for low-income parents. The Hispanic projects used all kinds of innovative ways to get parents to events, and so have other successful projects. One project used the school's buses. Some projects utilized escort services—picking up the parents and taking them home. Others provided the parents with money for trans-portation. Child care or babysitting was always provided if necessary. Try to anticipate what needs there might be and make changes if necessary.

High Visibility

Visibility will help sustain the effort to implement parent involvement activities. Hester suggests formal presentations and progress reports to parent organizations, teachers, and the school board, plus media coverage recognizing the special efforts of parents and teachers, as ways to attain recognition for the program.

FOUR INNOVATIVE PROGRAMS

Family Math (at numerous sites nationwide) is a program that brings together children in kindergarten through eighth grade and their parents to participate in problem-solving and hands-on math activities to reinforce and complement the school curriculum. The program was developed in 1981 at the Lawrence Hall of Science, University of California at Berkeley, to help children and their parents see mathematics as an enjoyable and active pursuit. Weekly classes lasting about an hour are held in four- to six-week cycles and are taught by teachers and parents who have received training to be Family Math instructors.

Kuban Parent Involvement Program (Phoenix, Arizona) was designed by the school administration and teaching staff to increase parent involvement in school activities and encourage home learning in an innercity school district where the dropout rate is nearly 65 percent. Teachers run the program for parents of students in kindergarten through third grade. Parents attend quarterly training sessions that focus on the skills students learn in school, classroom objectives, and ways parents can help at home. Teachers also make home visits as needed.

Parents in Touch (Indianapolis, Indiana) is run by the Indianapolis Public Schools and consists of a range of activities to increase parent involvement and improve home-school communication, including activity calendars for children; student/teacher/parent contracts and work folders; dial-a-teacher telephone line available five nights a week to provide help with homework; parent line/communicator where parents can hear a recorded message about school activities; and a series of workshops on parent education. In addition, the district has implemented the Family Math as well as the TIPS-Math and TIPS-Science programs.

TIPS-Math (at numerous sites nationwide) was developed by researchers at Johns Hopkins University to involve parents in their children's mathematics homework, to increase communication between the home and school about mathematics work, and to improve students' mastery of mathematical skills. The structured materials include information for parents from teachers about classroom activities as well as a set of activities for families to complete at home.

Source: Goodson and others (1991)

Chapter 27

THE RECRUITMENT PROCESS

*H*ow do you get parents to that first event or meeting? Here are ideas on the recruitment process from Nicolau and Ramos (1990) and other sources.

Assign a Recruiter

The recruiter might be called a project coordinator or home-school liaison. He or she should be someone who understands the culture and background of the parents and is sincerely interested and dedicated. Give the recruiter time to do the job.

Survey Your Community

Get a clear picture of what kinds and how many different groups of families you have. Questions you might ask include:

• What are their special interests, needs, and concerns?

• What at-risk groups do you have—and how many members are there in each group?

• What barriers might keep these groups from getting involved?

• To what organizations do they belong?

• Who are their spokespersons and leaders

• Where are their neighborhood centers?

• Where do they work?

It is crucial to find out who your school families are and the details of their family composition. As a first step in gathering information, you might survey parents when they register. As Nicolau and Ramos found, that may be the only time a "high risk or troubled parent will appear at school."

In areas with large numbers of ethnic groups, the national PTA gives grants for programs that encourage minority parents' participation in their children's education. In San Diego, California, PTA members go into Hispanic, Asian, and African-American communities to survey parents about their wants and needs (Decker and Decker 1988).

Use a Variety of Recruitment Techniques

It is important not to rely on just one recruitment strategy. Here are some examples of techniques used by innovative programs: "current or former participants recruiting others in their neighborhood; brochures or letters sent home with school children; visits by program staff; door-to-door recruitment; and posters in community locations" (Goodson and others 1991). Other methods they mention are Hispanic radio programs and neighborhood sound tracks.

Imaginatively designed printed materials can be effectively used to recruit families, Goodson and her colleagues say. For example, one program posts flyers and notices at several places of employment, churches, housing projects, gas stations, social service agencies, and kindergarten registration. Another program hangs banners from public buildings, announcing a name and telephone number to call.

Printed material should not require advanced literacy skills and should be available in languages other than English.

Arrange Home Visits

As has been pointed out in chapter 8, personal contact or communication is mandatory, at least for Hispanics, and that means talking face-to-face with the parents in their primary language at their homes or at school or wherever you can engage a parent.

Getting to know high-risk families (those with multiple and serious problems) is a must, and that also means home visits. It's important to remember, though, that a single visit may not do it. It may be necessary to make contact two or three times to convince parents to attend an activity. Many parents are suspicious of an invitation to become involved in school activities or feel nervous if they don't speak English.

Your home visits can be part of your community survey and carried out in conjunction with the survey. Here are questions Nicolau and Ramos suggest you find answers to during your visits so that you can understand who your partners are:

• Are they single parents, welfare parents, working mothers, intact families, large families, immigrant families, native-born families?

• Do they speak English?

• Who are the primary caretakers of the children—the mothers, the fathers, or the grandparents?

• Are the neighborhoods dangerous?

• Do the families live near or far from the school?

• Is transportation available?

• Do the fathers permit the mothers to go out alone?

• Are there places or institutions in the neighborhoods where the families gather or feel comfortable?

• Do many of the families appear troubled?

• What is the custody situation in each family?

• Why should you take the time to do this?

The decision about *whom* to invite to *which kind of affair* at *what* time is difficult if you do not know who your families are or how they live their lives. "The projects that took the time to know their families were the ones that succeeded," state Nicolau and Ramos.

Follow Up Visits or Invitations

Follow up a visit with a phone call. Even though this didn't work as well for Hispanic parents, at least at first you might encourage teachers to send notes home (in the family's primary language) or make phone calls to the parents. In the Hispanic projects, coordinators found that many parents didn't read or else chose not to open a letter from a school.

If you do send a followup invitation or notice, make it nonintimidating and appealing. Don't, for instance, send it on official school stationery. Do follow up invitations to activities with a phone call one or two days before the event.

In Project Home Visit in Los Angeles, a tWG person team visits the homes of students in cases where teachers' phone calls and notes have not been effective. The teams work on facilitating a partnership between parent and teacher (Council of Chief State School Officers 1989).

Post Teachers and Principals Outside the School

This way they can personally greet parents when the parents drop off or pick up their children

NONPROFIT ORGANIZATION RUNS PARENT INVOLVEMENT PROGRAM

The Parent Institute for Quality Education, a nonprofit organization located in San Diego County, California, is working with low-income Hispanic and ethnolinguistic populations to develop parent involvement, empowerment, action, and advocacy. The institute was established in the late 1980s by a Baptist minister and works jointly with the faculty of the Department of Policy Studies in Language and Cross Cultural Education.

The program begins with schools inviting a team of facilitators from the Parent Institute to dialogue with a core group of parents. This dialogue takes place for three to five weeks, during which time facilitators help parents identify their needs, wants, and concerns. These themes then become the focus of training workshops for parents. Thus each workshop addresses a concern or issue identified by the parents themselves. Over one thousand concerns have been documented so far and grouped into four workshop areas: student development, family interaction, school-home accountability, and school culture.

Parents are trained in groups of twenty to thirty to allow for interaction. The workshops use diverse methods and are delivered in the primary languages of the school communities. Field assignments are given, which can consist of gathering facts and information at the local level, thus relating the theme to specific applica-

tions in the actual home-community setting. Generally three to six themes are covered in a series of training workshops.

During a two-year period, the Parent Institute has trained over 2,800 parents, who have participated in at least four thematic workshops. "The vision of such training," says Alberto M. Ochoa (1990), "is to nurture the development of parents from a level of understanding of their role and advocacy in the education of their children to a level in which they become the trainers of other parents."

In its two years of operation, the Parent Institute has worked with twenty-three school communities, including eighteen elementary schools, four junior highs, and one high school. The majority of these schools have a history of very low parent participation. In addition, these schools are large and overcrowded, with over 80 percent of students ethnically diverse (predominantly Hispanic) and as many as 50 percent from single parent homes.

"Our initial work and research," says Ochoa, "has convinced us that not only are low income parents interested, willing, and socially responsible for improving the quality of education provided to their children, but that a vision exists for making schooling a truly democratic and empowering institution."

Source: Adapted from Albert M. Ochoa (1990)

This is an effective icebreaker and makes the staff more "real" to the parents.

Use Parents to Recruit Other Parents

Build parent networks. If some Hispanic parents, for example, are already involved in school activities, encourage them to bring their neighbors or friends to school events. Use a nucleus of involved at-risk parents to serve as the motivational core for organizing other at-risk families. These parents are most effective when they re-

ceive special leadership training on program objectives and school procedures.

Post parent volunteers at the school gates or in the hallways to greet other parents personally or give them information about upcoming events.

Ask Parents What They Would Be Interested in Doing

Make your first event something that parents are interested in—something that's on *their* agenda, not yours. Often they will want to start with things that the school doesn't. Follow their interests first, say Nicolau and Ramos, and soon they will follow yours.

Also build on what parents are good at and where they will feel needed. For instance, asking Hispanic parents to help make costumes and scenery for a production of *Snow White was* not only a great icebreaker, but an activity where the parents felt needed (Nicolau and Ramos).

Don't Hold Your First Activity at School

Choose a site within the neighborhood, perhaps even use a neighborhood home. Good examples from the Hispanic projects are ones that initially met at McDonald's, then later at the public housing project where many of the families lived. Another project operated much like a Tupperware party in parents' homes, where the principal, teacher, school nurse, and counselor came to the home. Eventually, when parents feel comfortable with the teachers, meetings and activities can be held at school.

Make the First Event Fun

Don't start off with a formal meeting or conference as your first activity. Such events are scary for many low-income parents. And don't load your first meeting with serious information or talk "at" parents—they will not return. The initial activity, say Nicolau and Ramos, must be warm, comfortable, and beneficial for the parents. Otherwise, it will be the last one they will attend.

Start with a social event or some kind of icebreaker. Social gatherings tend to make people relaxed and approachable. Hispanic parents—and other at-risk parents—need to learn to feel at home with teachers, and this takes time.

Use the First Event to Capture the Parents' Attention

Design the initial event around an activity or issue with broad appeal. One goal for this event is to ease parents' nervousness. Then, for the next event, offer some carefully considered options that correspond to their expressed needs and wants. Make it plain that you really care about their participation.

The real job, say Nicolau and Ramos, begins after the first meeting: holding parents' attention, maintaining their attendance, and gaining their participation in the partnership.

Chapter 28

KEEPING PARENTS INVOLVED

*H*ow do you maintain parents' attendance and hold their attention at meetings? After all, as one Hispanic coordinator said, "Not every meeting can be a party" (Nicolau and Ramos 1990).

To sustain a sense of commitment, Nicolau and Ramos say, every meeting has to respond to some need or concern of the parents. "Parents will come when they believe they are getting something out of the activities, when their feelings are respected, and that they are a needed and valued resource," they explain.

Here are twenty ideas for keeping parents involved:

Give parents a sense of ownership by consulting with them

Isn't this what partnership is really all about? Make the agenda the parents' agenda, not yours, at least in the beginning. The Hispanic projects that planned an agenda of meetings and then imposed issues and formats on the parents found that attendance was low or fluctuated from meeting to meeting. The projects that had higher rates of attendance were those that spent time asking the parents what was important to them, then offering them options, and, finally, presenting them with school needs that only the parents could meet.

Survey parents' interests on subject matter. A review of parents' interests in a Hispanic project found that the first issues parents wanted to tackle were AIDS, teen pregnancy, drugs, spouse and child abuse, and ESL classes. The schools admitted that if they hadn't asked the parents' advice, they would have begun the program with homework, good study habits, discipline, and communication. What is important is that they did eventually get to those issues, and parents' interest and attendance was high. But first they had to establish trust and demonstrate respect for parents' concerns.

Pay attention to format

Many low-income parents are not comfortable in a formal meeting or conference setting. Informal settings are less intimidating. Make events as participatory as possible: people like to be involved, make things, go places, and generally be active.

Small groups are more effective than large ones, and role playing and discussion are more successful than lectures. Meetings that require parents to passively listen to a speaker are seldom effective.

Establish a caring environment

This is the manner in which the subject matter is presented and the event conducted. Coordinators of the Hispanic projects indicated that making parents feel comfortable and welcome at activities was essential in maintaining attendance.

Here are some of the things coordinators

• Talk *with* parents, not *at* them.

• Share personal experiences that you've had with your own children.

• Refrain from asking questions that can be seen as having "wrong answers" or that may make parents appear foolish; never expose adults' ignorance in front of their peers; never judge parents or make them feel judged.

• Provide child care, interpreters, and transportation when necessary.

• Offer refreshments, however modest, at all events, unless the events take place in the classroom.

• Recognize the efforts of parents.

• Set aside a parents' room in the school that has a living room atmosphere where parents can meet informally.

• Stock the parents' room with applications and forms that relate to parents' needs (such as license renewal forms, food stamp forms, voter registration cards) and provide someone at specific hours who can help parents fill out the forms.

• Make it easy for parents to develop new friendships and social support.

Choose different times to schedule events

Do the scheduling with consideration for parents' availability. This is essential. Working parents can't attend in the day; single parents may not want to attend in the evening. Most Hispanic women can't attend when it is time to feed their families.

Prepare staff with inservice workshops

Do this before parents arrive for events or meetings so that everyone understands the community they are serving. But don't stop there. All the successful programs identified by Goodson and others provide regular inservice training, either weekly or biweekly.

Involve parents in activities they can later duplicate and share with their children

For instance, offer trips, picnics, and cultural and social events. Find ways to include families in programs to enrich their child's educational experience. Develop a list of suggestions and give families tips they can use at home.

Organize special interest groups or other popular projects

These might be sewing, gardening, or crafts clubs. Hispanic projects that were popular included parent activity centers in children's classrooms (this helped parents better understand their children's school day); "Make and Take" workshops where parents learned to make educational games and activity boxes and how to use these materials at home; and community projects, such as planting gardens, building playground equipment, or organizing to obtain sidewalks in their neighborhoods.

Also popular were tutoring and homework centers where students received assistance with homework and parents attended workshops and parenting classes, and informal workshops on issues first identified by the parents, then by the schools, as priorities (Nicolau and Ramos). Krasnow (1990) also suggests scheduling events that involve children's performances, as parent attendance is usually higher at these events.

Discover what parents are good at

After discovering parents' talents and abilities, find a way to use them at school. And when they contribute, let the rest of the community know. "If Mrs. Rios plants flowers in front of the school, we send a letter home with all the students

ILLINOIS URBAN EDUCATION PARTNERSHIP GRANTS

The majority of programs that have been funded by the Illinois Urban Education Partnership Grants program have included one or more types of parent involvement. Here are examples:

Improving Language and Writing Skills. An Illinois innercity elementary school was awarded an Urban Partnership Grant. Most of its students are Hispanic and most have limited skills in speaking and writing English. Parent involvement has been limited.

The main focus of the grant proposal was to improve the language and writing skills of the students in the primary grades through a whole language approach.

The grant included support for students to go on field trips to museums, the zoo, and other educational events. A group of parents accompanied the students and teachers on these trips. Back at the school after the trips, the students told stories of their experiences to the parents, who encouraged students to give as much detail as possible and acted as scribes, writing down what the children said in Spanish or English. Parents who were not able to go on the field trips were encouraged to write down stories for their own children at home. Each child's dictated work was collected throughout the year and compiled into a portfolio.

"By the end of the school year," says Warren Chapman (1991), "one could see that in virtually every instance students were telling stories in greater detail, using larger vocabularies, and creating sentences more complex than had been the case at the beginning of the school year." What's more, the parents improved their own vocabulary and writing skills. Most important, parents learned how to assist their own children in learning at home.

Improvement Contracts. Another school established "improvement contracts" for individual students. Each student met with a counselor to draw up a contract in which the goal was to raise report card grades in three subject areas. The contract was then signed by the student, the teacher or teachers involved, and the student's parent(s).

"These contracts proved very influential in establishing meaningful communication between teachers and parents," says Chapman. "The structure they established gave parents a reason to monitor both homework and schoolwork regularly. Parents, teachers, and students received immediate feedback about the students' academic progress."

Other Projects. Some funded projects helped improve the school newsletter; others provided translators for parents who didn't understand English. Still others made use of the telephone as a way of communicating with parents. One school used trained parent volunteers in a homework center, and several schools organized parent volunteers to work in classrooms with at-risk students or with those lacking English proficiency. Parent volunteers in some schools served as translators at meetings of the parent teacher organization (Chapman 1991).

---

telling parents about Mrs. Rios' generosity," says Bruce C. Davis (1989).

Delegate responsibilities to parents

Don't dictate what parents should do or how. Use parent observers on your evaluation teams.

Don't tell parents they should change the way they are rearing their children

Instead of criticizing parents' child-rearing practices, tell them they should consider building on their traditions by adding practices that will better prepare their children for U.S. schools. Praise parents for the positive qualities they bring to their parenting, such as a strong sense of family loyalty, discipline, and respect.

Be generous with recognition and awards

"Incorporate tangible rewards for participation, ceremonies and rituals, and products with the program's logo or motto," say Goodson and others. Examples are stickers, balloons, pins, refrigerator magnets, pencils, bookmarks, t-shirts, and coffee mugs advertising the program's name, logo, or motto.

Recognize both parents and students in newsletters and on school bulletin boards. Make "good news" telephone calls and establish a tone of shared celebration to help set the stage for ongoing communication.

One of the keys to parent involvement at the Ralph Waldo Emerson School in Rosemead, California—where 44 percent of the families are limited-English speaking, nineteen different languages or dialects are represented, and 38 percent are on welfare—is appropriate recognition.

Every week each teacher picks two students from his or her classroom to honor as Student of the Week and Super Reader of the Week. Teachers present these awards at assemblies and then phone the parents and tell them (in the parents' native language) why their child received the award, how proud they are of the child. The school has been doing this for nine years and says those 13,230 calls make a difference: If your child has attended Emerson for seven years, chances are you have received at least seven to fourteen positive calls during that period.

It's hard to resist a plea for involvement when the school has acknowledged your child. After all, if your child is doing so many things right, and the school can see it, then your parental skills have been validated. Most of us like to help people who give us positive recognition (Davis).

Communicate frequently and positively

The other key to Emerson's successful parent involvement program with its at-risk population is "constant communication" with the families of its 650 students. Teachers send thank you notes and letters of praise to the students, but only when they are deserved. Parents receive letters praising them for their participation and support, but, again, only when deserved. And this is all done in four languages (meetings are conducted in six, simultaneously).

In the letters, teachers ask for feedback about Emerson in the parents' native language and say it's routine for 61 to 67 percent of the parents to respond to their letters. Then they translate the parents' responses and report back to the parents on what they plan to do about the parents' suggestions. "Parents tell us we keep them well informed," says Davis, "and that they feel no detail is too small to warrant our attention."

If a meeting, workshop, or other event is deemed essential for parents, then the schools must find other ways to get that information to those parents who cannot be there, say D'Angelo and Adler (1991). They suggest videotaping a workshop or sending a short summary home in the next newsletter.

According to Ziegler (1987), research shows that home visits—that is, ongoing face-to-face contact between parents and teachers—may be necessary to sustain the effects of parent involvement programs.

Try new ideas and projects

Being innovative provides variety and renews interest.

For example, a unique approach to parent involvement was tried with Hispanic parents in Texas, with great success. One of the components was called "Rewards" and involved giving gift certificates redeemable at local stores. The idea behind the rewards was to motivate parents by rewarding them and their children with tangible items for fullfilling specific obligations (attending parent meetings, conferring with teachers, supporting teachers in classrooms). The teachers' cooperation was also rewarded (Nicolau and Ramos).

These rewards drew parents to the activities, but once parents felt comfortable about coming to school, they began forgetting to collect the entry forms—an indication that the reward had ceased to be a reason for participating.

Remember, flexibility is the key

Be prepared to alter program operations to respond to families' changing needs. It may be necessary to adjust meeting schedules or places, for example, to accommodate the reentry of program families.

To remain flexible, it is often necessary to engage in creative problem-solving. Here's an example:

The School Neighborhood Consortium in Pittsburgh, which is an advisory committee of businesses, agencies, foundations, and local government, found themselves faced with problems of distance, sprawling school buildings, time constraints, and unpleasant school experiences for the parents.

The result? They decided to focus activities at an active neighborhood house in a predominately low-income, minority community. The consortium offers an afterschool homework program, parent meetings, transportation for parents who want to volunteer at the school, and home visits. Parents receive weekly calls from the Homework Center coordinator and regular reminder calls about school activities. Future plans include seminars for parents at the neighborhood center (Snowden 1988).

Keep a record of events

Take pictures of events, make displays, and raise expectations for further parent involvement.

When ready, involve parents in decisionmaking groups

Some parents might be interested in your parent advisory committee, the PTA, or task forces. Sometimes they will need leadership training in order to feel ready to be involved in this way.

Organize retreats

When a strong core group of parents has emerged, retreats create cohesion, stimulate positive dynamics, and clarify the goals and objectives of your parent program.

Establish a network of contacts with community resources

Find contacts who are sensitive to the needs of your at-risk groups. Building a strong relationship with a community-based agency in the neigh-borhood may be the most efficient way of helping parents—and thus the children—of high-risk families lies. Schools need to be in a position to provide referrals, and a central person needs to coordinate help for families.

Continue to offer easy-access programs

Always welcome new faces, even after a leadership group has emerged.

Don't give up if the initial response isn't overwhelming

Under the best of circumstances, it takes : to generate interest. "Program development is not quick," says Epstein (1991). Partnership programs often require a considerable investment of time and sensitive work before progress is evident. She cites examples of programs that needed a long time for real progress in partnerships: fifteen years in Indianapolis, seven years in San Diego, three years for developing a state policy in California, and between two and three years to see "small but real" steps in the Schools Reaching Out (SRO) demonstration sites.

Also, don't expect everyone at every event. People will choose what works for them. Different tactics work with different groups; remember that not everything works for everyone. If you can attract a core group of parents and then keep them coming, word will spread.

Nicolau and Ramos conclude: "Little by little, others will dare to join. They will discover that it is a rewarding experience and will tell their friends. Keep up the effort, and one day you will find that you can't keep the parents away."

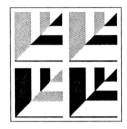

CONCLUSION

"*7*he reforms of the last five years may pale against the requirements of the next 10," says the statement on at-risk students from the Forum of Educational Organization Leaders. "In fact, many predict that the task will require nothing short of a fundamental reordering of the institution called school" (Reeves 1988). Some of this restructuring will necessitate links with the larger community, including parents.

And it will require more money. "Any plan for major improvements in the development and education of disadvantaged children that does not recognize the need for additional resources over a sustained period is doomed to failure," says Reeves. That includes money specifically for parent involvement programs with at-risk families.

Principles of Organizational Change

Davies (1989) reminds us of several points worth remembering when developing programs for at-risk families and the schools:

Organizational change is a gradual process

School reform requires changes of everyone, not just teachers, administrators, and families, but of communities and social service agencies. Change in the school structure as a whole is often a difficult dilemma.

Davies points out that his Schools Reaching Out (SRO) project builds high expectations on the part of teachers and policymakers for change and dramatic results. Yet urban schools are often plagued by poor conditions, skepticism about the viability of new ideas, bureaucratic and financial constraints, as well as the lethargy of tradition and suspicion about or fear of change.

Organizational change requires collaboration

Davies says (in a preface to Krasnow 1990) that school reform should be seen as "a slow, collaborative developmental process." He adds that for schools to change in their ability to share the responsibility for children's development with families—and especially at-risk families and communities—individuals must become more connected to one another. Thus collaboration between schools and other community and human service agencies is necessary to help at-risk children and their families.

Outside pressure and organization are needed for change to occur

Without external pressure, says Davies, the builtin inertia of the school system is likely to defeat change. By outside *pressure* he means laws, mandates, citizen protests, and citizen organizations demanding change.

"Without public dissatisfaction," he emphasizes, "politicians are unlikely to make substantial shifts in the allocation of public resources. This points to the need for...work outside the schools by grassroots parent and community organizations to press for school reform and improved results." He also stresses that this has to be citizen-initiated and controlled, not dependent on the support or financing of school officials.

Parent involvement with at-risk families must not be seen as an end in itself or the only component

Davies' nightmare is that advocates of parent involvement will succeed too well, that there will be an upswell of interest, books, and reports—and also perhaps activities in the schools—and yet 5 or 35 percent of our children will still be failing and leaving school ill-prepared.

"The point is," he maintains, "that parent involvement should not be viewed in any way other than as one of many needed connections between schools, families, and communities which might contribute to social and academic success for all children."

Is It Worth the Effort?

Well, the Hispanic Policy Development Project certainly concluded it was (Nicolau and Ramos 1990).

They found that parents who became involved and attended school activities became familiar with the school system; their discomfort and fear then evaporated and they began to feel they belonged. With this belonging, they became more deeply involved in their children's education. "The involved parents," say Nicolau and Ramos, "repeatedly remarked how good it felt to be able to help their children learn."

Project coordinators noted some of the changes they saw in the attitude and behavior of parents. For instance, more parents telephoned schools to make inquiries and ask for homework assistance with their children. Parents no longer visited the school only when their kids were in trouble but began dropping by to share problems, express concerns, or ask for advice—and they no longer waited to be asked to come in. Many initiated visits and communication with teachers. Parents said they felt more self-confident in general and felt appreciated by the school staff. Some requested additional activities (such as education training for their husbands, relatives, and friends). These are indeed wonderful changes in these once reluctant parents!

Schools reaped benefits as well. These changes enabled teachers to do their jobs better. They learned how to communicate cross-culturally and found that doing things in new ways need not be threatening. The ultimate satisfaction, of course, was that teachers experienced that the students were *learning*!

Nicolau and Ramos conclude with a quote from Justice Holmes, which suggests what these school-parent partnerships discovered. "As the mind, once expanded..., never returns to its original size," said Holmes, so Hispanic parents, once exposed to school involvement, never revert to their original ways of thinking. They begin to alter their parenting styles, which is greatly encouraging for their children's success.

Isn't that progress? And isn't that worth, in addition to the changes in parents and children, the time, patience, and creativity that must go into such a partnership?

APPENDIX
ORGANIZATIONS CONCERNED
WITH AT-RISK FAMILIES

*F*or aditional information about the issues discussed in this report, you may wish to consult the following organizations whose missions embrace at-risk youth and family involvement in schools.

✦ **ASPIRA: Hispanic Community Mobilization for Dropout Prevention** (Janie Petrovich, National Executive Director), ASPIRA Association, Inc., National Office, 1112 16th Street NW, Suite 340, Washington, DC 20036. (202) 835-3600. ASPIRA focuses on creating community awareness and providing practical information to Hispanic parents to help them be more effective participants in their children's education. ASPIRA collaborates with other Hispanic community organizations. The national office provides technical assistance, training, and materials to enhance strategies and models for parent participation.

✦ **Hispanic Policy Development Project** (Siobhan Nicolau, President), 36 E. 22nd Street, 9th Floor, New York, NY 10010. (212) 529-9323. HPDP has published the booklet *Together Is Better: Building Strong Partnerships Between Schools and Hispanic Parents* and also has an appealing pamphlet for Hispanic parents (with one page in English, one in Spanish).

✦ **The Home and School Institute, Inc.** (Dorothy Rich, President), Special Projects Office, Suite 228, 1201 16th Street NW, Washington, DC 20036. (202) 466-3633. Offers publications and help on how parents can get involved in their children's education; has had success in working with at-risk families.

✦ **Institute for Responsive Education** (Don Davies, President), 605 Commonwealth Avenue, Boston, MA 02215. (617) 353-3309. IRE is a nonprofit public interest organization that is studying new approaches to improving relations among schools, parents, and the community. Publishes reports, handbooks, and other publications, including the magazine *Equity and Choice*.

✦ **The Language Minority Program** (Richard Duran and Alejandro Portes, Codirectors), Johns Hopkins University, 3505 North Charles St., Baltimore, MD 21218. (301) 338-7570. The goal of the program is to identify, develop, and evaluate effective learning programs for disadvantaged Hispanic, American Indian, Southeast Asian, and other language minority children. The program focuses on rigorous evaluations of practical, replicable programs that can increase the language skills of language minority children in their home language and in English and can accelerate their learning in traditional school subjects.

✦ **Mexican American Legal Defense and Educational Fund** (Antonia Hernandez, President and General Counsel), 634 South Spring Street, 11th Floor, Los Angeles, CA 90014. (213) 629-2512. This civil rights organization conducts a Parent Leadership Program for promoting the participation of Latino parents as leaders at their children's schools. The program involves a twelve-week course, including parent-teacher conferences and meetings with school district officials.

✦ **National Black Child Development Institute** (Evelyn K. Moore, Executive Director), 1023 15th Street NW, Suite 600, Washington, DC 20005. Operates a comprehensive tutoring and mentoring program for low-income, elementary school age black children entitled "Each One, Reach One: The Spirit of Excellence" in Greensboro, North Carolina, and Detroit, Michigan. The goal of the project is to instill the values and teach the basic skills that children need for academic success and serve as a bridge between home and school.

✦ **National Coalition of Title I/ Chapter I Parents** (Robert Witherspoon, Executive Director), National Parent Center, Edmonds School Building, 9th and D Streets NE, Washington, DC 20002. (202) 547-9286. This organization provides a voice for Chapter I parents at the federal, regional, state, and local levels. The coalition publishes a newsletter, provides training, and sponsors conferences.

✦ **National Committee for Citizens in Education** (Carl Marburger and William Rioux, Codirectors), 10840 Little Patuxent Parkway, Suite 301, Columbia, MD 21044. (301) 997-9300 or 1-800-NETWORK. NCCE seeks to improve public education for all children through increased involvement of parents and citizens in the community.

✦ **National Council of La Raza** (Raul Yzaguirre, President), 810 First Street NE, Suite 300, Washington, DC 20002. (202) 289-1380. This research and advocacy organization works on behalf of the U.S. Hispanic population and provides technical assistance to community-based organizations. NCLR's Project EXCEL is a national education demonstration project that includes tutoring services and parental education.

✦ **National Research and Development Center on Families, Communities, Schools, and Children's Learning** (Don Davies and Joyce Epstein, Codirectors), Boston University, 605 Commonwealth Avenue, Boston, MA 02215. (617) 353-3309. Funded in 1990 by the U.S. Department of Education's Office of Educational Research and Improvement in cooperation with the U.S. Department of Health and Human Services, the center will carry out research in family involvement and related issues.

✦ **The National Rural Development Institute** (Doris Helge, Executive Director), Western Washington University, Miller Hall 359, Bellingham, WA 98225. (206) 676-3576. The institute has recently published a study, *The National Study Regarding Rural, Suburban, and Urban At-Risk Students*, which shows that rural children are more likely to be at risk than their counterparts in cities and suburbs.

✦ **Parent Training and Information Centers, and Technical Assistance to Parent Projects** (Mildred Winter, Executive Director), 95 Berkeley Street, Suite 104, Boston, MA 02116. (617) 482-2915. The Office of Special Education Programs supports a network of sixty Parent Training and Information Centers in all fifty states and Puerto Rico to enable parents to participate more effectively with professionals in meeting the educational needs of children with disabilities. Technical Assistance to Parent Projects (TAPP) provides technical assistance and coordination to the sixty PTICs and to developing minority programs in urban and rural locations.

✦ **Tucson Dropout Prevention Collaborative** (Ralph Chavez, Coordinator), TUSD Starr Center, 102 N. Plumer, Tucson, AZ 85719. (602) 798-2047. The Tucson Dropout Prevention Collaborative functions as an advisory board to the district's dropout prevention coordinator. Part of the collaborative is the innovative parent leadership program called Commadre Network.

BIBLIOGRAPHY

M any of the items in this bibliography are indexed in ERIC's monthly catalog *Resources in Education (RIE)*. Reports in *RIE* are indicated by an "ED" number. Journal articles, indexed in ERIC's companion catalog, *Current Index to Journals in Education*, are indicated by an "EJ" number.

Most items with an ED number are available from ERIC Document Reproduction Service (EDRS), 7420 Fullerton Rd., Suite 110, Springfield, VA 22153-2852.

To order from EDRS, specify the ED number, type of reproduction desired—microfiche (MF) or paper copy (PC), and number of copies. Add postage to the cost of all orders and include check or money order payable to EDRS. For credit card orders, call 1-800-443-3742.

Alexander, Shirley, and Terry Lovelace. *Lafayette Parish Early Childhood Project: 1987 - 1988 Academic Year. Evaluation Report.* Lafayette, Louisiana: Lafayette Parish School Board, 1988. 96 pages. ED 299 051.

Almy H. "Day Care and Early Childhood Education." In *Day Care: Scientific and Social Policy Issues,* edited by E. Zigler and E. Gordon. 476-96. Boston: Auburn House, 1982.

Amundson, Kristen J. *First Teachers: Parental Involvement in the Public Schools.* Alexandria, Virginia: National School Boards Association, 1988. 57 pages. ED 302 883.

Ascher, Carol. "Improving the School-Home Connection for Poor and Minority Urban Students." New York: Institute for Urban and Minority Education, Columbia University. ERIC/CUE Trends & Issues Series 8 (December 1987): 1-21. ED 300 484.

Austin, Susan, and Gail Meister. *Responding to Children at Risk: A Guide to Recent Reports.* Philadelphia, Pennsylvania: Research for Better Schools, 1990. 71 pages. ED 322 271.

Bauch, Patricia A. "Family Choice and Parent Involvement in Inner-City Catholic High Schools: An Exploration of Psycho-Social and Organizational Factors." Revision of paper presented at the annual meeting of the American Educational Research Association, Washington, DC, April 1987. 45 pages. ED 302 950.

Baum, Jerry. "Parent Involvement: The LEF and a University Work Together in Baltimore." *PEForum* 3, 3 (Fall 1988): 2.

Becher, Rhoda McShane. *Parent Involvement: A Review of Research and Principles of Successful Practice.* Urbana, Illinois: ERIC Clearinghouse on Elementary and Early Childhood Education, 1984. 71 pages. ED 247 032.

Becker, Henry Jay, and Joyce L. Epstein. "Parent Involvement: A Survey of Teacher Practices." *Elementary School Journal* 83, 2 (November 1982): 85-102. EJ 273 072.

Berlin, Gordon, and Andrew Sum. "Toward a More Perfect Union: Basic Skills, Poor Families, and Our Economic Future." *Occasional Paper* 3. New York: Ford Foundation, 1988. 110 pages. ED 297 037.

Berman, Douglas, and others. "Extending the Home-School Partnership—Starting a Parent Support Group." *NASSP Bulletin* 71, 499 (May 1987): 123-125.

Bloom, Benjamin. *Developing Talent in Young People.* New York: Ballantine Books, 1985.

Bradley, Ann. "High-School Graduation Rates for Blacks Up, Census Finds." *Education Week* XI, 5 (October 2, 1991): 5.

Brandt, Ron. "On Parents and Schools: A Conversation with Joyce Epstein." *Educational Leadership 47,* 2 (October 1989): 24-27. EJ 397 732.

Bronfenbrenner, Urie. "Is Early Intervention Effective?" *Teachers College Record* 76, 2 (1972): 279-301.

Center for Research on Elementary and Middle Schools. "STaR Preschool Program Emphasizes Oral Language Development and Comprehension." *CREMS* (June 1989): 1-14.

Chapman, Warren. "The Illinois Experience." *Phi Delta Kappan* 72, 5 (January 1991): 355-58. EJ 419 904.

Chavkin, Nancy F., and David L. Williams. "Critical Issues for Teacher Training for Parent Involvement." *Educational Horizons* 66, 2 (Winter 1988): 87-89. EJ 364 525.

Chrispeels, Janet H. "District Leadership in Parent Involvement: Policies and Actions in San Diego." *Phi Delta Kappan* 22, 5 (January 1991): 367-71. EJ 419 907.

The City College. *Successful Schooling for the At-Risk Student: Conference Report and Recommendations.* New York: Author, June 1988. ED 303 560.

Clark, Reginald M. *Family Life and School Achievement: Why Poor Black Children Succeed or Fail.* Chicago: University Press, 1983. 249 pages.

_____. "Home Learning Activities and Children's Literacy Achievement." *Sociological Studies of Child Development* 3. Greenwich, Connecticut: JAI Press, 1987.

Cochran, Moncrieff, and Charles R. Henderson, Jr. *Family Matters: Evaluation of the Parental Empowerment Program. A Summary of a Final Report to the National Institute of Education.* Ithaca, New York: Cornell University, 1986. 81 pages. ED 280 577.

Cohen, Deborah L. "Conferees Find Problems, Solutions for At-Risk Children Are Universal." *Education Week* IX, 21 (February 14, 1990): 6.

_____. "In Early-Years Programs, New Focus Is on Families." *Education Week* X, 13 (November 28, 1990): 8.

_____. "Parents as Partners." *Education Week* IX, 33 (May 9, 1990): 13-14, 16-20.

_____. "Parents as Partners: More Businesses Are Training Employees to Be Better Parents." *Education Week* IX, 33 (August 1, 1990): 26-27.

Coleman, James S. "Families and Schools." *Educational Researcher* 16, 6 (August-September 1987): 32-38. EJ 363 043.

Comer, James P., and others. "School Power: A Model for Improving Black Student Achievement." *The Urban League Review* 11, 1-2 (Summer-Winter 1987-88): 187-200. EJ 377 109.

Constable, Robert, and Herbert Walberg. "School Social Work: Facilitating Home, School, and Community Partnerships." *Urban Education* 22, 4 (January 1988): 429-43. EJ 369 757.

The Council of Chief State School Officers. *Family Support: Education and Involvement: A Guide for State Action.* Washington, DC: Author, November 1989. 63 pages. ED 319 112.

Cross, Christopher T., and others. "The FIRST Grants: Federal Leadership to Advance School and Family." *Phi Delta Kappan* 72, 5 (January 1991): 383-88. EJ 419 910.

D'Angelo, Diane A., and Ralph C. Adler. "Chapter 1: A Catalyst for Improving Parent Involvement." *Phi Delta Kappan* 72, 5 (January 1991): 350-54. EJ 419 903.

Darnton, Nina. "A Mother's Touch." *Newsweek* (Fall/Winter 1990 special issue): 60-61.

Davies, Don. "Low-Income Parents and the Schools: A Research Report and a Plan for Action." *Equity and Choice* 4, 3 (Spring 1988): 51-57. EJ 374 512.

_____. "Parent Involvement in the Public Schools: Opportunities for Administrators." *Education and Urban Society* 19, 2 (February 1987): 147-63. EJ 351 804.

_____. "Poor Parents, Teachers, and the Schools: Comments about Practice, Policy and Research." Paper presented at the annual meeting of the American Educational Research Association, San Francisco, California, March 27-31, 1989. ED 308 574.

_____. "Schools Reaching Out: Family, School, and Community Partnerships for Student Success." *Phi Delta Kappan* 72, 5 (January 1991): 376-82. EJ 419 909.

Davis, Bruce C. "A Successful Parent Involvement Program." *Educational Leadership* 47, 2 (October 1989): 21-23. EJ 397 731.

Decker, Larry E., and Virginia A. Decker. *Home/School/Community Involvement.* Arlington, Virginia: American Association of School Administrators, 1988. 147 pages. ED 298 610.

Dornbusch, S. M., and P. L. Ritter. "Parents of High School Students: A Neglected Resource." *Educational Horizons* 66 (1988): 75-77.

Dornbusch, Sanford, and others. "The Relation of Parenting Style to Adolescent School Performance." *Child Development* 58, 5 (October 1987): 1244-57. EJ 362 728.

Education Commission of the States. *Securing Our Future: The Report of the National Forum for Youth At Risk.* Denver, Colorado: Author, 1988. 57 pages. ED 305 207.

Elling, Sue. "Parent Involvement: Focus on Parents in Dayton-Montgomery County." *PEForum* 3, 3 (Fall 1988): 4.

Epstein, Joyce. *Effects on Parents of Teacher Practices of Parent Involvement.* Baltimore: Center for Social Organization of Schools, Johns Hopkins University, 1983. 59 pages.

_____. *Single Parents and the Schools: The Effect of Marital Status on Parent and Teacher Evaluations.* Baltimore: The Johns Hopkins University, Center for Social Organization of Schools, 1984.

_____. "Parents' Reactions to Teacher Practices of Parent Involvement." *Elementary School Journal* 86, 3 (January 1986): 277-94. EJ 337 873.

_____. "Paths to Partnership: What We Can Learn from Federal, State, District, and School Initiatives." *Phi Delta Kappan* 72, 5 (January 1991): 344-49. EJ 419 902.

Freedberg, Louis. "Don't Remediate, Accelerate: Can Disadvantaged Students Benefit from Fast-Forwarded Instruction?" *Equity and Choice* 5, 2 (March 1989): 40-43. EJ 390 061.

Fullan, Michael. *The Meaning of Educational Change.* New York: Teachers College, Columbia University, 1982. 326 pages.

Goodson, Barbara Dillon, and others. *Working with Families: Promising Programs to Help Parents Support Young Children's Learning.* Executive Summary. Cambridge, Massachusetts: Abt Associates, Inc., February 1991. (Prepared for the Office of Planning, Budget, and Evaluation.)

Gotts, Edward E. *HOPE Revisited: Preschool to Graduation, Reflections on Parenting and School-Family Relations.* Occasional Paper 28. Charleston, West Virginia: Appalachia Educational Laboratory, February, 1989. 21 pages. ED 305 147.

Guthrie, Larry F., Claudia Long, and Grace Pung Guthrie. *Strategies for Dropout Prevention.* San Francisco, California: Far West Laboratory, Students At Risk Program, 1989. 36 pages.

Hamilton-Lee, Muriel. "Home-School Partnerships: The School Development Program Model." Paper presented at the annual meeting of the American Psychological Association, Atlanta, Georgia, August 12-16, 1988. 20 pages. ED 303 923.

Hart, Thomas E. *Involving Parents in the Education of Their Children.* OSSC Bulletin. Eugene: Oregon School Study Council, November 1988. 42 pages. ED 300 930.

Haycock, Kati, and Luis Duany. "Developing the Potential of Latino Students." *Principal* 70, 3 (January 1991): 25-27. EJ 419 922.

Heleen, Owen. "Involving the 'Hard to Reach' Parent: A Working Model." *Equity and Choice* 4, 3 (Spring 1988): 60-63.

Helge, Doris. *A National Study Regarding At-Risk Students.* Bellingham, Washington: National Rural Development Institute, 1990. 26 pages.

Helping at Home 1,1. Seattle School District No. 1 (September 1989).

Henderson, Anne, ed. *The Evidence Continues to Grow: Parent Involvement Improves Student Achievement. An Annotated Bibliography.* Columbia, Maryland: National Committee for Citizens in Education, Special Report, 1987. 84 pages. ED 315 199.

_____. *Parent Participation—Student Achievement: the Evidence Grows.* Columbia, Maryland: National Committee for Citizens in Education, 1981. ED 209 754.

_____. "Parents Are a School's Best Friends." *Phi Delta Kappan* 70, 2 (October 1988): 148-53. ED 377 529.

Hester, Harold. "Start at Home to Improve Home-School Relations." *NASSP Bulletin* 73, 513 (January 1989): 23-27. EJ 382 018.

The Home and School Institute. "What People are Saying about the New Partnerships/Megaskills Curriculum." Washington, DC: Author, undated.

Jennings, Lisa. "Network Created to Share Ideas on the Parent-School Connection." *Education Week* IX, 21 (February 14, 1990): 8.

_____. "Parents as Partners." *Education Week* IX, 33 (August 1, 1990): 23-32.

_____. "States Should Require Schools to Craft Family-Support Plans, Chiefs Propose." *Education Week* IX, 21 (February 14, 1990).

_____. "Studies Link Parental Involvement, Higher Student Achievement." *Education Week* IX, 28 (April 4, 1990): 20-24.

_____. "Union Locals Join to Encourage Parent-School Ties." *Education Week* IX, 32 (May 2, 1990).

Jonas, Edward D. *The Atlanta Dropout Prevention Plan.* Atlanta, Georgia: Atlanta Public Schools, November, 1987. 26 pages. ED 299 331.

Jones, Judith E. "Changing Needs for a Changing Future: The Need for Educational Leadership." New York: National Center for Children in Poverty. Keynote address before the Leadership Seminar on Special Programs of the Texas Education Agency, Austin, Texas, June 14, 1989. 23 pages. ED 318 079.

Kamminger, Kenneth. "Early Intervention with Children at Risk: Marquette County's Strategy to Increase School Success and Reduce Social Service Cost." October 1988. 10 pages. ED 314 825.

Kelly, Joan, and Judith Wallerstein. *Surviving the Breakup: How Children and Parents Cope with Divorce.* New York: Basic Books, 1979, reissued 1990.

Kneidek, Tony. "Parent Involvement Can Empower Children." Northwest Regional Educational Laboratory. *Northwest Report* (July/August 1990): 6-7.

Krasnow, Jean. *Building Parent-Teacher Partnerships: Prospects from the Perspective of the Schools Reaching Out Project.* Boston: Institute for Responsive Education, 1990. 66 pages. ED 318 817.

Kurtz, P. David. "Social Work Services to Parents: Essential to Pupils at Risk." *Urban Education* 22, 4 (January 1988): 444-59. EJ 369 758.

Lareau, Annette. "Social Class Differences in Family-School Relationships: The Importance of Cultural Capital." *Sociology of Education* 60, 2 (April 1987): 73-85. EJ 353 123.

Leler, H. "Parent Education and Involvement in Relation to the Schools and to Parents of School-Aged Children." In *Parent Education and Public Policy,* edited by R. Haskins and D. Adamson. Norwood, New Jersey: Ablex, 1983. 385 pages.

Levy, Janet E., with Carol Copple. *Joining Forces: A Report from the First Year.* Alexandria, Virginia: National Association of State Boards of Education, 1989. 53 pages. ED 308 609.

Lightfoot, Sara Lawrence. *Worlds Apart: The Relationship Between Families and Schools.* New York: Basic Books, 1978. 257 pages.

Lindle, Jane C. "Five Reasons to Prepare Your Staff for Parent Involvement." *The School Administrator* 47, 6 (June 1990): 19-22, 24. EJ 410 177.

McAfee, Oralie. "Improving Home School Relations: Implications for Staff Development." *Education and Urban Society* 19, 2 (February 1987): 185-89. EJ 351 806.

McCormick, John. "Where Are the Parents?" *Newsweek* (Fall/Winter 1990, Special Issue): 54-58.

McLaughlin, Milbrey, and Patrick Shields. "Involving Low-Income Parents in the Schools: A Role for Policy?" *Phi Delta Kappan* 69, 2 (October 1987): 156-60. EJ 359 353.

The Metropolitan Life Survey. *The American Teacher 1987: Strengthening Links Between Home and School.* New York: Louis Harris and Associates, Inc., 1987. 123 pages. ED 289 841.

Moles, Oliver C. "Disadvantaged Parents' Participation in Their Children's Education." Paper presented at the annual meeting of the American Educational Research Association, Boston, Massachusetts, April 16-20, 1990. 19 pages.

Montolvo, F. "Making Good Schools from Bad." In *Make Something Happen: Hispanic and Urban High School Reform.* Washington, DC: National Commission on Secondary Education for Hispanics, 1984.

Morrow, Robert D. "The Challenge of Southeast Asian Parental Involvement." *Principal* 70, 3 (January 1991): 20-22. EJ 419 921.

National Urban League. *What Students Need to Know.* National Urban League Education Institute Tool Box. New York: Author, 1989. 152 pages. ED 316 636.

Newman, Joan A. *Helping Parents to Help Their Children Succeed in School: What Research Says About Supplementary Home Instruction,* 1989. 19 pages. ED 307 674.

New York State Department of Education. *The Time for Assertive Action: School Strategies for Promoting the Education Success of At-Risk Children.* Report of the Commissioner's Task Force on the Education of Children and Youth At-Risk. Albany, New York: Author, 1988. 35 pages. ED 303 534.

Nicolau, Siobhan, and Carmen Lydia Ramos. *Together Is Better: Building Strong Partnerships Between Schools and Hispanic Parents.* New York: Hispanic Policy Development Project, Inc., 1990. 76 pages. ED 325 543.

Nicolau, Siobhan, and others. *Dear Parents: In The United States...It's Our School Too.* New York: Hispanic Policy Development Project, Inc., 1990. 25 pages. ED 325 542.

Ochoa, Alberto M. "Parents as Equal Collaborators of Their Children's Education: Towards Transformational Empowerment." Paper presented at the annual meeting of the American Educational Research Association, Boston, Massachusetts, April 16-20, 1990. 40 pages. ED 323 614.

Olson, Lynn. "Parents as Partners: Redefining the Social Contract Between Families and Schools." *Education Week* IX, 28 (April 4, 1990):17-24.

Orleans Parish School Board. *Educating Black Male Youth: A Moral and Civic Imperative.* New Orleans, Louisiana: Author, 1988. 57 pages. ED 303 546.

The Parent Institute. "Practical Ideas for Parents to Help Their Children." *Parents Make the Difference!* (Special Issue, 1989): 4 pages.

The Parent Institute. "Practical Ideas for Parents to Help Their Children." *Parents Make the Difference!* (Sample Issue, 1990): 4 pages.

Peck, Nancy L., and Raymond G. Eberhard. *Dropout Prevention Strategies.* Reston, Virginia: National Association of Secondary School Principals, 1988. 8 pages. ED 302 897.

Price, Laura. "The Game of Success." *What's Happening,* Eugene, Oregon. (March 14, 1991): 5.

Raspberry, William. "Things You Can Do to Help Your Kids Learn." *The Washington Post* (September 7, 1988).

Reeves, M. Sandra. "Self-Interest and the Common Weal: Focusing on the Bottom Half." *Education Week* III, 31 (April 27, 1988).

Rich, Dorothy. "The Community Gap in Education Reform." *PEForum* (April 1986): 2-3.

_____. *The Forgotten Factor in School Success—The Family. A Policymaker's Guide.* Washington, D.C.: Home and School Institute, 1985. 75 pages. ED 263 264.

_____. *Megaskills: How Families Can Help Children Succeed in School and Beyond.* Boston, Massachusetts: Houghton Mifflin, 1988.

_____. "Testimony of Dr. Dorothy Rich, The Home and School Institute." *Congressional Record* 133, 79 (May 15, 1987).

Richardson, Barbara B. *Negotiating Your Child's Experience in the Public Schools: A Handbook for Black Parents.* Washington, DC: National Black Child Development Institute, 1989. 31 pages. ED 321 876.

Rothman, Robert. "New Study Confirms Income, Education Linked to Parent Involvement in Schools." *Education Week* IX, 31 (April 25, 1990): 10.

Rupp, J. "Attitudes and Expectations of Indochinese Parents." Paper presented at the National Conference on Indochinese Education and Social Services, Arlington, Virginia, 1980.

Sandfort, James A. "Putting Parents in Their Place in Public Schools." *NASSP Bulletin* 71, 496 (February 1987): 99-103. EJ 349 133.

Sarkees, Michelle D. "Developing Effective Assistance Programs for Parents of At Risk Students. Parent Involvement Is Critical." *Journal for Vocational Special Needs Education* 11, 2 (Winter 1989): 17, 19-21. EJ 386 664.

Sattes, B.D. *Parent Involvement: A Review of the Literature.* Charleston, West Virginia: Appalachia ory, 1985.

Schmidt, Peter. "Parents as Partners: English-Literacy Classes Help Avert Family Rifts." *Education Week* IX, 33 (August 1, 1990): 29.

Seeley, David S. "A New Paradigm for Parent Involvement." *Educational Leadership* 47, 2 (October 1989): 46-48. EJ 397 741.

_____. "Education Through Partnership." *Educational Leadership* 40, 2 (November 1982): 42-43. EJ 272 575.

Slaughter, Diana T., and Valerie Shahariw Kuehne. "Improving Black Education: Perspectives on Parent Involvement." *The Urban League Review* 11, 1-2 (Summer/Winter 1987-88): 59-75. EJ 377 100.

_____. "Is a New Dawn Breaking? Status Report on School Reform." *Youth Policy* (May 1987): 9-11.

Smith, Mildred B. "We Must Involve Parents." *Instructor* (August/September 1970).

Snowden, Marcia. "Parent Involvement: Pairing a School and Its Distant Community in Pittsburgh." *PEForum* 3, 3 (Fall 1988): 3.

Solomon, Zelma P. "California's Policy on Parent Involvement." *Phi Delta Kappan* 72, 5 (January 1991): 359-62. EJ 419 905.

Sorohan, Erica. "More School Systems Establishing PreSchools." *School Board News* (February 3, 1988).

Statistical Abstracts of the U.S. 1990. Washington, DC: U.S. Government Printing Office, 1990.

Stedman, James B. *The Educational Attainment of Select Groups of "At Risk" Children and Youth.* Washington, DC: Library of Congress Congressional Research Service, 1987. 67 pages. ED 292 927.

Stedman, Lawrence C. "It's Time We Changed the Effective Schools Formula." *Phi Delta Kappan* 69, 3 (November 1987): 215-24. EJ 360 782.

Strand, Paul J. *Indochinese Refugees in America: Problems of Adaptation and Assimilation.* Durham, North Carolina: Duke University Press, 1985. 182 pages.

Swap, Susan McAllister. *Parent Involvement and Success for All Children: What We Know Now.* Boston: Institute for Responsive Education, 1990. 85 pages. ED 321 907.

Tan, Amy. *The Joy Luck Club.* New York: Putnam, 1989.

Texas Education Agency Dropout Information Clearinghouse. "Information Is a Key to Dropout Prevention." In *Parent and Community Involvement Series.* Austin, Texas: Author, 1989. 23 pages.

Toomey, Derek. "Home-School Relations and Inequality in Education" Paper presented at a Conference on Education and the Family, Provo, Utah, February 4-6, 1986. 43 pages. ED 269 495.

Tran, X. *The Factors Hindering Indochinese Parent Participation in School Activities.* San Diego: Institute for Cultural Pluralism, 1982.

U.S. Bureau of the Census. Current Population Reports, Series P-60, No. 175. *Poverty in the United States: 1990.* Washington, DC: U.S. Government Printing Office, August 1991. 221 pages.

Vanderslice, V. "Empowerment: A Definition in Process." *Human Ecology Forum* 14, 1 (1984).

Walberg, Herbert J. "Families as Partners in Educational Productivity." *Phi Delta Kappan* 65, 6 (February 1984): 397-400. EJ 293 132.

West Virginia Association of School Administrators and Appalachia Educational Laboratory. *Parent Involvement Seminar. Rationale: Why Parent Involvement?* Charleston, West Virginia: Author, October 1990.

Western Interstate Commission for Higher Education and The College Board. *The Road to College: Educational Progress by Race and Ethnicity.* Boulder, Colorado: Author, July 1991. 102 pages.

Williams, David L., and Nancy Feyl Chavkin. "Essential Elements of Strong Parent Involvement Programs." *Educational Leadership* 47, 2 (October 1989): 18-20. EJ 397 730.

Wolf, Joan S., and Thomas M. Stephens. "Parent/Teacher Conferences: Finding Common Ground." *Educational Leadership* 47, 2 (October 1989): 28-31. EJ 397 733.

Ziegler, Suzanne. *The Effects of Parent Involvement on Children's Achievement: The Significance of Home/School Links.* Toronto, Canada: Toronto Board of Education, 1987. 72 pages. ED 304 234.

Printed in the United States
1384100001B/92